LIBRARY OF NEW TESTAMENT STUDIES

427

Formerly Journal for the Study of the New Testament Supplement Series

Editor
Mark Goodacre

READING ACTS TODAY

Essays in Honour of
Loveday C.A. Alexander

edited by

Steve Walton
Thomas E. Philips
Lloyd K. Pietersen
F. Scott Spencer

t & t clark

Published by T&T Clark International
A Continuum imprint
The Tower Building, 11 York Road, London SE1 7NX
80 Maiden Lane, New York, NY 10038

www.continuumbooks.com

British Library Cataloguing-in-Publication Data
A catalogue record for this book is available from the British Library

ISBN: HB: 978-0-567-23813-9

Typeset and copy-edited by Forthcoming Publications Ltd. (www.forthpub.com)
Printed and bound in Great Britain

For our dear friend and colleague, Loveday Alexander,
with love, respect and thanks.

Loveday C.A. Alexander

CONTENTS

Part II
READING THEMES IN ACTS

PREFACE

Steve Walton, Thomas E. Phillips, Lloyd K. Pietersen
and F. Scott Spencer

The book of Acts invites thoughtful engagement, but offers great challenges to its explorers. This ancient-but-modern book has been the stimulus to much fascinating study and reflection over the centuries, and this collection of essays provides a fresh and stimulating window into the 'state of the art' in studies of Acts in the early twenty-first century. This introduction sketches the wider range of areas where we seek to contribute to the study of Acts in honour of our valued friend and colleague, Loveday Alexander, who has herself provided so much stimulus and helpful study of Acts.

Acts is an ancient book, and thus it behoves us to locate it within its world and to seek to understand how it would have been heard by ancient hearers and readers. Loveday Alexander has herself contributed greatly to this discussion, as many of the contributors to this volume note, and in particular to the question of the genre of Acts. Richard Burridge seeks to offer a fresh perspective on this much-discussed question by bringing to the question the tools which he developed in studying the genre of the canonical Gospels.

In addition, there are a number of specific questions which arise from studying Acts in the contexts of the ancient world. Thomas Phillips reads the 'swaddling clothes' of Luke's infancy narrative in the light of Euripides' *Ion* to provide a fresh angle on a puzzling phenomenon, and then to reflect on Luke's view of the Roman empire, much debated in recent times. Dennis MacDonald argues that Luke made use of the writings of Papias, Bishop of Hierapolis in the early second century, in composing his account of Judas' death. Scott Spencer faces one of the most difficult stories in Acts, the deaths of Ananias and Sapphira, and seeks to hear how this shocking account is informed by Aristotle's understanding of rhetoric and ethics. Barry Matlock considers how we might hear the Acts accounts of Paul's Damascus Road experience in the light of the evidence we can glean from Paul's own letters about that encounter with the exalted Christ.

Acts offers other opportunities for thoughtful and engaging study in considering major themes which run through the book, and how these might inform those who regard Acts as Christian Scripture. Joel Green revisits the key question of the relationship of Acts and Luke's Gospel, a question recently re-opened in interesting ways by the work of a number of scholars. James Dunn picks up the question of Luke's portrait of Paul and offers a fresh angle by following up clues left by Olof Linton, which lead Dunn to suggest that Luke and Paul may be offering us different geographical and ideological perspectives. Heidi Hornik and Mikeal Parsons reflect on the way in which the story of Pentecost has stimulated Christian art, and consider how such artists read that story from the sixth to the sixteenth century. Howard Marshall provides a fresh contribution to debate on Luke's understanding of the death of Jesus, focusing on one of the clearest 'atonement' verses in Acts, namely, 20.28. Daniel Marguerat gives a fine, clear exposition of the various forms which witness to the resurrection of Jesus takes in Acts. Steve Walton seeks to understand what picture of spirituality, that is, life with God, the book of Acts offers.

These essays offer models of a variety of approaches to Acts: reading Acts with other ancient (extra-biblical) literature (Burridge, Phillips, MacDonald, Spencer); reading a theological theme in Acts (Marshall, Marguerat, Walton); reading Acts with other parts of the New Testament (Green: Luke's Gospel; Dunn, Matlock: Paul's letters); reading Acts through the eyes of later Christian readers and considering its reception history (Hornik and Parsons); literary/narrative approaches (Spencer, Green, Walton); historically-focused approaches (MacDonald, Matlock, Dunn, Marshall); and theological readings (Marshall, Marguerat, Walton). We are seeking to demonstrate the value of reading Acts from this wide variety of angles in order to enrich our reading of this key document of early Christianity.

This book, in other words, responds to the invitation to engage with the book of Acts with alacrity—and these essays offer windows into the book and its scholarly study which will stimulate, help, provoke and cause readers to think further, and read further, for themselves. We are delighted to offer this collection with great affection and respect to our friend and admired colleague Loveday Alexander.

Finally, the editors would like to thank the office of the Provost at Point Loma Nazarene University which provided a grant to cover the cost of editing this volume. Also, we would like to thank Ms Andrea Phillips and Dr Duncan Burns for their meticulous work in helping to prepare the manuscript for publication.

ABBREVIATIONS

AB	Anchor Bible
ABD	David Noel Freedman (ed.), *The Anchor Bible Dictionary* (6 vols.; New York: Doubleday, 1992)
ANTC	Abingdon New Testament Commentaries
BBB	Bonner biblische Beiträge
BBR	*Bulletin for Biblical Research*
BETL	Bibliotheca ephemeridum theologicarum lovaniensium
Bib	*Biblica*
BibInt	*Biblical Interpretation*
BNTC	Black's New Testament Commentaries
BSL	Biblical Studies Library
BZNW	Beihefte zur Zeitschrift für die neutestamentliche Wissenschaft und die Kunde der älteren Kirche
CBET	Contributions to Biblical Exegesis and Theology
CBQ	*Catholic Biblical Quarterly*
CBR	*Currents in Biblical Research*
CNT	Commentaire du Nouveau Testament
CQ	*Classical Quarterly*
DPL	G.F. Hawthorne and R.P. Martin (eds.), *Dictionary of Paul and His Letters* (Downers Grove: InterVarsity Press, 1993)
EDNT	H. Balz and G. Schneider (eds.), *Exegetical Dictionary of the New Testament* (3 vols.; Grand Rapids: Eerdmans, 1990–93)
EKK	Evangelisch-katholischer Kommentar zum Neuen Testament
EvQ	*Evangelical Quarterly*
EVV	English versions
EWNT	H. Balz (ed.), *Exegetisches Wörterbuch zum neuen Testament* (3 vols.; Stuttgart: Kohlhammer, 1978)
ExpTim	*Expository Times*
FRLANT	Forschungen zur Religion und Literatur des Alten und Neuen Testaments
HKNT	Handkommentar zum Neuen Testament
HR	*History of Religions*
HTR	*Harvard Theological Review*
ICC	International Critical Commentary
ITQ	*Irish Theological Quarterly*
JBL	*Journal of Biblical Literature*
JETS	*Journal of the Evangelical Theological Society*
JHS	*Journal of Hellenic Studies*

JPTSup	Journal of Pentecostal Theology Supplement Series
JR	*Journal of Religion*
JSNT	*Journal for the Study of the New Testament*
JSNTSup	Journal for the Study of the New Testament Supplement Series
JSOTSup	Journal for the Study of the Old Testament Supplement Series
JTS	*Journal of Theological Studies*
KEK	H.A.W. Meyer (ed.), Kritisch-exegetischer Kommentar über das Neue Testament
LCL	Loeb Classical Library
LD	Lectio divina
LNTS	Library of New Testament Studies
LPS	Library of Pauline Studies
NIDB	K.D. Sakenfeld (ed.), *New Interpreter's Dictionary of the Bible* (5 vols.; Nashville: Abingdon Press, 2006)
NIDNTT	C. Brown (ed.), *New International Dictionary of New Testament Theology* (4 vols.; Grand Rapids: Zondervan, 1975–85)
NIGTC	New International Greek Testament Commentary
NovT	*Novum Testamentum*
NovTSup	Novum Testamentum Supplements
NRSV	New Revised Standard Version
NTS	*New Testament Studies*
OBT	Overtures to Biblical Theology
PBM	Paternoster Biblical Monographs
RevExp	*Review and Expositor*
RevQ	*Revue de Qumran*
SBLDS	Society of Biblical Literature Dissertation Series
SBLMS	Society of Biblical Literature Monograph Series
SBLSP	*Society of Biblical Literature Seminar Papers*
SBLSymS	Society of Biblical Literature Symposium Series
ScEs	*Science et Espirit*
Sem	*Semeia*
SJT	*Scottish Journal of Theology*
SNTSMS	Society for New Testament Studies Monograph Series
SNTSU	Studien zum Neuen Testament und seiner Umwelt
SNTW	Studies of the New Testament and its World
SP	Sacra Pagina
SR	*Studies in Religion*
StBL	Studies in Biblical Literature
StSp	*Studies in Spirituality*
TynBul	*Tyndale Bulletin*
WBC	Word Biblical Commentary
WUNT	Wissenschaftliche Untersuchungen zum Neuen Testament
ZKT	*Zeitschrift für Theologie und Kirche*
ZNW	*Zeitschrift für die neutestamentliche Wissenschaft und die Kunde der älteren Kirche*

LIST OF CONTRIBUTORS

Richard A. Burridge is Professor of Biblical Interpretation and Dean of King's College London.

James D.G. Dunn is Emeritus Lightfoot Professor of Divinity, University of Durham.

Joel B. Green is Associate Dean for the Center for Advanced Theological Studies and Professor of New Testament Interpretation, Fuller Theological Seminary, Pasadena, CA.

Heidi J. Hornik is Professor of Italian Renaissance and Baroque Art History, Baylor University, Waco, TX.

Dennis R. MacDonald is John Wesley Professor of New Testament and Christian Origins, Claremont School of Theology, and Professor of New Testament, Claremont Graduate University, Claremont, CA.

Daniel Marguerat is Professor Emeritus of New Testament, University of Lausanne, Switzerland.

I. Howard Marshall is Professor Emeritus of New Testament, University of Aberdeen.

R. Barry Matlock is Lecturer in Biblical Studies, University of Tennessee at Chattanooga.

Mikeal C. Parsons is Kidd L. and Buna Hitchcock Macon Chair in Religion, Baylor University, Waco, TX.

Thomas E. Phillips is Professor of New Testament and Early Christian Studies, Point Loma Nazarene University, San Diego, CA.

Lloyd K. Pietersen is Senior Lecturer and Research Coordinator in New Testament Studies, University of Gloucestershire.

F. Scott Spencer is Professor of New Testament and Preaching, Baptist Theological Seminary at Richmond, VA.

Steve Walton is Senior Lecturer in Greek and New Testament Studies, and Director of Research, London School of Theology.

INTRODUCTION:
THE HONOUREE—LOVEDAY ALEXANDER

Lloyd K. Pietersen

The Reverend Canon Professor Loveday Alexander is Professor Emerita in Biblical Studies at the University of Sheffield. She came to the Department of Biblical Studies at Sheffield in 1986 having taken her first degree in classics in the Faculty of Literae Humaniores at Oxford and her DPhil in the Faculty of Theology there on the preface to Luke's Gospel. She has served on the Council of the Society of Biblical Literature, was previously Chair of the Social World of the New Testament Seminar at the British New Testament Conference and Secretary/Treasurer of the British New Testament Society for five years. She serves on the editorial boards of the *Journal of Biblical Literature*, the *Journal for the Study of the New Testament* and *New Testament Studies*. She was also an associate editor of *The Oxford Bible Commentary*. She was appointed as Canon Theologian at Chester Cathedral in 2003. Her background in Classics, her doctoral research on Luke's preface and her church commitment have informed her teaching and scholarship throughout her illustrious career.

Loveday's first article, derived from her thesis and anticipating her first monograph, was published in 1986. Prior to the publication of the monograph in 1993, a further article, an edited volume, a couple of chapters in edited volumes and several dictionary articles appeared, all of which demonstrated her interest not only in Luke–Acts and Graeco-Roman literature but also Paul.[1] However, it was the publication of *The Preface to Luke's Gospel*, in conjunction with the 1986 article, which set the trajectories for Loveday's subsequent work. As she herself states: 'My initial work on the Lukan preface set out two primary research trajectories: the question of Luke's social location, and the question of the literary classification of his work'.[2] A number of subsequent articles, primarily pursuing the second of these trajectories, were collected together in *Acts in its Ancient Literary Context*, published in 2005. Loveday's on-going research

---

1. See the detailed bibliography below.
2. *Acts in its Ancient Literary Context: A Classicist Looks at the Acts of the Apostles* (LNTS, 298; London/New York: T&T Clark International, 2005), p. 6.

continues to involve 'an open-ended process of learning to read Acts alongside a multiplicity of ancient readers, with a variety of reading competencies formed within distinct cultural locations'.[3] The fruit of this research is due to be published in 2012 as *Acts and the Ancient Reader: Genre, Paideia, and the Reading of Luke's Acts*.

1. *Personal Recollections*

I first met Loveday when I came to Sheffield initially to do a Graduate Diploma in Biblical Studies in 1992. I was immediately impressed by her evident interest in my own Christian journey and my expressed desire to do further study beyond the Diploma. Initially as a Diploma student and subsequently as a Masters student, I attended modules given by her on 'Images of Empire', 'The Corinthian Correspondence', 'Advanced New Testament Greek' and 'Christian Origins'. She proved to be a very able teacher as well as an excellent scholar. The range of modules taught by her demonstrates that she is by no means simply interested in Luke–Acts—the area of scholarship for which she is renowned. For example, her course on Corinthians was marked by a keen awareness of what was happening in what was then the newly emerging field of the use of social-scientific methods in New Testament scholarship.

It was my introduction to these methods by her that led to my own interest in sociological approaches, an interest I developed in my subsequent doctoral thesis. Indeed, Loveday's attention to methodological rigour meant that she insisted that I enrolled on the induction programme for doctoral students in sociology, so that I had an appropriate theoretical foundation for engaging in interdisciplinary work. Furthermore, during the course of my doctoral studies, she encouraged me to attend and present a paper at a professional gathering of sociologists of religion. As a biblical scholar it was a profoundly unnerving, yet necessary, experience to have one's tentative work in another discipline scrutinized by experts in that discipline![4] I remain very grateful to Loveday, as my supervisor, for pushing me outside my comfort zone. She also has an amazing ability to make one feel completely at ease in a supervision session whilst actually drawing out the best from one in a series of penetrating questions. Her dedication and expertise as a supervisor can readily be seen from the list of her successful doctoral students, many of whom have gone on to secure their own place in the academy.

3. Alexander, *Ancient Literary Context*, p. 20.
4. Later published as L.K. Pietersen, 'Despicable Deviants: Labelling Theory and the Polemic of the Pastorals', *Sociology of Religion* 58.4 (1997), pp. 343-52.

2. *Loveday the Teacher*

As stated above, I have first-hand experience of Loveday's abilities as a teacher. In this section I will simply mention two of her modules which I took. Her class on 1 Corinthians introduced undergraduates to a wide range of primary and secondary sources, and Loveday's extensive knowledge of Graeco-Roman literature was readily apparent in the range of comparative materials she encouraged her students to read. Furthermore, each class session combined detailed exegesis of the passage under discussion with insights drawn from the social sciences. The class reading list was extensive and every student who engaged with the material would have come away with a very good overall appreciation of scholarship on 1 Corinthians. This amount of detail was combined with Loveday's excellent ability as a teacher in class, meaning that each session was informative, lively and interactive. The handouts and detailed notes that I took then still inform my own lectures on 1 Corinthians today.

Loveday's class on 'Images of Empire' provided fascinating insight into various attitudes to the Roman Empire portrayed both in the biblical text and in contemporary Graeco-Roman literature. Fully informed by the edited volume published in 1991 with the same title, this class introduced students to the range of possible responses to imperial rule and highlighted various ambiguities. As such, it anticipated subsequent debates in the scholarly literature, as exemplified, for example, in the works of Richard Horsley,[5] Christopher Bryan,[6] Warren Carter[7] and Seyoon Kim.[8]

III. *Loveday the Research Supervisor*

The following is a list of Loveday's successful doctoral students (some were jointly supervised with the Urban Theological Unit based in Sheffield). The range of successful dissertations, and the fact that many have been published, indicate Loveday's ability to engage with scholarship across a wide spectrum of texts and methodologies.

---

5. E.g. *Galilee: History, Politics, People* (Valley Forge, PA: Trinity Press International, 1995), and *Jesus and Empire: The Kingdom of God and the New World Disorder* (Minneapolis: Fortress Press, 2003).

6. *Render to Caesar: Jesus, the Early Church, and the Roman Superpower* (Oxford: Oxford University Press, 2005).

7. E.g. *Matthew and the Margins: A Sociopolitical and Religious Reading* (Maryknoll, NY: Orbis Books, 2000), and *The Roman Empire and the New Testament: An Essential Guide* (Nashville: Abingdon Press, 2006).

8. *Christ and Caesar: The Gospel and the Roman Empire in the Writings of Paul and Luke* (Grand Rapids: Eerdmans, 2008).

1990

David Neale, 'Sinners in the Gospel of Luke: A Study in Religious Categorization'.

1991

Ian Wallis, 'Faith in Jesus in Early Christianity'.

1993

Clinton Cozier, 'Oral Dynamics in Select Synoptic Parables'.

Pandang Yamsat, 'The *Ekklesia* as Partnership: Paul and Threats to *Koinonia* in 1 Corinthians'.

1994

Philip Kern, 'Rhetoric, Scholarship and Galatians: Assessing an Approach to an Epistle'.

1995

Derek Newton, 'Food Offered to Idols in 1 Corinthians 8–10: A Study of Conflicting Viewpoints in the Setting of Religious Pluralism at Corinth'.

1996

Dachollom Datiri, 'Finances in the Pauline Churches'.

Todd Klutz, 'With Authority and Power: A Sociostylistic Investigation of Exorcism in Luke–Acts'.

Cheol-Won Yoon, 'Paul's Citizenship and Its Function in the Narratives of Acts'.

1997

Steve Walton, 'Paul in Acts and Epistles: The Miletus Speech and 1 Thessalonians as a Test Case'.

1998

Steve Hunt, 'John 6.1-21 as a Test Case for Johannine Dependence on the Synoptic Gospels'.

1999

Andy Reimer, 'Miracle-workers and Magicians in the Acts of the Apostles and in Philostratus' *Life of Apollonius of Tyana*'.

2000

Hong Bum Kim, 'Parity or Hierarchy? Patterns of Church Leadership in the Reformed Churches and in the New Testament'.

Peter Phillips, 'The Prologue of the Fourth Gospel: An Exploration into the Meaning of a Text'.

Lloyd Pietersen, 'Teaching, Tradition and Thaumaturgy: A Sociological Examination of the Polemic of the Pastorals'.

John Tipei, 'The Laying on of Hands in the New Testament'.

2001

Stephen Smyth, 'Supporting Teachers in Catholic Schools: Working for the Personal, Spiritual and Professional Support and Development of a Volunteer Group of Teachers in Catholic Schools in the East End of Glasgow'.

2002

Greg Camp, '"Woe to You, Hypocrites": Law and Leaders in the Gospel of Matthew'.

Nelson Estrada, 'From Followers to Leaders: The Apostles in the Ritual of Status Transformation in Acts 1-2'.

Simon Samuel, 'A Postcolonial Reading of Mark's Story of Jesus'.

James Smith, 'Marks of an Apostle: Context, Deconstruction, (Re)citation and Proclamation in Philippians'.

2003

David Havea, 'Paul's Kinship Status and Duties in 1 Corinthians: A Cross-cultural Exegetical Study'.

Robbie Waddell, 'The Faithful Witness of a Pneumatic Church: The Role of the Spirit in the Apocalypse of John'.

Ian Williams, 'Rural Anglicanism: Roles and Relationships in Collaborative Ministry'.

2004

Joseph Aldred, 'Respect: A Caribbean British Theology'.

Alessandra Fusi, 'The Oral/Literate Model: A Valid Approach for New Testament Studies?'

Joseph Gouverneur, 'The Third Wave: A Case Study of Romantic Narratives within Late Twentieth Century Charismatic Evangelicalism'.

V.J. Samkutty, 'The Samaritan Mission in Acts'.

Simon Topping, 'Che Guevara and Revolutionary Christianity in Latin America'.

2005

Stephen Heap, 'An Evaluation of New Labour from the Perspective of Ecumenical Social Thought'.

2006

Mark Blackwell, 'Pauline Slave Texts: A Comparative Analysis of Modern Biblical Scholarship with Antebellum Commentaries'.

Deborah Herring, 'Contextual Theology in Cyberspace'.

2007

Joe Fantin, 'The Lord of the Entire World: Lord Jesus, a Challenge to Lord Caesar?'

Andrew Goodhead, 'A Crown and a Cross: The Origins, Development and Decline of the Methodist Class Meeting in Eighteenth-Century England'.

Stuart Ware, 'Theology of the Incarcerated: Views from the Underside'.

2008

Simon Bell, 'Drawing on the End of Life: Art, Therapy, Spirituality and Palliative Care'.

Rafael Rodríguez, 'Structuring Early Christian Memory: Jesus in Tradition, Performance and Text'.

Paul Shackerley, 'The Church in the City: Partnership and Hospitality'.

2010

James Chun, 'The Spirituality of the Lucan Jesus: A Challenge to Korean Protestant Spirituality'.

William Lamb, 'Voices from the Margins: An Exploration of the Christian Exegesis of Late Antiquity with reference to the Catena in Marcum Attributed to Victor of Antioch'.

4. *The Publications of Loveday Alexander*

The following is a comprehensive list (excluding book reviews) of Loveday's academic publications.

a. *Monographs*
1993
The Preface to Luke's Gospel: Literary Convention and Social Context in Luke 1:1-4 and Acts 1:1 (SNTSMS, 78; Cambridge: Cambridge University Press).

2005
Acts in its Ancient Literary Context: A Classicist Looks at the Acts of the Apostles (LNTS, 298; London/New York: T&T Clark International).

2006
Acts (The People's Bible Commentary; Oxford: Bible Reading Fellowship).

b. *Edited Volumes*
1991
Images of Empire: The Roman Empire in Jewish, Christian and Greco-Roman Sources (JSOTSup, 122; Sheffield: JSOT Press).

c. *Articles*[9]
1986
'Luke's Preface in the Pattern of Greek Preface-Writing', *NovT* 28, pp. 48-74.

1989
'Hellenistic Letter-form and the Structure of Philippians', *JSNT* 37, pp. 87-101.

1990
'The Living Voice: Scepticism Towards the Written Word in Early Christian and in Greco-Roman Texts', in D.J.A.Clines, S.E. Fowl and S.E.Porter (eds.), *The Bible in Three Dimensions* (JSOTSup, 87; Sheffield: Sheffield Academic Press), pp. 221-47.

---

9. Articles collected together and republished in *Acts in its Ancient Literary Setting* are marked with an asterisk.

1992

'Sisters in Adversity: Retelling Martha's Story', in George J. Brooke (ed.), *Women in the Biblical Tradition* (Studies in Women and Religion, 31; New York: Edwin Mellen Press), pp. 167-86.

1993

*'Acts and Ancient Intellectual Biography', in Bruce W. Winter and Andrew D. Clarke (eds.), *The Book of Acts in its First Century Setting.* I. *Ancient Literary Setting* (Grand Rapids: Eerdmans), pp. 31-63.

1995

*'"In Journeyings Often": Voyaging in the Acts of the Apostles and in Greek Romance', in C.M. Tuckett (ed.), *Luke's Literary Achievement: Collected Essays* (JSNTSup, 116; Sheffield: Sheffield Academic Press), pp. 17-49.

*'Narrative Maps: Reflections on the Toponymy of Acts', in M. Daniel Carroll R., D.J.A. Clines and P.R. Davies (eds.), *The Bible in Human Society: Essays in Honour of John Rogerson* (JSOTSup, 200; Sheffield: Sheffield Academic Press), pp. 17-57.

'Paul and the Hellenistic Schools: The Evidence of Galen', in Troels Engberg-Pedersen (ed.), *Paul in His Hellenistic Context* (Minneapolis: Fortress/Edinburgh: T. & T. Clark), pp. 60-83.

'The Relevance of Greco-Roman Literature and Culture to New Testament Studies', in Joel B. Green (ed.), *Hearing the New Testament* (Grand Rapids: Eerdmans/Carlisle: Paternoster Press), pp. 109-26.

1996

*'The Preface to Acts and the Historians', Ben Witherington III (ed.), in *History, Literature and Society in the Book of Acts* (Cambridge: Cambridge University Press), pp. 73-103.

1997

'Ancient Book-Production and the Circulation of the Gospels', in Richard J. Bauckham (ed.), *The Gospels for All Christians: Rethinking the Gospel Audiences* (Grand Rapids: Eerdmans), pp. 71-111.

1998

'"Better to Marry than to Burn?": St. Paul and the Greek Novel', in Ron Hock (ed.), *Ancient Fiction and Early Christian Narrative* (SBLSymS; Atlanta: Scholars Press), pp. 235-56.

*'Fact, Fiction, and the Genre of Acts', *NTS* 44, pp. 380-99.

'Marathon or Jericho? Reading Acts in Dialogue with Biblical and Greek Historiography', in D.J.A. Clines and S.D. Mooore (eds.), *Auguries: The Jubilee Volume of the Sheffield Department of Biblical Studies* (JSOTSup, 269; Sheffield: Sheffield Academic Press), pp. 92-125.

1999

*'The Acts of the Apostles as an Apologetic Text', in Mark Edwards, Martin Goodman, Simon Price and Christoper Rowland (eds.), *Apologetics in the Roman Empire* (Oxford: Oxford University Press), pp. 15-44.

'Formal Elements and Genre: Which Greco-Roman Prologues Most Closely Parallel the Lukan Prologues?', in David P. Moessner (ed.), *Jesus and the Heritage of Israel* (Harrisburg, PA: Trinity Press International), pp. 9-26.

'L'intertextualité et la question des lecteurs. Réflexions sur l'usage de la Bible dans les Actes des Apôtres', in D. Marguerat and A. Curtis (eds.), *Bible et Intertextualité* (Geneva: Labor et Fides), pp. 201-14.

*'Reading Luke–Acts from Back to Front', in Jos Verheyden (ed.), *The Unity of Luke–Acts* (BETL, 142; Leuven: Peeters Press), pp. 419-46.

'What if Luke had never met Theophilus?', *BibInt* 8, pp. 161-70.

2001

'IPSE DIXIT: Citation of Authority in Paul and in the Jewish and Hellenistic Schools', in Troels Engberg-Pedersen (ed.), *Paul Beyond the Judaism–Hellenism Divide* (Louisville, KY: Westminster John Knox), pp. 103-27.

2002

'"Foolishness to the Greeks": Jews and Christians in the Public Life of the Empire', in G. Clark and T. Rajak (eds.), *Philosophy and Power in the Graeco-Roman World: Essays in Honour of Miriam T. Griffin* (Oxford: Oxford University Press), pp. 229-49.

2003

'Mapping Early Christianity: Acts and the Shape of Early Christianity', *Int* 57, pp. 163-73.

*'New Testament Narrative and Ancient Epic', in Emmanuelle Steffek and Yvan Bourquin (eds.), *Raconter, Interpreter, Annoncer: Parcours de Nouveau Testament. Mélanges offerts à Daniel Marguerat pour son 60e anniversaire* (Le Monde de la Bible, 47; Geneva: Labor et Fides), pp. 239-49.

2004

*'Septuaginta, Fachprosa, Imitatio: Albert Wifstrand and the Language of Luke–Acts', in Cilliers Breytenbach and Jens Schröter (eds.), *Die Apostelgeschichte und die hellenistische Geschichtsschreibung* (Festschrift Eckhard Plümacher; Leiden: Brill), pp. 1-26.

'"This is That": The Authority of Scripture in the Acts of the Apostles', *Princeton Seminary Bulletin* NS 25, pp. 189-204.

2005

'The Four among Pagans', in Markus N A. Bockmuehl and Donald A. Hagner (eds.), *The Written Gospel* (Cambridge: Cambridge University Press), pp. 222-37.

2006

'God's Frozen Word: Canonicity and the Dilemmas of Biblical Studies Today', *ExpTim* 117, pp. 237-42.

'The Pauline Itinerary and the Archive of Theophanes', in John Fotopoulos (ed.), *The New Testament and Early Christian Literature in the Greco-Roman Context: Studies in Honor of David E. Aune* (Leiden: Brill), pp. 151-65.

'What is a Gospel?', in Stephen C. Barton (ed.), *The Cambridge Companion to the Gospels* (Cambridge: Cambridge University Press), pp. 13-33.

2007

'The Image of the Oriental Monarch in the Third Book of Maccabees' (with Philip S. Alexander), in Tessa Rajak, Sarah Pearce, J. K. Aitken and Jennifer M. Dines (eds.), *Jewish Perspectives on Hellenistic Rulers* (Berkeley/Los Angeles: University of California Press), pp. 92-109.

2008

'Community and Canon: Reflections on the Ecclesiology of Acts', in Anatoly Alexeev, Christos Karakolis and Ulrich Luz (eds.), *Einheit der Kirche im Neuen Testament: dritte europäische orthodox-westliche Exegetenkonferenz in Sankt Petersburg, 24.-31. August 2005* (Tübingen: Mohr Siebeck), pp. 45-78.

'The Passions in Galen and the Novels of Chariton and Xenophon', in John T. Fitzgerald (ed.), *Passions and Moral Progress in Greco-Roman Thought* (New York/London: Routledge), pp. 175-97.

d. *Dictionary Articles, etc.*

1992

'Novels, Greek and Latin', in *ABD*, IV, pp. 1137-39.

'Rome, Early Christian Attitudes to', in *ABD*, V, pp. 835-39.

'Schools, Hellenistic', in *ABD*, V, pp. 1005-11.

1993

'Chronology of Paul', in Gerald F. Hawthorne, Ralph P. Martin and Daniel G. Reid (eds.), *Dictionary of Paul and the Letters* (Leicester: InterVarsity Press), pp. 115-23.

2001

'Acts', in John Barton and John Muddiman (eds.), *The Oxford Bible Commentary* (Oxford: Oxford University Press), pp. 1028-61.

5. *Conclusion*

I am honoured to be able to present this brief introduction to Loveday's work and interests. On behalf of all her doctoral students and colleagues I wish her well and look forward to many years of continuing scholarly contributions.

Part I

READING ACTS IN ITS ANCIENT CONTEXT

THE GENRE OF ACTS—REVISITED

Richard A. Burridge

The genre of the Acts of the Apostles is much disputed. When I was researching Gospel genre, Loveday Alexander became a friend and colleague, as another classicist working on the New Testament. When my doctoral thesis was published,[1] she was the first to debate and review it.[2] The implications of my book for her work on Acts became clear in SBL sessions discussing both my and Gregory Sterling's work,[3] in which we all participated.[4] I am delighted to return the compliment by applying my original methodology for the genre of the Gospels to Acts as part of this collection in Loveday Alexander's honour.

I. *The Genre of Acts and Genre Theory*

a. *Commentaries and the Genre of Luke–Acts*

The importance of this topic is demonstrated by comparing the two Hermeneia Acts commentaries: the introduction to the 1987 translation of Conzelmann discusses the genre of Acts not at all, debating instead

---

1. Richard A. Burridge, *What are the Gospels? A Comparison with Graeco-Roman Biography* (SNTSMS, 70; Cambridge University Press, 1992); revised and updated second edition: Grand Rapids: Eerdmans, 2004, from which all subsequent quotation and page references are taken.

2. Loveday C.A. Alexander, 'Ancient Biography and the Social Function of Luke–Acts', paper given at the British New Testament Conference, University of Exeter, 19 Sept 1992; later published in *EvQ* 66 (1994), pp. 73-76, and reprinted in *European Journal of Theology* 3 (1994), pp. 84-86.

3. Gregory E. Sterling, *Self-Definition: Josephos, Luke–Acts and Apologetic Historiography* (NovTSup, 64; Leiden: Brill, 1992); Gerald Downing compared my work with Sterling's in his review of both in *JTS* NS 44 (1993), pp. 238-40.

4. Twelfth International Meeting of the Society of Biblical Literature, Leuven, 7-10 August 1994; papers were also given by Richard Pervo, Hubert Cancik, Albrecht Dihle and Adela Yarbro Collins, with Collins' paper published as 'Genre and the Gospels', *JR* 75 (1995), pp. 239-46.

Luke's authorship and 'view of history'.[5] However, in his 2009 Hermeneia commentary, Pervo devotes a section to genre which begins, 'genre is one of the most hotly contested topics in the study of Acts'.[6] The interest in Luke as an historian is evident in traditional commentaries (e.g. Bruce or Haenchen),[7] yet books as recent as Barrett's ICC or as different as Malina and Pilch discuss only history in their introductions.[8] On the other hand, commentators as disparate as Jervell and Witherington do both include significant treatments of the genre of Acts in their introductions.[9]

Another regular feature in commentary introductions is the relationship of Acts to Luke's Gospel. Since Cadbury's work in 1927, both books are often referred together as Luke–Acts.[10] However, treating them as a single work in two volumes is problematic for genre. Although Aune recognized that the other three Gospels were a form of ancient biography, he concluded that 'Luke does not belong to a type of ancient biography for it belongs with Acts, and Acts cannot be forced into a biographical mold'.[11] It is odd to accept Matthew, Mark and John as biographies, but not Luke. However, it is not obvious how a single work can have two volumes in two different genres. This difficulty would be eased if Luke–Acts is not a single work, as some have argued.[12]

---

5. Hans Conzelmann, *Acts of the Apostles* (Hermeneia; Philadelphia: Fortress Press, 1987 [translated from the second German edition of 1972; first edition: Tübingen: Mohr 1963]), pp. xl-xlviii.

6. Richard I. Pervo, *Acts of the Apostles* (Hermeneia; Minneapolis: Fortress Press, 2009), p. 14; see also pp. 14-18.

7. See F.F. Bruce, *The Acts of the Apostles* (London: Tyndale, 1951), pp. 15-18; Ernst Haenchen, *The Acts of the Apostles* (Oxford: Blackwell, 1971) pp. 90-112.

8. C.K. Barrett, *A Critical and Exegetical Commentary on the Acts of the Apostles* (ICC; 2 vols.; Edinburgh: T. & T. Clark, 1994, 1998), II, pp. xxxiii-cxviii; Bruce J. Malina and John J. Pilch, *Social-Science Commentary on the Book of Acts* (Minneapolis: Fortress Press, 2008), pp. 6-8.

9. Jacob Jervell, *Die Apostelgeschichte* (KEK; Göttingen: Vandenhoeck & Ruprecht, 1998), pp. 76-79; Ben Witherington III, *The Acts of the Apostles: A Socio-Rhetorical Commentary* (Grand Rapids: Eerdmans, 1998), pp. 2-39.

10. Henry J. Cadbury, *The Making of Luke–Acts* (New York: Macmillan, 1927).

11. David E. Aune, *The New Testament in Its Literary Environment* (Philadelphia: Westminster Press, 1987), p. 77.

12. See, for example, Richard I. Pervo, 'Must Luke and Acts Belong to the Same Genre?', in *SBLSP* (1989), pp. 309-16; M.C. Parsons and R.I. Pervo, *Rethinking the Unity of Luke and Acts* (Minneapolis: Fortress Press, 1993); Patricia Walters, *The Assumed Authorial Unity of Luke and Acts: A Reassessment of the Evidence* (SNTSMS, 145; Cambridge: Cambridge University Press, 2009).

Conversely, if one maintains a close relationship between Luke and Acts, then a search begins for their common genre, in either biography or historiography, or in something altogether different.[13]

b. *Acts and Historiography*

Insisting that 'Acts cannot be forced into a biographical mold', Aune treats Luke–Acts as a 'general history', thereby forcing the Third Gospel into that mould![14] In treating Luke as a kind of ancient historian, Aune stands with such scholars as Hengel and Dibelius.[15] Luke's setting within ancient historiography has been so well documented by writers such as Hemer that Marguerat refers to Luke as 'the first Christian historian'.[16] Others have defined Luke's form of historiography more precisely, as in Sterling's 'apologetic historiography', Yamada's 'rhetorical history', or Balch's 'political history'.[17] Palmer considers the genre of Acts alone and argues against other genres in favour of 'historical monograph' following Polybius,[18] while Schmidt prefers 'the rather wide spectrum of "Hellenistic historiography"'.[19] Meanwhile, Mealand's computer study of Acts'

13.   For a helpful, full and up to date survey, see Thomas E. Phillips, 'The Genre of Acts: Moving Toward a Consensus?', *CBR* 4 (2006), pp. 365-96; for a more historical survey, see also Joseph B. Tyson, 'From History to Rhetoric and Back: Assessing New Trends in Acts Studies', in Todd Penner and Caroline Vander Stichele (eds.), *Contextualizing Acts: Lukan Narrative and Greco-Roman Discourse* (SBLSymS; Atlanta: Scholars Press, 2003), pp. 23-42.

14.   Aune, *New Testament*, pp. 77-115; see Burridge, *Gospels*, pp. 98-99, for further discussion of Aune's position regarding Luke.

15.   Martin Hengel, *Acts and the History of Earliest Christianity* (London: SCM Press, 1979); Martin Dibelius, *Studies in the Acts of the Apostles* (London: SCM Press, 1956); updated edition edited by K.C. Hanson, *The Book of Acts* (London: SCM Press, 2004).

16.   Colin J. Hemer, *The Book of Acts in the Setting of Hellenistic History* (WUNT, 49; Tübingen: Mohr Siebeck, 1989); Daniel Marguerat, *The First Christian Historian* (SNTSMS, 121; Cambridge: Cambridge University Press, 2002).

17.   Sterling, *Self-Definition*; K. Yamada, 'A Rhetorical History: The Literary Genre of the Acts of the Apostles', in S.E. Porter and T.H. Olbricht (eds.), *Rhetoric, Scripture and Theology* (JSNTSup, 131; Sheffield: Sheffield Academic Press, 1996); David L. Balch, 'ΜΕΤΑΒΟΛΗ ΠΟΛΙΤΕΙΩΝ—Jesus as Founder of the Church in Luke–Acts: Form and Function', in Penner and Vander Stichele (eds.), *Contextualizing Acts*, pp. 137-86.

18.   Darryl W. Palmer, 'Acts and the Ancient Historical Monograph', in Bruce W. Winter and Andrew D. Clarke (eds.), *The Book of Acts in Its Ancient Literary Setting* (Carlisle: Paternoster Press; Grand Rapids: Eerdmans, 1993), pp. 1-29.

19.   Daryl D. Schmidt, 'Rhetorical Influences and Genre: Luke's Preface and the Rhetoric of Hellenistic Historiography', in David P. Moessner (ed.), *Jesus and the*

style demonstrated its relationship to both Hellenistic history and the Septuagint.[20]

c. *Novel and Epic*

Noting that Luke the historian is often criticized for his lack of historicity, Pervo compared Acts to the ancient novel, since it was clearly written to entertain as much as to edify. However, his definition that 'the novel = material + manner + style + structure' is rather vague for identifying genre.[21] He treats Acts separately from the Gospel—and indeed, he describes the whole book as 'Luke's Story of Paul', even though Paul is not significant until half way through.[22] Elsewhere, Pervo argues for Luke and Acts as two monographs, where 'Acts is a sequel rather than a second volume'.[23] Recently, Pervo has returned to attack historiography by arguing that the amount of direct speech in Acts (calculated at 51%) is larger than that in historians (usually below 30%) but equivalent to what he calls 'fiction' (46–61%).[24] In a comparable search for similar material in a different direction, MacDonald notes various parallels between Acts and the Homeric poems.[25] While both Pervo and MacDonald draw interesting comparisons between Acts and other ancient literature, these are not sufficient to identify genre, so unsurprisingly neither has convinced the majority of New Testament scholars about their proposed solution.

d. *Ancient Biography*

The only serious alternative to historiography for Acts' genre is ancient biography. In two influential books, Talbert argued that Luke–Acts is

Heritage of Israel: Luke's Narrative Claim upon Israel's Legacy (Harrisburg: Trinity Press International, 1999), pp. 27-60 (59).

20. David L. Mealand, 'Style, Genre, and Authorship in Acts, the Septuagint, and Hellenistic Historians', *LLC* 14 (1999), pp. 479-506.

21. Richard I. Pervo, *Profit with Delight: The Literary Genre of the Acts of the Apostles* (Philadelphia: Fortress Press, 1987), p. 114.

22. Richard I. Pervo, *Luke's Story of Paul* (Minneapolis: Fortress Press, 1990).

23. Richard I. Pervo, 'Israel's Heritage and Claims upon the Genre(s) of Luke and Acts: The Problems of a History', in Moessner (ed.), *Jesus and the Heritage of Israel*, pp. 127-43.

24. Richard I. Pervo, 'Direct Speech in Acts and the Question of Genre', *JSNT* 28 (2006), pp. 285-307.

25. Dennis R. MacDonald, *Does the New Testament Imitate Homer? Four Cases from the Acts of the Apostles* (New Haven: Yale University Press, 2003); see also his 'Paul's Farewell to the Ephesian Elders and Hector's Farewell to Andromache: A Strategic Imitation of Homer's *Iliad*', in Penner and Vander Stichele (eds.), *Contextualizing Acts*, pp. 189-203.

a biographical narrative with the first volume detailing the founder's life, while Acts is an account of his successors.[26] Subsequently, Talbert continued to argue strongly for a biographical approach.[27] Encouraged by him, others, including Barr and Wentling, follow a similar path.[28] In his 1990 *Introduction*, Bruce notes that 'Luke develops his theme biographically: he records what might be called the Acts of Stephen and Philip, the Acts of Peter, and the Acts of Paul'.[29] Marshall's treatment considered both Aune and Talbert, concluding that 'the whole work demonstrates affinities both to historical monographs and to biographies, but it appears to represent a new type of work, of which it is the only example'.[30] Meanwhile, I concluded my doctoral work on the genre of the Gospels with a brief consideration of Acts as either a biographical account of the subject's followers (as in Talbert) or as a *bios* of the church, in the manner of Dicaearchus' Περὶ τοῦ τῆς Ἑλλάδος βίου, a suggestion Talbert described as 'a novel one'.[31] I discussed the subsequent debate between history and biography ten years later in the second edition.[32] Porter's consideration of the ethical issues in Acts argues that not only are the Gospels 'forms of ancient biography, but the book of Acts [is] as well'.[33]

26.   Charles H. Talbert, *Literary Patterns, Theological Themes, and the Genre of Luke–Acts* (SBLMS, 20; Missoula: Scholars Press, 1974); see also his *What Is a Gospel? The Genre of the Canonical Gospels* (Minneapolis: Fortress Press, 1977; London: SPCK, 1978).

27.   Charles H. Talbert, 'The Acts of the Apostles: Monograph or *Bios*?', in Ben Witherington III (ed.), *History, Literature, and Society in the Book of Acts* (Cambridge: Cambridge University Press, 1996), pp. 58-72; Charles H. Talbert and Perry L. Stepp, 'Succession in Mediterranean Antiquity, Part 1: The Lukan Milieu' and 'Part 2: Luke–Acts', both in *SBLSP* (1998), pp. 148-68 and 169-79.

28.   David L. Barr and Judith L. Wentling, 'The Conventions of Classical Biography and the Genre of Luke Acts: A Preliminary Study', in Charles H. Talbert (ed.), *Luke–Acts: New Perspectives from the Society of Biblical Literature Seminar* (New York: Crossroad, 1984), pp. 63-88.

29.   F.F. Bruce, *The Acts of the Apostles: The Greek Text with Introduction and Commentary* (Leicester: Inter-Varsity Press; Grand Rapids: Eerdmans, 3rd edn, 1990), pp. 22-34; quotations from pp. 28 and 30.

30.   I. Howard Marshall, 'Acts and the "Former Treatise"', in Winter and Clarke (eds.), *The Book of Acts in its Ancient Literary Setting*, pp. 162-83 (178-80).

31.   Burridge, *Gospels*, pp. 237-39; see Talbert, 'Acts', p. 64.

32.   Burridge, *Gospels*, pp. 275-79.

33.   Stanley E. Porter, 'The Genre of Acts and the Ethics of Discourse', in Thomas E. Phillips (ed.), *Acts and Ethics* (New Testament Monographs, 8; Sheffield: Sheffield Phoenix Press, 2005), p. 13.

e. *Loveday Alexander's Contribution*

With her classics background, Alexander compared Luke's preface with those in scientific treatises in her doctoral work.[34] She applied this interest in Luke's prefaces to the question of the genre of Acts, where she argued that 'if Luke is writing history, the preface conventions he chooses would locate his work on the fringes of the genre, precisely where historiography overlaps with the broader enterprises of Ionian *historia*'.[35] Her classical expertise is evidenced by the collection of her major articles, subtitled *A Classicist Looks at the Acts of the Apostles*.[36] Remarkably, in the classification of scholarship above, I could have included examples of Alexander's work in every section. In the course of preparing her Black's commentary on Acts,[37] she has produced many articles, which concern the relationship of the genre of Acts to classical biography,[38] ancient novels and fiction,[39] and to historiography in its various forms,[40] as well as many other topics too numerous to detail here. Phillips concludes that her writing 'has done more to challenge the prevailing association of Acts with historiography than have any of the existing counter-proposals for

34. Loveday C.A. Alexander, *The Preface to Luke's Gospel: Literary Convention and Social Context in Luke 1.1-4 and Acts 1.1* (SNTSMS, 78; Cambridge: Cambridge University Press, 1993).

35. Loveday C.A. Alexander, 'Formal Elements and Genre: Which Greco-Roman Prologues Most Closely Parallel the Lukan Prologues?', in Moessner (ed.), *Jesus and the Heritage of Israel*, pp. 9-26 (23).

36. Loveday C.A. Alexander, *Acts in its Ancient Literary Context: A Classicist Looks at the Acts of the Apostles* (LNTS, 298; London: T&T Clark International, 2005).

37. See the foretaste of it in her excellent and accessible commentary, *Acts* (People's Bible Commentary; Oxford: Bible Reading Fellowship, 2006).

38. Loveday C.A. Alexander, 'Acts and Ancient Intellectual Biography', in Winter and Clarke (eds.), *The Book of Acts in Its Ancient Literary Setting*, pp. 31-63; reprinted in Alexander, *Acts in its Ancient Literary Context*, pp. 43-68.

39. Loveday C.A. Alexander, '"In Journeyings Often": Voyaging in the Acts of the Apostles and in Greek Romance', in C.M. Tuckett (ed.), *Luke's Literary Achievement* (JSNTSup, 116; Sheffield: Sheffield Academic Press, 1995), pp. 380-99; reprinted in Alexander, *Ancient Literary Context*, pp. 69-96.

40. Loveday C.A. Alexander, 'The Preface to Acts and the Historians', in Witherington III (ed.), *History, Literature, and Society in the Book of Acts*, pp. 73-103, reprinted in Alexander, *Ancient Literary Context*, pp. 21-42; *eadem*, 'Fact, Fiction and the Genre of Acts', NTS 44 (1998), pp. 380-99, reprinted in Alexander, *Ancient Literary Context*, pp. 133-64; *eadem*, 'Formal Elements and Genre'; *eadem*, 'Marathon or Jericho? Reading Acts in Dialogue with Biblical and Greek Historiography', in D.J.A. Clines and Stephen D. Moore (eds.), *Auguries: The Jubilee Volume of the Sheffield Department of Biblical Studies* (JSOTSup, 269; Sheffield: Sheffield Academic Press, 1998), pp. 92-125.

the genre of Acts.'[41] However, since none of these have provided a definitive solution for Acts' genre, it seems appropriate to make this my contribution to this volume in her honour.

f. *Genre Theogy and Acts*

In my original research, I noted that most proposals for Gospel genre failed to understand both genre theory and how genres functioned in the ancient world.[42] Genres are identified through a range of generic features, both external (form) and internal (content) and works sharing a 'family resemblance' belong to the same genre. Works of different genres may share similar features at a higher level of *mode*, so that books may be 'tragic' without obeying the conventions of being in verse and with actors and a chorus required for the genre of tragedy. Equally, MacDonald's parallels with Homeric epic or Pervo's comparisons with ancient romance may be illuminating at the modal level, but cannot determine the genre of Acts.

This leaves the perennial debate between historiography and biography. Previously, I demonstrated that ancient genres are flexible, and may overlap shared features, especially at the boundaries with *genera proxima*, as with history and biography.[43] Length is also determinative, with works and genres affected by what can be fitted on a single scroll—literally a mono-graph. Such works, usually 10,000–25,000 words long, required a uniting focus, such as an historical monograph about an event (e.g. the Catilinarian conspiracy), a geographical or ethnographical monograph about a place or people, a biography about a person, or other works, such as dialogue, romance, novel, or treatise. With such neighbouring or overlapping genres, it is extremely difficult to determine genres: thus I concluded that 'the generic boundaries of historiography, monograph and βίοι could get blurred even within one work'.[44] Momigliano notes that 'it is impossible to try and enforce a rigid separation of biography from the monograph centred on one man.'[45] Only by considering all the features together, especially with analysis of the subject and focus, can we distinguish between, for example, when Tacitus is composing

41. Phillips, 'Genre', p. 383.
42. Burridge, *Gospels*, p. 24, pp. 25-52 (Chapter 2) and pp. 53-77 (Chapter 3) were attempts to remedy these deficiencies.
43. Burridge, *Gospels*, pp. 62-67.
44. Burridge, *Gospels*, p. 239, which discusses Cicero, *Ad. Fam.* V.12.2-4 regarding Catiline, and also Diodorus Siculus on Alexander.
45. A. Momigliano, *The Development of Greek Biography* (Cambridge, MA: Harvard University Press, 1971), p. 83.

historiography (*Annals*), geographical-ethnographical monograph (*Germania*), or biography (*Agricola*). Therefore, we need to analyse Acts against all these features to see if this approach can determine its genre.

II. *The Generic Features of Acts*

a. *Opening Features*

1. *Title*. Titles are a key initial indicator of genre, but often ancient titles are not necessarily original to the work, as with the Gospels and the New Testament.[46] While the description of 'Acts', πράξεις, reflects Aristotle's view of history, they are still 'human deeds' (*Rhet.* 1.1360a.35). Quintilian agrees that history is 'the narration of a deed done' (*gestae rei expositio*, *Inst.* 2.4.2). Unlike many Acts commentaries, Fitzmyer begins with 'Title', noting that '*Praxeis* was a term designating a specific Greek literary form'. Against Talbert and Pervo, Fitzmyer understands *praxeis* to indicate the genre of 'historical monograph', but 'a biographical concern is not excluded'.[47] Given that the Latin equivalent, *Res Gestae*, was usually linked to a particular person, such as Augustus, this title puts us squarely on the biography–historiography boundary.

2. *Opening Formulae/Prologue/Preface*. Given that titles are rarely original, the opening words often gave the first indication of an ancient work's genre, sometimes through a prologue or preface. Some ancient biographies had one of these, but often the first words were or included the subject's name; the Gospels also have this mixture of prefaces and the name of Jesus.[48] The opening words of Acts refer to 'what Jesus began to do and teach' (ὧν ἤρξατο ὁ Ἰησοῦς ποιεῖν τε καὶ διδάσκειν), giving us clear biographical indicators of both the subject's name and the reference to his deeds and words. While this refers to the 'first book', the Gospel, 'began' (ἤρξατο) suggests a continuation of Jesus' deeds and words in the second volume. Significantly, Acts also ends with Paul 'teaching about the Lord Jesus Christ', τὰ περὶ τοῦ κυρίου Ἰησοῦ Χριστοῦ, providing a verbal echo back to the end of Luke, 24.19. Equally, the preface to Acts, 1.1-2, refers us back to the original preface to the Gospel, intending to provide a 'narrative', διήγησιν, for the reader (Lk. 1.1-4). Once again, therefore, this opening feature indicates a narrative genre, like historiography, but with a strong biographical focus.

---

46. See Burridge, *Gospels*, pp. 108-109, 129, 156-57, 186-88, 215.

47. Joseph A. Fitzmyer, SJ, *The Acts of the Apostles: A New Translation with Introduction and Commentary* (AB, 31; New York: Doubleday, 1998), pp. 47-49.

48. See Burridge, *Gospels*, pp. 109, 129-30, 157-58, 188-89, 215-16.

b. *Subject*

1. *Analysis of Verbal Subjects.* Central to my original study of the genre of the Gospels was their subject, given the previous scholarly consensus that the Gospels were 'not really about Jesus'. Using linguistic and structuralist theories, I analysed the subjects of all of a text's verbs to build up a picture of the overall subject of the book in one of two main ways: the most accurate was manual analysis of the Greek or Latin text, looking at all the verbs, both in subordinate clauses as well as main clauses, including other forms such as infinitives and participles. By counting them all, one can ascertain the distribution of the different subjects of a work and discover whether any person or topic dominated the statistics.

This is very time consuming, and not really practical for larger works, such as Homer, Herodotus or Thucydides. However, with such authors, through the Oxford University Computing Service, I undertook pioneering work using cumbersome mainframes to analyse early computer tapes of the *Thesaurus Linguae Graecae*. Making use of the inflected nature of Latin and Greek, searches were made for the frequency of proper names, revealing how often a character was mentioned, with appearances in the nominative case denoting that the person was the subject of a verb. While this doctoral research took place in the mid-1980s, I repeated the exercise on a desktop in the early 1990s for publication.[49] Now, of course, such analysis can be easily checked, even on a mobile telephone!

This research showed that in most narrative literature, especially larger works, there is a wide range of subjects. Thus in the *Iliad*, the most frequent names are Hector and Achilles, together with Zeus. However, each only occur in 4–5% of the sentences, and are the subject in the nominative of 2.0–2.4%. Similar results were obtained from prose works like Herodotus' *Histories*. However, Homer's focus on one main character skewed the analysis of the *Odyssey*, with Odysseus appearing in 8.8% of the sentences and as the subject in the nominative in 4.8%, twice as often as anyone else. This, however, is dwarfed by computer analysis of biographical works such as Plutarch's *Parallel Lives*, which revealed that the eponymous subject of each *Life* is named in 30–50% of all sentences, and is the subject in the nominative of about 10%, while other key characters are named in about 10%, and the subject of only 2–3%.

Such computer analysis by proper names and nominatives is a blunt instrument. Accurate counting of them all by hand picks up frequencies missed by the computer, such as where the subject is not named, but contained within the verb, or is the subject of constructions such as participles, genitive-absolutes or accusative-infinitives. In addition, many

---

49. See Burridge, *Gospels*, pp. 110-112 for an account of this method.

ancient narrative genres use speeches and quotations; ancient *Lives* displayed the great deeds and words of their subjects, so the verbs contained in speeches placed on the subject's lips also had to be counted. Thus manual analysis of Satyrus' *Life of Euripides* noted that Euripides was the subject of 25.8% of the verbs, while a further 17.5% occurred in quotations from his plays. Similarly, Lucian's account of Demonax made him the subject of 33.6%, with his sayings and teachings accounting for another 19.7%. This demonstrated that around half the verbs in ancient biographies were given to the deeds and words of their subject, a concentration not seen in other genres, and particularly useful for distinguishing *bioi* from neighbouring genres, such as historical monograph where many different subjects would share the limelight.[50]

Similar manual analysis of the canonical Gospels discovered the same verbal concentrations within their structure. Thus Mark had Jesus as the subject of 24.4% of the verbs, with another 20.2% given to Jesus' teachings, saying and parables—a similar result to that of Satyrus. Matthew, Luke and John, like Lucian, devoted just over a half to Jesus' deeds and words: Matthew's and Luke's use of the double teaching tradition ('Q') occupied 42.5% and 36.8% of their verbs, with Jesus himself as the subject of 17.2% and 17.9% respectively. The results for John were in between Mark and Matthew/Luke, with Jesus as the subject of 20.2% and 34% in his teaching and discourses.[51] These statistical results, so close to those found in *bioi*, became a key argument that the Gospels were written in the genre of ancient biography.

In my original conclusions in 1992, computer analysis of Acts revealed that God appeared in 17% of the sentences, with Paul named in 14.5%, Jesus in 7% and Peter in 6%.[52] In the revised edition of 2004, I noted that Steve Walton used my method of computer analysis to argue that the main actor in Acts was actually God himself.[53] Walton argued that various factors, including verbs of divine action, the focus of the speeches and the development of the mission in Acts led to the conclusion that 'God is the key actor'.[54] Using a computer to look for subjects in the nominative case, Walton revealed 65 occurrences of θεός, 6.7% of all nominatives in Acts;

---

50. See Burridge, *Gospels*, pp. 130-31, 158-59 for discussion, and pp. 308-17 (Appendix I) for statistical pie charts and full results.

51. See Burridge, *Gospels*, pp. 189-191, 216-17 for discussion, and pp. 318-21 for statistical pie charts.

52. Burridge, *Gospels*, p. 238.

53. See Burridge, *Gospels*, p. 279; this was later published by Steve Walton, 'The Acts—of God? What is the "Acts of the Apostles" All About?', *EvQ* 80 (2008), pp. 291-306.

54. Walton, 'The Acts—of God?', p. 303.

only Paul came close with 63 occurrences, 6.5%, with others lagging behind, such as Peter on 3.8%, 'Lord' on 2.5%, brother on 2.7%, Spirit on 2.3% and everyone else having 1% or less. If Walton is correct, this raises questions about the genre of Acts: is it perhaps a 'biography of God'?! However, he does note that 'a full analysis would require examining each of the clauses of Acts by hand, as Burridge does for the canonical Gospels. Hence the results below should be regarded as preliminary, pending further detailed examination of Acts.'[55]

Therefore, I have undertaken that examination for this article. In analysing by hand all the verbs in Acts, I have followed the methods I used originally to get the best comparison with my results for the Gospels. As with the Gospels, I have noted all the occurrences when any person or group of people are the subject of a verb. I have also counted all the verbs placed upon anyone's lips in speeches, including the letter about the Apostolic Decree (Acts 15.23-29) and the letter of Claudius Lysias the tribune to the governor Felix (Acts 23.26-30).

What has emerged from this analysis is rather striking. Unsurprisingly, Paul scores more than anyone else, being the subject of 11.4% of the verbs and speaking a further 11.2%, giving him almost a quarter of the total. The second highest is 'the disciples' as a group, whose score of 18% includes all the named individuals other than the apostles, plural subjects such as 'Peter and John', 'Paul and Barnabas', as well as the general 'the disciples', 'the brethren' and simply 'they', referring to disciples. The only other significant individuals are Peter (3.7%, plus 6.8% for his speeches), Stephen (0.5% plus 4.6% for his speech, Acts 7.2-53) and James (0.1%, plus 0.5% for his speech, Acts 15.13-21, and a further 0.5% for the Apostolic Decree, Acts 15.23-29).

For Walton's claim that God is the 'key actor', God's score of 0.7% is disappointing. Together with Jesus (1.2%), 'the Lord' (0.6%) and the Spirit (0.5%), the Trinity still only makes up a total of 3% all together. Further analysis of every instance of θεός in the nominative may explain the contrast between Walton's results and mine: the vast majority occur in the speeches of Peter, Stephen and Paul, rather than being subjects of the narrative; here, therefore, they count as the words of Peter, Stephen and Paul. Furthermore, most of the other occurrences are in indirect speech, as Paul and others relate 'all that God had done' (Acts 14.27; 15.4, 12; 21.29). Three other instances relate to visions, the voice from heaven to Peter (10.15), or the Macedonian inviting Paul to Europe (16.10), and Paul's vision in the ship that God has granted them safety (27.24).

---

55. Walton, 'The Acts—of God?', p. 293.

Table 1. Acts: Analysis of Verb Subjects

Acts chapters	1	2	3	4	5	6	7	8	9	10	11	12	13	14	15	16	17	18	19	20	21	22	23	24	25	26	27	28	Totals	%	Group %
Jesus	21																4	2	1										43	1.15	2.90
The Lord	3	1				2	4					3	3	1		2		3							2				22	0.59	
God	1			7	5					2	1								1		1	1	1				1		26	0.70	
Holy Spirit	1	2						4	4				2					1	2								1		17	0.46	
Disciples	30	24	2	39	30	9		19	55	41	34	13	39	35	42	54	19	12	15	34	58						26	17	647	17.38	57.05
Peter	2	7	9	2	5			2	20	51	6	30																	136	3.65	
Peter's Speeches	25	68	47	15						35	49				14														253	6.80	
Stephen						6	11																						17	0.46	
Stephen's Speech							170																						170	4.57	
Philip								22																					22	0.59	
Paul							1	5	56				7	11	6	17	17	45	26	41	48	14	23	6	34	17	19	30	423	11.36	
Paul's Speech													77	11			39			58		83		36		77		35	416	11.17	
James															2														2	0.05	
James' Speech															20														20	0.54	
Decree letter																18													18	0.48	
Minor characters	1			22	33	1		48	5	20		33	18	10		42	1	23	22		21	21	36	15	50	11	49	15	499	13.40	14.91
Minor speech & letter																			37				19						56	1.50	
Jewish Leaders				31	34	17	10		4				10	12			20				16	1	36	4	18			6	226	6.07	6.50
Jewish Speech																								16					16	0.43	
Indefinite	1	26	6	9	36	5	2	19	11	6	2	7	1	9	13	6	11	7	25	1	8	14	6	2	9	2	28	14	286	7.68	18.64
Impersonal	1	1	2	3	3	1				8	3	1	2	2	2	3	1	1	4	1	4	2	2		3	1	7	2	61	1.64	
Miscellaneous	6	12	3	13	19	6	1	22	13	19	11	27	15	3	3	39	16	4	22	5	15		24	2	2	2	31	11	347	9.32	
TOTALS	92	141	91	121	165	47	199	142	183	181	104	113	174	96	124	165	128	105	155	140	172	135	149	82	118	110	161	130	3723	100.00	100.00
Verses	26	47	26	37	42	15	60	40	43	48	30	25	52	28	41	40	34	28	41	38	40	30	35	27	27	32	44	31	1007		

The sole occurrence of θεός in the nominative as the subject of actual narrative is Acts 19.11: 'God did extraordinary miracles through Paul'.

Walton goes on to discuss God as the 'focus of attention in the speeches', concluding that 'there is thus a consistent pattern that God is the focus of the speeches' and 'God is the central subject in speech after speech'.[56] However, this does not mean that God is the subject of the book itself. In fact, God is the subject of the main narrative only once, in 'the exception that proves the rule' of Acts 19.11. Overall, the Godhead accounts for only 3% of Acts' verbs. Thus Luke, as author, does *not* depict God doing things as the 'key actor'; rather, he depicts his key actors, namely Peter, Stephen, Paul and the other disciples, *interpreting* what is happening as the activity of God.

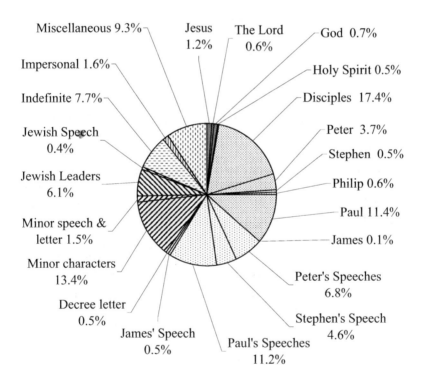

Table 2. *Pie Chart of Verb Subjects in Acts*

56. Walton, 'Acts–of God?', pp. 296-99.

Finally, what is most striking is how much the results resemble my original study of Luke's Gospel.[57] First, there is a remarkable coincidence of frequencies for the three categories of impersonal verbs (1.6% in Acts, cf. 1.7% in Luke), indefinite subjects such as 'they', 'the crowd' and so on (7.7% in Acts, cf. 7.3% in Luke), and miscellaneous subjects (9.3% in Acts, cf. 9.1% in Luke). These categories are an unconscious result of a writer's style, and the close relationship of these scores between Acts and Luke might be a further indicator that these books do share the same author, especially since the scores for these three categories in Matthew, Mark and John are quite different.[58] The Jewish leaders score 6.1% plus 0.4% for Tertullus' speech (Acts 24.2-8), compared with 3.4% in Luke's Gospel, reflecting their larger role as opponents throughout Acts. Other minor characters' deeds and words, including the speeches of Demetrius and the town clerk of Ephesus (Acts 19.25-27, 35-40) and the letter of Claudius Lysias (Acts 23.26-30), account for 14.9% of the total of Acts, compared with 14.4% devoted in the Gospel to other subjects including those who received ministry from Jesus.

Most important, however, is what this analysis reveals about the main subject of the book of Acts. My previous research demonstrated how ancient biography was dominated by the deeds and words of the main character, so that Jesus is the subject of 17.9% of the verbs in Luke, with a further 36.8% given to his teachings and sayings, totalling 54.7% for his deeds and words. Acts is not an account of a single person, but it is concerned with the deeds and words of a particular group of people, namely the early disciples with their leaders, especially Peter and Paul. If we add the totals for the activities of the disciples and named apostles together with the totals of their speeches, we find that *just over 57% of the verbs of Acts are devoted to the deeds and words of the first Christians.* Since this is a group subject, rather than an individual, it indicates that the genre of Acts is more like a monograph than a biography. Yet the similarity between the total of Jesus' deeds and words, and those of his early followers, could also suggest that Acts is a biography of the early church or the first Christians. If the Gospel is what Jesus 'began to do and teach' (Acts 1.1), then Acts is what he *continues* 'to do and teach', through his disciples.

---

57. Compare the pie chart for Luke in Burridge, *Gospels*, p. 320, with that for Acts here in Fig. 1.

58. Compare their pie charts in Burridge, *Gospels*, pp. 318, 319, 321.

2. *Allocation of Space.* If verbal analysis reveals the overall subject, analysis of the allocation of space clarifies how this subject is treated— whether all aspects or periods are given equal attention, or whether one particular element dominates. Thus the extensive allocation of space in the Gospels to Jesus' last days, arrest, trial, passion and death was often cited as a reason why they were not biographies, especially given modern biography's tendency to treat all periods equally. However, I demonstrated that the allocation of space within Graeco-Roman biography was rarely even-handed: early years were passed over briefly en route to the public debut, while particular periods (revealing the subject's virtues or his major speech) would receive disproportionate attention. Thus the two years of Agesilaus' Persian campaign occupied 37.4% of Xenophon's account, while the battle of Mons Graupius takes up 26.1% of Tacitus' *Agricola*, including the speeches of Calgacus, the native leader, and Agricola himself. Much greater space was devoted to the hero's final days, especially if any trial was involved, leading to a detailed account of their death and the aftermath: thus Plutarch gives 17.3% to Cato's last supper, death and honours in the *Cato Minor*, while Philostratus uses over 26% to describe Apollonius of Tyana's imprisonment, trial before the emperor, death, honours and even appearances to his disciples![59]

In this light, the Gospels' accounts of Jesus do not seem dissimilar. They also either ignore the birth and early years (Mark and John) or have a brief account (Matthew and Luke) before beginning the main narrative with Jesus' baptism. All four concentrate on Jesus' last supper, trial, passion, death and resurrection: Matthew 15.1%, Mark 19.1%, Luke 15.6%, while John devotes 17.6% to the last supper and final discourse of Jesus plus 15.7% to the trial, death and resurrection, making 33.3% in total. In between his public debut and his death, the material can be arranged topically, oscillating between narrative and discourse, as in Matthew, or geographically, as in Luke's account of ministry in Galilee (Lk. 4.14–9.50), journeying down the Jordan to Jerusalem (9.51–19.27), and final events there (19.28–24.53).

Most Acts commentaries begin with an analysis of its structure, noting the summary statements at the end of each part, often giving a geographical indicator: thus 6.7 concludes the Jerusalem section, 9.31 references Judaea, Galilee and Samaria, and 19.21 points towards Macedonia and Achaea, leading Paul eventually to Rome; 12.24 and 16.5 note how the word of God was growing and the churches strengthened. Using these summaries gives the following allocation of space:

---

59. See Burridge, *Gospels*, pp. 112-13, 131-33, 159-63.

References	Topic and key actors	Verses	%
1.1–6.7	Early church in Jerusalem: Peter, John	185	18.4
6.8–9.31	Judaea and Samaria: Stephen, Philip, Paul	139	13.8
9.32–12.24	'Acts of Peter' take the gospel to Gentiles	114	11.3
12.25–16.5	Paul's missionary journeys in Asia	127	12.6
16.9–19.20	Paul's missionary journeys in Greece	117	11.6
19.21–28.31	Paul's return to Jerusalem, trials, to Rome	325	32.3

This immediately demonstrates Luke's choices about what to include in how much space, choices that are determined both *geographically* and *biographically*. Presumably, he had more material about what happened in Jerusalem after the early years, or other places such as Syria, and about what other people did. Given the geographical pattern in the Gospel from Galilee down Jordan to Jerusalem, the programmatic statement of Acts 1.8, 'you shall be my witnesses in Jerusalem and in all Judaea and Samaria and to the end of the earth', reveals that Acts' geographical movement from Jerusalem across the ancient Mediterranean to Rome is similarly deliberate—and makes another connection to the Third Gospel.

Acts also reflects Luke's biographical interest, but, as the verbal analysis demonstrated, provides the deeds and words of several early Christian leaders, rather than one character as in the Gospel. However, the focus on Peter in the first half and on Paul through the second half does compare to Luke's treatment of Jesus in the Gospel. Equally, the large concentration of 32.3% of Acts to Paul's final journey, including his trials, is not unlike that found in ancient biographies, and is extremely close to John's allocation of 33% to Jesus' final hours, trial, death and resurrection. In both cases, to devote a third of the space available to the final journey or trial of the subject is a clear indicator of biographical genre.

I have allocated a disproportionate amount of space to analysis of the verbs and the allocation of space since these are two major generic indicators which might suggest that Acts has a different genre from the Gospels. I now turn to consider the other generic features used as indicators in my previous study. They are divided into *external features* revealing the form, construction and appearance of the text, and *internal features* describing its content.[60] These features are not confined to biography, but apply across most ancient genres. However, my previous study noted how the general profile from these features was shared by both ancient biography and the Gospels, and was related to other neighbouring genres, such as monograph. We might therefore expect a similar pattern to emerge for Acts.

60. See Burridge, *Gospels*, p. 107.

c. *External Features*

1. *Mode of Representation.* This refers to whether a work is for oral or written presentation, whether it is in prose or verse, narrative, dialogue or drama, how continuous it is, or whether it was all in one voice. Ancient biography was usually in continuous prose narrative, in the third person and containing speeches, sayings or other reported material. While some describe the Gospels in dramatic terms, such as tragedy, this is more modal than genre, since they are not written in verse for actors. Like ancient *Lives*, they are also in continuous prose narrative, in the third person with sayings and discourses.[61] The same is true for Acts' mode of representation, which is continuous prose narrative throughout. The first person appears in the singular in the dedication to Theophilus (Acts 1.1) and in the plural in 'we-passages' such as Acts 16.10-17, but this can happen similarly in both biography and historiography. Like these genres and the Gospels, Acts contains direct speeches through which the story is advanced and meaning elucidated. So, this is a link to the Gospels, as well as to several possible genres.

2. *Size and Length.* Aristotle says that 'having a certain size', τι μέγεθος, is an indicator of genre (*Poetics* 6.1450b.25). Previously, I noted that length could be categorized in broad terms as long, medium or short. Medium length is what could be written in a single scroll: scrolls tend to be 8–12 inches high and 30–35 feet long and contain between 10,000 and 25,000 words, depending on the size of handwriting and layout. Significantly, a scroll contained what could be read out aloud to an audience at a single sitting. Major genres, such as historiography, epic, philosophy, could run into hundreds of thousands of words requiring several scrolls—hence their divisions into 'books'. Shorter length works below 10,000 words, such as poems, hymns, epigrams, idylls, tragedies and comedies, would be grouped into one scroll. Medium-length works tended to be in the genres of monograph, romance, or dialogue. Most notably, ancient *Lives* also were of this length.[62]

The Gospels also display this range: Mark contains 11,242 words, Matthew and Luke are similar at 18,305 and 19,428 words respectively, and John has 15,416 words. Acts, which contains 18,382 words, is very similar in length to Matthew and Luke. Significantly, the rest of the New Testament books are shorter: Revelation is next longest (9,834), while even the longest epistles, Romans, 1 and 2 Corinthians (7,105, 6,811 and

---

61. See Burridge, *Gospels*, pp. 113, 134, 163-64, 193, 218 for full analysis.
62. See Burridge, *Gospels*, pp. 114-15, 134-35, 164-65 for full analysis.

4,469 words respectively) are considerably shorter, with the others ranging between 1,000 and 2,000 words.[63] Thus Acts, like the Gospels, could be written on its own scroll and performed in one sitting, unlike the rest of the New Testament, which would have been gathered into collections of several books in one scroll.

3. *Structure.* This concerns how a work is organized: thus drama consists of various scenes with choral odes interposed, while rhetorical genres follow a conventional sequence. Material may be organized chronologically, topically or geographically, and the flow may be continuous or disjointed. While structure does not determine genre, works of the same genre tend to exhibit similar structures. As noted above, ancient biographies did not treat their subject's life in equally balanced sections. After a brief account of origins, birth or a childhood story, the narrative quickly moves to the public debut, and ends with an extended treatment of the final period of the person's life, death and aftermath. In between, material can be organized chronologically, for example, for statesmen or generals such as Evagoras, Cato or Agricola; however, lives of philosophers, poets and teachers such as Euripides or Demonax are more thematically or topically arranged. The Gospels similarly begin with Jesus' arrival on the public scene and end with his arrest, trial, passion, death and resurrection. In between, they are structured with sequences of stories, anecdotes, teachings and discourses. There is a geographical progression towards Jerusalem, most clearly in Luke, while both Matthew and John oscillate between narrative and discourse.[64]

Acts' overall structure begins with the church coming to public notice through Jesus' ascension and the coming of the Spirit at Pentecost, and ends with Paul in Rome, awaiting trial but preaching the Gospel 'unhindered' (Acts 28.31). In between, it was noted above how Acts has a geographical structure with journeys moving away from Jerusalem which balances the Gospel's move towards Jerusalem. The narrative is structured through episodes, containing both action and speeches, which reflect upon the spread of the Gospel through the deeds and words of the first Christian leaders, particularly Peter and Paul. In this respect, Acts is similar to many single-scroll works, especially historical monograph and biography.

---

63. Statistics are taken from Robert Morgenthaler, *Statistik des neutestamentlichen Wortschatzes* (Zurich: Gotthelf, 1958), Table 3, p. 164; see also Burridge, *Gospels*, pp. 194, 219.

64. See Burridge, *Gospels*, pp. 115, 135-36, 165-66, 194-96, 219-20 for full analysis.

4. *Scale.* This concerns how broad a canvas the author uses: wide-ranging, as in historiography, or narrowly focussed on a single topic, as in monograph, or person, as in biography. Attention is required to what is omitted as well as included. The concentration upon the deeds and words of a single person noted in the analysis above gives most biographies a relatively narrow scale. Even with notable republicans such as Cato, or Atticus, other civil war leaders, such as Caesar or Pompey, appear only in passing. Significantly, works with a larger scale, such as the role of Britain in the *Agricola*, or the travels of Apollonius of Tyana, are seen as on the fringes of biography, bordering on history, travelogue or ethnography. The Gospels are on a narrow scale, focussing on Jesus' deeds and words, leading to his death.[65]

Acts is obviously written on a broader canvas, as the narrative follows the deeds and words of different leaders, notably Peter and Paul. The geographical scale is wider as it covers the eastern ancient Mediterranean. However, considering what is omitted makes us realize that the scale is still limited. The controversies over taking the gospel to the Gentiles which dominate Paul's letters are only alluded to in the Council of Jerusalem and decree (Acts 15). Equally, while client kings, governors, clerks and military officers appear, the narrative is not set in the context of the wider scale of what was happening in the eastern Roman empire at the time. So, while Acts is on a larger scale than the Gospels, it is still limited, being closer to biography and monograph than to historiography, such as Herodotus or Thucydides.

5. *Literary Units.* Texts comprise various literary units, such as prologues, speeches, dialogues, anecdotes, maxims, proverbs, catalogues, stories, songs, descriptions and so on, either carefully interwoven or loosely strung together. Many units appear in various genres, but examples of the same genre often exhibit similar literary units. Ancient biographies use anecdotes, sayings, stories, speeches, discourses, personal or geographical description and particularly accounts of people's last days or death. While most are carefully constructed from such units into a coherent narrative, as in *Lives* by Plutarch or Tacitus, others, such as Lucian's *Demonax*, are more loosely connected. The Gospels contain similar literary units, giving rise to Form Criticism, identifying different forms such as apophthegms, sayings, stories, anecdotes, parables and speeches—but these are all common to ancient biographies. While Mark's units may be more loosely connected, the other evangelists, such

---

65. See Burridge, *Gospels*, pp. 116, 137, 166-67, 196, 220 for full analysis.

as Luke, have moulded their units into the narrative very carefully.[66] Exactly the same is found in Luke's second volume, where similar units—anecdotes, stories, speeches, sermons, dialogues, descriptions—are connected into a well-constructed narrative. Furthermore, parallel stories, events or speeches happening to Peter, Stephen and Paul, as with Jesus, makes another generic link between Acts and Luke's Gospel.

6. *Use of Sources*. Ancient writers used a wide variety of written and oral sources for their works. As with other generic features, sources cannot determine genre, but works of the same genre utilize comparable sources similarly: thus epic poems use oral formulae, while the sources found in historiography are quite different. Writers of ancient biographies drew upon a wide variety of oral traditions and written sources, but notably they use and select their sources for their chosen portrait, omitting what is embarrassing or unhelpful: thus Isocrates glosses over Evagoras' ignominious death at his own people's hands at the end lest it weaken his encomium! Equally, Plutarch uses the same sources to describe the same events differently in different *Lives* to depict each particular character as he wishes.[67]

Luke's preface mentions both written accounts, διήγησιν, and oral eye witnesses, αὐτόπται, used for his 'orderly account', καθεξῆς...γράψαι (Lk. 1.1-4). The literary relationships between the Synoptic Gospels and 'Q', and questions about possible sources and editions behind John, are issues too complex to debate here, but what they reveal is how the evangelists are creative artists, using oral and written sources to paint their particular portrait of Jesus' deeds and words.[68] Equally, Luke makes a similar selection of sources for his account in Acts of the deeds and words of the first Christian leaders. The 'we-sections' in the first person plural throughout the second half suggest either the author's personal experience accompanying Paul, or use of an eye-witness account. On the other hand, others have noted potential sources from Homer to romance for the sea-voyage and shipwreck in Acts 27. Whatever conclusions one may come to, the use of sources in Acts appears to be consonant with that in ancient biographies, monographs and in the Gospels.

---

66. See Burridge, *Gospels*, pp. 116, 137-38, 167-68, 196, 220-21 for full analysis.
67. C.B.R. Pelling, 'Plutarch's Method of Work in the Roman Lives', *JHS* 99 (1979), pp. 74-96; *idem*, 'Plutarch's Adaptation of his Source Material', *JHS* 100 (1980), pp. 127-40; *idem*, 'Truth and Fiction in Plutarch's Lives', in *Antonine Literature* (Oxford: Oxford University Press, 1990), pp. 19-52.
68. See Burridge, *Gospels*, pp. 116, 138-39, 168-70, 198-99, 221-22 for full analysis.

7. Methods of Characterization. The absence of direct analysis or psychological assessment was another supposed contrast between the Gospels and biography. While such techniques may be found in modern biography, ancient *Lives*—and Graeco-Roman literature generally—employed more indirect methods. Instead of direct analysis, the ancients built up portraits through depiction of a person's deeds and words, and this was very true in *bioi*. As Halliwell notes, Isocrates is typical in relying 'primarily on descriptive and narrative means of characterization'.[69] Thus Plutarch distinguishes between history, ἱστορία, and *bioi*, in that while history is concerned for famous actions and great events, such as sieges and battles, *bioi* are more interested in people's character as revealed by 'little things', πρᾶγμα βραχύ, such as a phrase or jest (*Alexander* 1.1-3). My previous study demonstrated that the evangelists' methods in building up the character of Jesus are very similar.[70] Luke makes this concern for the subject's deeds and words explicit in Acts 1.1, 'all that Jesus began to do and to teach', thus implying that this will continue throughout Acts. I have already noted this combination of stories and speeches in the analysis of verb subjects. Furthermore, the main characters, including Peter and Paul, are gradually portrayed through the wider narrative, including 'little things', like Peter not realizing that his release by an angel was actually real (Acts 12.9) or Paul being bitten by a snake (28.3-6). On the basis of Plutarch's distinction between history and biography in *Alexander* 1.1-3, Acts inclines towards the latter in this generic indicator.

Thus, regarding most external generic features, Acts appears very closely linked to both ancient biographies and the Gospels in its mode of representation, size, structure, literary units, use of sources and methods of characterization. Its scale is larger than that of the Gospels and ancient *bioi*, but even here it is still more limited than in true historiography. Therefore, this study of external generic features indicates that Acts is in the same area as ancient biography and monograph, and it only remains to examine its internal features.

d. *Internal Features*
1. *Setting.* Some settings indicate genre (such as fields for pastoral, or battles for epic), but many genres combine various geographical or historical settings, as well as dramatic settings regarding who is centre stage or what action takes place. The geographical settings found within

69. Stephen Halliwell, 'Traditional Greek Conceptions of Character', in C.B.R. Pelling (ed.), *Characterization and Individuality in Greek Literature* (Oxford: Oxford University Press, 1990), pp. 32-59 (58).
70. See Burridge, *Gospels*, pp. 117, 139-40, 170-72, 199, 222-23 for full analysis.

ancient biographies vary enormously, but are determined by their dramatic setting with the focus always upon their subject. Equally, while the Gospels' settings move around Galilee and end up in Jerusalem, we move there by following Jesus at the centre of the action, to whom others come for dialogue or ministry.[71] Exactly the same is found in Acts, where we move to various geographical settings between Jerusalem and Rome, because the narrative follows the early Christian leaders going there. On the few occasions when they are not centre stage, or are outside, others discuss what to do about them (Acts 4.16-17; 5.21-26, 35-39; 19.23-40; 23.12-15; 25.13-22; cf. similar passages especially in John's Gospel). This feature is thus comparable to both ancient *bioi* and to the Gospels.

2. *Topics.* Certain topics recur in some genres, such as the abandoned infant in New Comedy or the excluded lover in *paraclausithyron*. However, many *topoi* appear in various genres, but usually examples of a genre include the same mixture of motifs, confirming generic assignation. Ancient *bioi* usually contain some standard biographical topics, such as ancestry or birth, but move swiftly to the public debut, which together with the *topos* of his death provides the framework for his great deeds and words. The Gospels also contain a similar mix of topics.[72] Like Mark and John, Acts contains no ancestry or birth stories, but the Ascension and Pentecost are like a birth and public debut rolled into one, as the infant church comes into being and public notice at the same moment (Acts 1–2). Thereafter, the usual mixture of great deeds and words exemplifying the subjects' virtues are all seen in the stories of the early leaders, especially Peter and Paul. Admittedly, there is no narrative of a death or its consequences, but we do have various tests and trials. Thus Acts includes many *topoi* found in ancient biography and monographs.

3. *Style.* Style is roughly characterized as high, middle or low, and can be subjective. It, too, varies in genres, but plays its part in determining genre. Many ancient biographies tended towards a more literary style, but my study demonstrated that stylistic variety was possible, including the more popular, as in Satyrus and Lucian. The Koiné Greek used in the Synoptic Gospels and the mixture of Hellenism and Aramaisms in the

---

71. See Burridge, *Gospels*, pp. 117-18, 140-41, 172-73, 200, 223-24 for full analysis.

72. See Burridge, *Gospels*, pp. 118, 141-42, 173-75, 200-202, 224-25 for full analysis.

Fourth Gospel also reflect this more popular style.[73] The style and language of Acts has often been commentated upon: Bruce notes how the author varies his style between the more Semitic opening chapters in Jerusalem with Aramaisms, and the more Attic, literary style used by Paul in Athens or in his defence before Felix (Acts 17.21ff.; 24.10-21), while Witherington analyses his use of rhetoric.[74] Thus style not only links Acts to the Third Gospel, but also to the genres of biography, monograph and historiography.

4. *Atmosphere.* My previous study used this feature for aspects such as tone, mood, attitude and values. Again, while these vary within and between works, examples of the same genre breathe a similar atmosphere. Ancient *bioi* tended to be respectful and serious, especially in their attitude towards the subject, although some, such as Lucian and Satyrus, could be lighter. The Gospels also shared the generally respectful and serious atmosphere, which awe could even make worshipful.[75] This is also true of the tone, mood, attitude and values of Acts, both in its respect for the early church leaders such as Peter and Paul, as well as for how they interpret everything as the activity of God. Thus, the atmosphere of Acts is reminiscent of that found in *bioi*.

5. *Quality of Characterization.* If characterization's method is an external feature, the resulting quality of characterization of the subject belongs with the internal features. I noted previously the importance of not using modern concepts of character, personality development and change as understood in our post-Freudian world.[76] The portraits of people's deeds and words in ancient biography could often appear typical, even stereotypical, such as the strategic general (Agesilaus, Agricola), shrewd financier (Nepos) or brilliant speaker (Demonax, Apollonius), even if a more real 'feel' sometimes emerged through anecdotes. The similar tension between the real and stereotype in the Gospels' portrayals of Jesus is another indicator of shared genre with ancient *bioi*.[77] The same is true of the narrative of Acts: some aspects of Peter and Paul can appear typical,

---

73. See Burridge, *Gospels*, pp. 119, 142-43, 175-76, 203-204, 226 for full analysis.

74. Bruce, *Acts* (1951), pp. 26-29; Witherington, *Acts*, pp. 39-46.

75. See Burridge, *Gospels*, pp. 119, 143-44, 176-77, 204, 226-27 for full analysis.

76. See the essays appearing in Pelling (ed.), *Characterization and Individuality in Greek Literature*, for discussion across many Greek genres, especially Christopher Gill, 'The Character–Personality Distinction', pp. 1-31. See also Gill's 'The Question of Character-Development: Plutarch and Tacitus', *CQ* 33 (1983), pp. 469-87.

77. See Burridge, *Gospels*, pp. 120-21, 144, 177-79, 205, 227 for full analysis.

as in the debate about how Luke's portrait of Paul compares with the human writer of the letters. Yet some of the others, especially minor characters, such as the Ethiopian eunuch, the Philippian jailer, or the Ephesian town clerk, all seem at home in ancient biography.

6. *Social Setting and Occasion*. Some ancient texts reveal their function and original production, such as tragedy and comedy within Athenian festivals. Often, we have to find internal clues for a work's social setting or occasion. While most ancient *Lives* were written within literary, political elites, there are also hints of wider and more popular audiences, especially in authors like Lucian or Philostratus. The various settings and occasions suggested for the Gospels indicate that there is not sufficient internal evidence to locate them in space, time or society, but a general setting within the urban middle class with some education from a mixed Jewish-Hellenistic background seems likely, and this places the Gospels among ancient *bioi*.[78] Suggestions about the original setting and occasion for Acts range from being the brief for Paul's defending counsel at his trial to debates about the legality of the new religion, the delay of the Parousia or controversy around Paul's mission to the Gentiles.[79] Once again, the only sensible conclusion to draw from this variety is that Acts does not reveal its specific setting and occasion; however, generally it belongs with the Gospels, in the wider group of ancient biography and monograph.

7. *Authorial Intention and Purpose*. The author's purpose is essential to some genres, such as encomium, while others have a range of purposes; however, similar works of the same genre exhibit similar purposes. I have demonstrated this for ancient *Lives*, displaying various purposes, including encomiastic, to praise the subject (*Evagoras* 8; 11; *Agricola* 3.3), and

78. See Burridge, *Gospels*, pp. 121, 145, 179-80, 205-207, 228-29; see also *idem*, 'About People, by People, for People: Gospel Genre and Audiences', in Richard Bauckham (ed.), *The Gospels for All Christians: Rethinking the Gospel Audiences* (Grand Rapids: Eerdmans, 1998), pp. 113-45; and also *idem*, 'Who Writes, Why and for Whom?', in D.A. Hagner and M. Bockmuehl (eds.), *The Written Gospel* (Cambridge: Cambridge University Press, 2005), pp. 99-115.

79. See, for example, A.J. Matill, Jr, 'The Purpose of Acts: Schneckenburger Reconsidered', in W. Ward Gasque and R.P. Martin (eds.), *Apostolic History and the Gospel* (Exeter: Paternoster Press, 1970), pp. 108-22; see also his 'The Jesus–Paul Parallels and the Purpose of Luke–Acts', *NovT* 17 (1975), pp. 15-46. See further Robert Maddox, *The Purpose of Luke–Acts* (Göttingen: Vandenhoeck & Ruprecht, 1982); and W.W. Gasque, *A History of the Criticism of the Acts of the Apostles* (Tübingen: Mohr, 1975).

exemplary, to provide examples to become better people (*Evagoras* 73-81; *Agesilaus* 10.2; Plutarch, *Cato Minor* 24.1; 37.5). Other *bioi* were intended to be informative or to entertain (Satyrus and Lucian), and to preserve the memory of the subject (Philo, *Moses* 2.292; *Agricola* 46.3; *Demonax* 2; 67), often with elements of didactic, apologetic or polemic (*Agricola* 42.4; *Apollonius of Tyana* 1.3). As with these *bioi*, we cannot restrict the Gospels to a single purpose, or one authorial intention. However, they contain a similar range of purposes, to praise Jesus, to provide an exemplar to follow and imitate, to inform the reader about him, as well as to pass on his great deeds and words in a didactic manner designed both to defend his life and ministry as well as to attack misunderstandings of him.[80]

Once again, this is true of Acts. As just noted, the possible occasions for Acts suggest that the author's intention cannot be restricted to a single purpose. Yet Luke's concentration, as demonstrated in the verbal analysis, on the early church in general and its leaders, in particular Peter and Paul, means that he includes elements of encomium in providing the apostles as examples for Christians to imitate in following Jesus, as well as basic information about how the early church began, grew and developed, with didactic, apologetic and polemic about its leaders and their relationships with each other, with the Jewish hierarchy and Roman officials. Last but not least, Luke's literary ability to write in an entertaining and interesting way is clearly demonstrated in the voyage and shipwreck in Acts 27.

Thus, as with its external generic features, so also in its internal features Acts is closely related both to ancient biographies and to the Gospels, especially in its setting and range of topics, as well as its varied style, respectful atmosphere and the quality of its leading characters. The possible social settings and occasions proposed, together with its range of different purposes, all fit within those expected and indicative of ancient biography and monograph.

III. *Conclusion*

My previous work argued that the Gospels share a similar profile of generic features and indicators with a wide range of ancient biographies, and differed from this no more than the *bioi* did from one another. Applying the same criteria to the Acts of the Apostles has also produced a similar profile, demonstrating that Acts shares similar generic indicators

---

80. See Burridge, *Gospels*, pp. 121-22, 145-47, 180-83, 208-10, 229-31 for full analysis.

from its opening features as well as its external and internal features with those found in ancient medium-length prose works, such as monograph and ancient biography. Previously, I demonstrated that 'the borders between the genres of historiography, monograph and biography are blurred and flexible',[81] and the present study of Acts has borne that out.

The work differs from ancient biography in its title, 'Acts', and in its wider range of subjects revealed by verbal analysis, its allocation of space and broader focus and scale. However, these features are still not as broad or wide-ranging as found in ancient historiography proper, but remain tightly focussed upon the early church and its leaders, especially Peter and Paul. Not only are Luke's Gospel and the Acts of the Apostles closely related works, but their genres are also close within the sphere of single-scroll works, with Luke as a form of ancient biography and Acts a form of monograph. Where biography and history overlap in monographs, it is extremely difficult to distinguish them, but previously features such as verbal analysis enabled us to do that, especially with Tacitus' *Agricola*. It is notable that, like the Gospels, the opening words of Acts include the name of Jesus, normally a clear indicator of biography, along with the reference to his deeds and words. Biographical features and indicators recur through the concentration upon such people as Peter and Paul, with the result that over half of the verbs are taken up with the deeds and words of the first Christians, exactly comparable to how Jesus' deeds and words dominate the Gospels.

Unlike the Gospel of Luke, Acts is not a biography of one person, although it could be interpreted as a biography of the early church, in the manner of Dicaearchus' biographical work on Greece, Περὶ τοῦ τῆς Ἑλλάδος βίου. Acts' generic features are also very close to historical monograph, but without the wider focus, scale and variety of verbal subjects found in historiography. Its concentration upon early church leaders, especially Peter and Paul, suggests that it is best described as a 'biographical monograph'. If Luke's first volume (Τὸν μὲν πρῶτον λόγον) is all about 'what Jesus *began* to do and teach' in his life and ministry (ὧν ἤρξατο ὁ Ἰησοῦς ποιεῖν τε καὶ διδάσκειν), then the second part is what Jesus *continues* 'to do and teach' through the deeds and words of Peter, Paul and the early church.

---

81. Burridge, *Gospels*, p. 237.

Why Did Mary Wrap the Newborn Jesus in 'Swaddling Clothes'? Luke 2.7 and 2.12 in the Context of Luke–Acts and First-Century Literature

Thomas E. Phillips

While preaching on Mars Hill in Athens, the Paul of Acts quoted a line ('for we too are his offspring') from an unnamed poet whom the speech identified as 'one of your own poets' (17.28). This direct appeal to a piece of non-LXX Greek literature is unusual. Neither the Paul of Acts nor the Paul of the undisputed letters offers any other direct citation of non-biblical Greek literature. The uniqueness of the citation has placed this reference in the center of inquiries about Paul's and Luke's familiarity with—and possible mastery of—the Greek literary tradition. On one level, the issue is largely settled. The cited line was originally penned by Aratus, a fourth-century BCE Stoic, although it probably made its way into Acts from Aristobulus, a second-century BCE Jewish writer.[1] However, on another level, the issue remains quite unsettled. Does the poetic reference reflect an authentic memory of Pauline preaching to non-Jews, or is the poetic reference attributable to Lukan redaction alone? While we can have only limited confidence in the various attempts to extricate an authentic Pauline voice from this specific speech—or similar attempts to segregate authentic Pauline thoughts from their Lukan redaction elsewhere in Acts—I want to suppose for the moment that the reference could have come from Luke.[2] And I want to suggest that there is one other (often overlooked) example where Luke also makes a pretty direct

---

1. See Mark J. Edwards, 'Quoting Aratus: Acts 17,28', *ZNW* 83 (1992), pp. 266-69. Also see Michel Gourges, 'La Literatura Profana en el Discourse de Atenas (He 17,16-31): ¿Expedient Cerrado?', *Anámnesis* 13.2 (2003), pp. 15-45.

2. For my own preliminary comparison of the extent of Paul's education and Greco-Roman enculturation in Acts and in Paul's letters, see Thomas E. Phillips, *Paul, His Letters, and Acts* (LPS; Peabody, MA: Hendrickson, 2009), pp. 84-87, 107-11, 122-24.

appeal to non-biblical Greek literary traditions. That example is the 'sign' of Jesus' swaddling clothes in Luke's birth narrative.

Probably no biblical tradition is better known than the Lukan tradition of the newly born Jesus being wrapped in 'swaddling clothes' (σπαργα-νόω, Lk. 2.7, 12). Critical scholars of the nineteenth and early twentieth centuries commonly interpreted Mary's swaddling of the baby Jesus either as indicating the holy family's impoverished condition[3] or as foreshadowing Jesus' body being wrapped in cloth after his crucifixion.[4] Such interpretations are now largely abandoned in favor of reading the swaddling clothes as a simple expression of the culturally appropriate parental care for a newborn in the ancient world.[5] Indeed, such a reading is well supported by references to the swaddling of infants in a wide array of other ancient writings (Ezek. 16.4; Wis. 7.4-5; Plato, *Leg.* 7.5; Euripides, *Tro.* 759; Dio Chryostom, *Tyr.* 16; Strabo, *Geogr.* 3.4.17; Galen, *De loc. aff.* 7.27; Philo, *Aet.* 12; Plutarch, *Mor.* 2.3.638; *Quaest. Conv.* 2.3; *Cat. Maj.* 20.2; *Lyc.* 16.3—the latter of which even finds it unusual that Spartans do not swaddle their children).[6]

While the Lukan reference to swaddling is consistent with typical parent care in the ancient world, the angel's announcement in the story is significant: καὶ τοῦτο ὑμῖν τὸ σημεῖον, εὑρήσετε βρέφος ἐσταργανωμένον καὶ κείμενον ἐν φάτνῃ ('and this is the sign to you, you will find a newborn swaddled and lying in a manger', 2.12). By explicitly referring to Jesus' attire and the place of his repose as a 'sign' (σημεῖον, 2.12), Luke seems to be inviting the reader to reflect more deeply upon the significance of these two data. Ironically, even though the reference to Jesus' swaddling clothes precedes the reference to the manger, recent scholarship has

---

3. E.g. M. Baily, 'The Shepherds and the Sign of a Child', *ITQ* 31 (1964), pp. 1-23 (4-7); M.F. Sadler, *The Gospel According to St. Luke* (New York: James Pott, 1890), p. 46; and F.W. Farrar, *The Gospel According to St Luke* (Cambridge: Cambridge University Press, 1910), p. 66.

4. E.g. E. LaVerdiere, 'Wrapped in Swaddling Clothes', *Emmanuel* 90 (1984), pp. 542-46. From antiquity, see Clement of Alexandria, *Paed.* 1.6.

5. E.g. Raymond E. Brown, *The Birth of the Messiah* (Anchor Bible Reference Library; New York: Doubleday, updated edn, 1993), pp. 418-19; Joseph A. Fitzmyer, *The Gospel According to Luke I–X* (AB, 28; New York: Doubleday, 2nd edn, 1981), p. 408; John Nolland, *Luke 1–9:20* (WBC, 35a; Dallas: Word, 1989), I, p. 105; and Michael Wolter, *Das Lukas-Evangelium* (HKNT; Tübingen: Mohr Siebeck, 2008), p. 125.

6. For a detailed description of the process of, and the supposed benefits from, swaddling, see Soranus's late first-century medical textbook on pre-natal, natal and post-natal care of mothers and infants (*Gyn.* 2.14-19, 31-42). Soranus has more references to swaddling than any other ancient writer.

focused almost exclusively upon the place of Jesus' birth, and not upon his attire, as the indicated sign. For example, J. Duncan M. Derrett's musings are typical of New Testament scholarship. He inquired: 'The Manger is quite obviously (and indeed explicitly) a ṣiymān, a symbol, a catchword—but a symbol of what?'[7] For Derrett, the significance of the swaddling clothes simply drops out of consideration as he leaps directly to an inquiry about the symbolic significance of the manger. However, I want to avoid what I regard as Derrett's premature disregard of the swaddling clothes as the intended Lukan sign.

If the reader were intended to reflect upon the child's swaddling clothes as a sign, then the question should arise: Of what were they a sign? The word σπαργανόω had a long history of symbolic use by the time that Luke wrote in late first or early second century. At a most basic level, the word was commonly used to refer to the time of one's infancy or early childhood, with a meaning very comparable to the contemporary English expression 'from the cradle' (Aeschylus, *Cho.* l. 529; *Ag.* 1606; Sophocles, *Oed. Tyr.* 1035; Longinus, *Subl.* 44.3; Plutarch, *Alex. fort.* 2.5; Longus, *Daphn.* 2.1). Such use is particularly common in Luke's near contemporary Philo (*Sacr.* 4.15; *Ebr.* 13.51; *Somn.* 2.2; *Abr.* 2.2; *Mos.* 1.15; *Leg.* 1.57, 60; 2.63; 4.11, 28; *Prob.* 16; *Legat.* 26).[8] However, in this investigation, I want to move beyond this most basic level of symbolic meaning. I want to explore a set of frequently overlooked symbolic uses of swaddling clothes in ancient narrative, drama, and poetry. Specifically, I want to suggest three ideas. First, the Lukan reference to Jesus being wrapped in 'swaddling clothes' may stand within a rich literary tradition surrounding the family life of the gods. Second, when Luke's reference is read against this ancient literary background, it likely draws upon this tradition to highlight Jesus' divine origin. Third, this reference to the sign of the swaddling clothes may help to establish Luke's familiarity with—and Luke's willingness to draw upon—broader non-biblical Greek literary traditions.

---

7. J. Duncan M. Derrett, 'The Manger at Bethlehem: Light on St. Luke's Technique from Contemporary Jewish Religious Law', in his *Studies in the New Testament* (2 vols.; Leiden: Brill, 1978), II, pp. 39-47 (47). Also see Baily, 'The Shepherds and the Sign of a Child', and J. Duncan M. Derrett, 'The Manger: Ritual Law and Soteriology', in his *Studies in the New Testament*, II, pp. 48-53. This tradition of emphasizing the manger at the expense of the swaddling clothes extends back at least as far as Origen (*Cels.* 1.51).

8. Plutarch reported that the young Mithridates was struck by lightning which burned away his swaddling clothes without hurting the child, an apparent metaphor for Zeus's decision to have Mithridates leave childhood behind at an early age (*Quaest. Conv.* 1.6.2).

I. *Symbolic Swaddling in Pre-First-Century Greek Literature*

The word σπαργανόω does not appear frequently in extant pre-first-century Greek literature. In fact, just two documents, Euripides' *Ion* and the Homeric *Hymn to Hermes*, account for nearly one fourth of all extant occurrences of the word before the first century.[9] Each document uses the term six times (*Hymn to Hermes* 151, 237, 268, 301, 306, 388; *Ion* 32, 918, 955, 1351, 1490, 1598). The references within these texts are important for two reasons. First, no other extant pre-first-century text uses this term as frequently as do these two well-known texts. Second, the references to swaddling clothes in each of these texts help a divine son to establish his place within the divine family.

We begin with Euripides, the author of the most widely read and performed plays in the Greek world, and his play, *Ion*.[10] When Ion, the lead character, initially enters the play, he is completely unaware of his divine identity as the son of Apollo and grandson of Zeus. The play is set during Ion's late teen years as he discovers his divine origin. The central conflict of the play revolves around Ion's discovery of his divine identity, an identity which the reader knows from the play's preface where Hermes, the play's narrator, explained that Ion was Apollo's 'own son' (69, cf. 78).[11]

9. According to the *TLG*, σπαργανόω occurs 51 times in pre-first-century Greek texts. Eight of these occurrences appear in Euripides (6 in *Ion*) and six of these occurrences appear in the *Hymn to Hermes*.

10. *Ion* is widely available in English translation. Some of the most important translations are by David Kovacs, 'Ion', in *Euripides* (LCL; Cambridge, MA: Harvard University Press, 1999); Ronald Frederick Willetts, 'Ion', in *Eurpides* (Complete Greek Tragedies, 3; Chicago: University of Chicago Press, 1992); and Anne Pippen Burnett, *Ion* (Greek Drama Series; Englewood Cliffs, NJ: Prentice-Hall, 1970). Unless otherwise stated, the Burnett translation is quoted here. For a brief introduction to Euripides' work, see Ian C. Story and Arlene Allan, *A Guide to Ancient Greek Drama* (Malden, MA: Blackwell, 2005), pp. 131-51.

11. The play sometimes refers to Apollo by his alternative names, Phoebus and Loxias, but each of these names refers to the same god. See W.K.C. Guthrie, *The Greeks and Their Gods* (Boston: Beacon, 1950), pp. 73-87, and Burnett, *Ion*, pp. 22 n. 5, 26 n. 37. On Euripides' attitude toward the gods in general, see G.M.A. Grube, 'Euripides and the Gods', in Erich Segal (ed.), *Euripides* (Englewood Cliffs, NJ: Prentice-Hall, 1968), pp. 34-50, and Jon D. Mikalson, 'The Tragedians and Popular Religion', in *Greek Drama* (Bloom's Period Studies; Philadelphia: Chelsea House Publishers, 2004), pp. 277-87.

Ion was born after Apollo raped Ion's mother, Creusa.[12] In her desperation, Creusa exposed the child and left him facing the prospect of death (15-18). Ion undoubtedly would have died except for the immediate intervention of Hermes, Apollo's brother. At Apollo's request, Hermes picked up the exposed child (βρέφος) in his swaddling clothes (σπαργανόω) and delivered him to Apollo's temple where a priestess retrieved the child and raised him as a temple servant (30-56). The child's ignorance of his divine nature is central to the play's plot, and so Hermes reminds the audience that 'to this day the boy himself is ignorant of his line' (50-51).

After Ion's birth, Creusa married Xuthus, the king of Athens. After seventeen years of childless marriage, the seemingly childless mother and her teenage son were brought back together. Initially, the mother and her son met without becoming aware of their relatedness (82-509). In contrast, however, Xuthus sought out Ion because he honestly, but mistakenly, believed that Ion was his son through Xuthus's pre-marital escapade with one of the Bacchae at a long-ago feast (550-55). Xuthus then revealed his paternal claims to Ion and was able to convince Ion that Xuthus was in fact Ion's father (558-60). When Creusa learned of her husband's newfound 'son', she grew increasingly remorseful over what she mistakenly believed to be the death of the son whom she exposed while he was still wearing his swaddling clothes [918, 955].[13] Eventually, Creusa's grief became mixed with an overwhelming fear about her future status in a household where her husband had (mistakenly) recognized a

---

12.   On the rape of Creusa and the role of sexual violence in this play, see J.H. Kim On Chong-Gossard, *Gender and Communication in Euripides' Plays: Between Song and Silence* (Boston: Brill, 2008), pp. 49-50; Charles Segal, 'Euripides' Ion: Generational Passage and Civic Myth', in Mark W. Padilla (ed.), *Rites of Passage in Ancient Greece: Literature, Religion, Society* (Lewisburg: Bucknell University Press, 1999), pp. 42-66, 74-77; and Katherina Zacharia, *Converging Truths: Euripides' Ion and the Athenian Quest for Self Definition* (Boston: Brill, 2003), pp. 82-83.

13.   Euripides portrays Creusa's exposure of the infant as an act of love. She exposed the child because she 'thought the god would save his son' (965). She expected Apollo to intervene and spare the child the shame of being raised by an unwed mother. Not even Ion blames Creusa for exposing the child. Ion refers to his own exposure as a 'brave and terrible act' (1496). Apparently, women often exposed their children with the expectation that the child would be raised by another family. Many of these children were eventually reintegrated back into their biological families. Such pseudo-exposures (that is, exposure as a form of giving up a child for temporary adoption) were apparently common in antiquity. See Lynn H. Cohick, *Women in the World of the Earliest Christians* (Grand Rapids: Baker Academic, 2009), pp. 37-43.

son by another woman. As a result of these fears, Creusa and an accomplice created a plot to poison Ion (1028-38). The plot's failure and the discovery of her role within the attempted assassination forced Creusa to seek sanctuary from Ion's vengeance in the temple of Apollo (1250-70).

The confrontation between Creusa and Ion in the temple serves as the setting for the story's climax, as the couple learned that they were mother and son. The symbol of swaddling clothes plays a crucial role at this climatic point in the drama. As Ion was trying to extricate Creusa from the safety of the temple's altar, the goddess Pythia appeared with the cradle from which the infant Ion had been retrieved years earlier (1320-40). Pythia explained that Apollo had given her that cradle and the swaddling clothes within it for safe keeping after Ion was delivered to Apollo's temple (1350-53). Creusa immediately recognized the cradle and the swaddling clothes as those which belonged to her exposed child. She therefore quickly realized that Ion was her own son, the son whom she conceived with Apollo and subsequently exposed (1396-400). In light of Pythia's revelation of Ion's swaddling clothes, Creusa rediscovered her long-lost maternal sentiments toward Ion and began trying to convince Ion that she was his mother. However, her maternal claims were met with Ion's open scorn. Not surprisingly, Ion—who was at that moment seeking lethal vengeance upon Creusa—demanded proof of her maternal claims. Creusa, who had woven the swaddling clothes with her own hands, provided this proof by describing the swaddling clothes in detail while Ion held them out of her sight (1417-38). This demonstration convinced Ion that Creusa was indeed his mother ('Mother!', 1437), but Ion, even after accepting Creusa's maternal claims, remained reluctant to accept her claims that he was 'Apollo's secret son!' (1487). Ion stubbornly, but understandably, viewed Creusa's claims of his divine origin as too grandiose to be true and he made no effort to hide his disbelief. He quipped back, 'Oh lovely, welcome words, if they be true!' (1488).

In response to Ion's disbelief, Creusa again explained the entire story of how she had swaddled him as an infant and left him for others to raise (1488-96). Creusa continued insisting: 'Your father was no mortal man! It was the god, the very one who brought you up—Apollo Loxias!' (1530-31). Ion was, she insisted, 'Apollo's son' (1534). Joyous over discovering his mother, but reluctant to accept her claims about his divine origin, Ion mused, 'My heart is confounded, mother, in this uncertainty' (1538-39). Ion's uncertainty about his father's identity was finally overcome by yet another theophany, when the goddess Athena confirmed Creusa's story. Athena assured Ion that 'Apollo was your sire!' and that 'Phoebus fathered you' (1560, 1568). The swaddling clothes are mentioned for the sixth and final time as the goddess Athena again recounted the stories of

Ion's exposure in the swaddling clothes and of Apollo's maneuver to secure Ion's future by placing him in the custody of his own temple (1598-600). With his identity as Creusa's son confirmed by the evidence of the swaddling clothes, and with his identity as Apollo's son confirmed by two theophanies, Ion accepted his identity and proclaimed, 'I am sprung from Loxias and this queen!' (1608).

The six occurrences of σπαργανόω in Euripides' *Ion* play a central role in establishing Ion's divine origin and identity.[14] This alone would be suggestive as a background text against which to read the Lukan sign of the swaddling clothes. But Ion does not stand alone in employing swaddling clothes to confirm the assertion of one's place within the divine family.

The Homeric *Hymn to Hermes* recounts Hermes's extraordinary adventures on the night and first day after his 'glorious birth' (59), while he was still a 'newborn' (νεογνός, 406), 'new child' (παῖδα νέον, 271, 331) and 'infant child' (τέκνος νήπιον, 151-52, 163-64).[15] Within 24 hours of his birth, Hermes both invented the lyre and, more importantly for our purposes, stole a herd of cattle from his brother, Apollo.[16] After stealing Apollo's entire herd and single-handedly slaughtering two of the cattle,

14. Pindar's *Odes* recounts the story of Jason the Argonaut with a plot that roughly parallels Ion's story. Jason was exposed as a swaddled infant (*Pyth.* 4.114), was spared from death and raised by a representative of the gods, and was eventually able to reassert his parentage, his birth rights, and his identity as the son of god (4.101-115).

15. The Homeric hymns, though almost universally recognized both in antiquity and today as not composed by Homer, were attributed to Homer and were widely known from at least the fifth (and likely the sixth) century BCE. The best introduction to the provenance of the hymn is Norman O. Brown, *Hermes the Thief* (New York: Norton, 1947), pp. 69-105, and, more recently, N.J. Richardson, 'The Homeric Hymn to Hermes', in P.J. Finglass, C. Collard and N.J. Richardson (eds.), *Hesperos* (New York: Oxford University Press, 2007), pp. 83-91. Also see Martin L. West, *Homeric Hymns Homeric Apocrypha Lives of Homer* (LCL; Cambridge, MA: Harvard University Press, 2003), pp. 3-6, 12-14, and Jenny Strauss Clay, *The Politics of Olympus: Form and Meaning in the Major Homeric Hymns* (Princeton: Princeton University Press, 1989), pp. 3-16. In addition to the translation by West, other excellent translations exist: Apostolos N. Athanassakis, *The Homeric Hymns: Translation, Introduction, and Notes* (Baltimore: The Johns Hopkins University Press, 1976), and Daryl Hine, *Works of Hesiod and the Homeric Hymns* (Chicago: University of Chicago Press, 2005). Translations are from Athanassakis unless otherwise noted.

16. On Hermes's place within the pantheon, see Guthrie, *Greeks and Their Gods*, pp. 87-94. For a survey of other ancient traditions about Hermes as a thief, see Brown, *Hermes the Thief*, pp. 3-68, and Adele Haft, 'The Mercurial Significance of Raiding', *Arion* 4 (1996), pp. 27-48 (44 n. 6).

the newborn Hermes returned to his cradle and cloaked himself in swaddling clothes in order to feign child-like innocence (150-52). Hermes's mother, Maia, was not fooled by his implied claims of innocence and asked him, 'What is this, you weaver of schemes?' (155). In spite of his self-administered swaddling clothes, his mother insisted that his deeds that night had left him 'clothed in shamelessness' (156). A few minutes later, when Hermes's brother Apollo entered the room to investigate Hermes's role in the theft, Hermes again 'snuggled into his sweet-scented swaddling clothes' in yet another effort to deflect any allegations against him (235). In his defense speech, in which he attempted to counter his brother's (just) accusations, Hermes underscored the symbolic import of the newborn's swaddling clothes with which he had cloaked himself. The guilty Hermes insisted to his brother: 'I surely do not resemble a hardy rustler of cattle... I have cared for sleep, and milk from my mother's breast, and for swaddling-clothes wrapped round my shoulders, and a warm bath' (265-68). Even though Apollo apparently recognized that such clothing would normally imply innocence, he remained convinced of Hermes's guilt and sarcastically addressed Hermes as a 'swathed child' even while insisting that Hermes return his cattle (301-303).

Although Hermes's claims of innocence have convinced neither his mother nor his brother, he twice more used his swaddling clothes as supposed proof of his innocence. First, with his swaddling clothes wrapped around his shoulders, Hermes insisted to his brother, 'Surely, I neither stole the cows—whatever cows are—nor saw another man do it' (310-11). Second, while standing before his father Zeus with his swaddling clothes on his arm, Hermes insisted, 'I was born but yesterday...in no way do I resemble a hard man or a cattle-rustler' (376-77, 388). Zeus, like Hermes's brother Apollo and his mother Maia, was not fooled by Hermes's lies.[17] However, Zeus was impressed and 'laughed out loud when he saw the mischievous child (κακομηδέα παῖδα) denying so well and so adroitly any connection with the cattle' (389-90). With all of Hermes's claims of innocence rejected, Zeus ordered Hermes to lead Apollo to where the stolen cattle were hidden. The narrator informs the reader 'the beautiful children of Zeus both hurried away' to where the cattle where hidden (397). Once they arrived at the location of the stolen cattle, Hermes earned even Apollo's respect. Upon discovering the hides of the two slaughtered cattle, Apollo was forced to praise his brother's

---

17. On Hermes as a liar and deceiver, see Brown, *Hermes the Thief*, esp. pp. 78-89, and Judith Fletcher, 'A Trickster's Oaths in The *Homeric Hymn to Hermes*', *American Journal of Philology* 129 (2008), pp. 19-46.

maturity and strength, announcing 'How could you, you clever rogue, have slaughtered two cows, being still a new-born infant? Even I myself look back and admire your strength; no need for you to grow up for long, O Kyllenian son of Maia' (405-408).[18] With Hermes's identity confirmed by the words of both Zeus and Apollo, Hermes cemented his place within the divine family by giving Apollo his newly created lyre as restitution for the two slaughtered cattle.[19]

In this hymn, as in the play *Ion*, swaddling clothes take on important symbolic significance as a divine son establishes his identity as a true son of god. Both the concentration of references to swaddling clothes and clearly symbolic significance of these references within the pseudo-Homeric *Hymn to Hermes* and Euripides' *Ion* mark these documents as particularly important for understanding the symbolic significance of swaddling clothes in classical literature. However, these two texts are not the only relevant texts for thinking about the implications of the Lukan sign. Classical literature contains two other tales about swaddling clothes and divine origins: the story of Zeus's birth and the story of Heracles's childhood battle with deadly snakes. Each tale appears repeatedly in ancient literature, but the earliest of the stories are found in Hesiod's *Theogony* and Pindar's *Odes*.

Hesiod's *Theogony* recounts how the earlier god Kronos was a dim-witted and petty deity who feared that he would someday be replaced by some brighter and more cunning deity.[20] Therefore, in order to ensure his monopoly on divine power, Kronos would consume his own children as soon as they were born (459-65). However, Gaia, Zeus's mother, under-standably wanted to protect her child from this divine cannibalism, and so she conceived a plan to spare her child from such gruesome infanti-cide. Immediately after giving birth to Zeus, Gaia wrapped a stone in swaddling clothes and handed the stone to Kronos who quickly ingested it (486). After Zeus's mother's cunning use of swaddling clothes spared

18. The remainder of the hymn recounts how Hermes also won his brother's respect through his skilled use of the lyre.

19. On this story as a coming of age story in which the young Hermes earns Zeus' respect and his position within the divine family, see Adele Haft, 'Mercurial Significance', pp. 27-48, and Peter Walcot, 'Cattle Raiding, Heroic Tradition, and Ritual', *HR* 18 (1979), pp. 326-51 (343-48).

20. The best critical introductions to, and commentary on, the *Theogony* are Glen W. Most, *Hesiod: Theogony, Works and Days, Testamonia* (LCL; Cambridge, MA: Harvard University Press, 2006); M.L. West, *Hesiod Theogony* (Oxford: Clarendon Press, 1966); and Kathryn Stoddard, *The Narrative Voice in the Theogony of Hesiod* (Boston: Brill, 2004), pp. 1-59.

him from a grizzly death by parental consumption, Zeus went on to establish himself as the supreme god and as patriarch of his divine family. As distasteful as this story is to modern readers, it was certainly widely known among ancients through Hesiod's widely read *Theogony*.[21] The story was even repeated in the first century by Luke's near contemporary, Lucius Annaeus Cornutus (*Nat. d.* 6.4).

Pindar and Euripides each relate another story about the exploits of another of Zeus's sons being wrapped in swaddling clothes. Pindar's poetry celebrates how Heracles's jealous mother, Hera, threw venomous snakes in his crib to attack 'this son of Zeus' (*Nem.* 1.40-46).[22] Even though Heracles was still a swaddled infant (1.40), he tore the heads off his attackers and lived to accomplish many extraordinary deeds. Euripides places the same story on Heracles's lips in a dramatic monologue (*Hera.* 1265-70).[23] The tale of the child's extraordinary feats, like the tales of Hermes' extraordinary feats in the Homeric Hymn, establishes the child's divine status.

Given the extensive symbolic use of swaddling clothes in myth, hymn, drama and poetry before the first century,[24] it seems culturally appropriate to interpret the Lukan 'sign' of the swaddling clothes against the background of the literary motif of a divine son establishing his place within the divine family in a mode related to the actions of Ion, Zeus, Hermes and Heracles.

21.   Hesiod's influence was so profound that Herodotus credited Homer and Hesiod with being 'the poets who composed our theogonies and described the gods for us' (2.53; translation from Aubrey de Sélincourt, *Herodotus: The Histories* [Baltimore: Penguin, 1954]). In antiquity, Hesiod's popularity was second only to Homer's popularity, as demonstrated by the second-century text, *The Contest of Homer and Hesiod in Homeric Hymns, Homeric Apocrypha, Lives of Homer* (trans. Martin L. West; LCL; Cambridge, MA: Harvard University Press, 2003).

22.   For a critical introduction to, and a complete translation of, Pindar's *Odes*, see Roy Arthur Swanson, *Pindar's Odes* (Library of Liberal Arts; New York: Bobbs-Merrill, 1974). On Pindar's life, poetry, and influence, see William H. Race, *Pindar* (Twayne World Author Series, 773; Boston: Twayne Publishers, 1986); G.P. Goold, *Pindar I* (LCL; Cambridge, MA: Harvard University Press, 1997), pp. 1-42; and more recently Anne Pippin Burnett, *Pindar* (Ancients in Action; London: Bristol Classical Press, 2008).

23.   Many ancient writers make allusions to this famous scene, but these two early writers are important because their stories include references to Heracles's swaddling clothes.

24.   The references in the *Homeric Hymn to Hermes*, in Euripides' *Ion*, in Pindar's *Odes*, and in Euripides' *Heracles* account for 15 of the 51 references to swaddling clothes before the first century.

II. *The Sign of Jesus' Swaddling Clothes*
in the Lukan Context

While the symbol of the swaddling clothes, like any symbol, is highly evocative and can be legitimately interpreted in several ways, I want to emphasize one plausible inference that can be drawn from this Lukan sign. The sign of the swaddling clothes could be read as a Christian challenge to the mythology and theology of the imperial cult.

In the first decade of the twenty-first century, scholars swarmed around anti-imperial readings of the Matthew, Paul and Revelation.[25] In spite of the prominence of Roman trials and of overtly political characters in Luke–Acts, Lukan scholars were late in coming to biblical scholarship's anti-imperial party. Instead, until very recently, Lukan scholars have tended to follow late twentieth-century scholarship in assuming that Luke–Acts has a largely positive view of the Roman Empire.[26] Sometimes, Luke–Acts has even served as a foil for scholars who wish to contrast the anti-imperial Paul of the authentic Pauline

25. E.g. Warren Carter, *Matthew and Empire: Initial Explorations* (Harrisburg, PA: Trinity Press International, 2001); *idem, Matthew and the Margins* (New York: Orbis, 2001); *idem* (ed.), *Paul and Empire* (Harrisburg, PA: Trinity Press International, 1997); Richard A. Horsley (ed.), *Paul and Politics* (Harrisburg, PA: Trinity Press International, 2000); *idem* (ed.), *Paul and the Roman Imperial Order* (Harrisburg, PA: Trinity Press International, 2004); Leonard L. Thompson, *The Book of Revelation: Apocalypse and Empire* (Oxford: Oxford University Press, 1990); and Steven J. Friesen, 'Satan's Throne, Imperial Cults and the Social Settings of Revelation', *JSNT* 27 (2005), pp. 351-73.

26. The typical discussions within Lukan scholarship have been whether Luke's largely—though not entirely—positive view of the empire was designed to legitimate Christianity to Roman readers (e.g. Paul W. Walaskay, *And So We Came to Rome* [SNTSMS, 49; Cambridge: Cambridge University Press, 1983]; Daniel R. Schwartz, 'The End of the Line: Paul in the Canonical Book of Acts', in William S. Babcock [ed.], *Paul and the Legacies of Paul* [Dallas: SMU Press, 1991], pp. 3-24; and Diane G. Chen, *God as Father in Luke–Acts* [StBL, 92; New York: Peter Lang, 2006]) or to legitimate the empire to Christian readers (e.g. J.H. Cadbury, *The Making of Luke–Acts* [London: SPCK, 2nd edn, 1958], pp. 308-15; Hans Conzelmann, *Theology of St. Luke* [trans. Geoffrey Buswell; San Francisco: Harper & Row, 1960], pp. 137-49; and Robert F. O'Toole, 'Luke's Position on Politics and Society in Luke–Acts', in Richard J. Cassidy [ed.], *Political Issues in Luke–Acts* [Maryknoll: Orbis, 1983], pp. 1-17). For superb overviews of recent discussions, see Steve Walton, 'The State They Were In: Luke's View of the Roman Empire', in Peter Oakes (ed.), *Rome in the Bible and the Early Church* (Carlisle: Paternoster; Grand Rapids: Baker Academic, 2002), pp. 1-41, and Alexandru Neagoe, *The Trial of the Gospel: An Apologetic Reading of Luke's Trial Narratives* (SNTSMS, 116; Cambridge: Cambridge University Press, 2002), pp. 175-87.

letters with the culturally compromised and imperially accommodated Paul of Acts.[27] However, in the closing years of the twenty-first century's first decade, several Lukan scholars have joined the forces allied against the empire and have given Luke–Acts an anti-imperial reading.[28] In spite of this rising tide of anti-imperial readings of Luke–Acts, I am becoming increasingly convinced that some of the potentially anti-imperial inferences of Luke's birth narrative continue to be overlooked.

Luke 2.1-14 contains two announcements—a proclamation from Caesar Augustus (2.1-7) and a proclamation from the heavenly hosts (2.8-14). Both announcements are laden with highly political language. Caesar issued a δόγμα (2.7), which was a technical term for an imperial action taken in consultation with the Roman Senate;[29] the heavenly hosts announced good news (εὐαγγελίζω, 2.10), another technical term for the proclamation of a new emperor.[30] Caesar's decree went out to the entire world that Rome had civilized (οἰκουμένην, 2.1); the heavenly hosts' decree went to the even broader 'all people' (παντὶ τῷ λαῷ, 2.10). Caesar's bland decree directed people to enroll in a census; the decree of the heavenly hosts called people to participate in a decisive eschatological event. The heavenly hosts' bold declaration co-opted the soteriological language shared by the Roman empire and the LXX, and then applied that soteriological language to the Christ event. This language is typically read against the background of the Old Testament, but it could also be read against the background of the empire. Consider the following themes as a challenge to Roman Imperial theology: the Lord's messenger (ἄγγελος κυρίου, 2.9) was surrounded by the glory of the Lord (δόξα κυρίου, 2.9) and the announcement was to bring great joy (χαρὰν μεγάλην, 2.10) because the Savior who is Christ the Lord (σωτὴρ ὅς ἐστιν χριστός κύριος, 2.11) was being born. The birth of this newborn Lord prompted

27. E.g. John Dominic Crossan and Jonathan L. Reed, *In Search of Paul: How Jesus's Apostle Opposed Rome's Empire with God's Kingdom* (San Francisco: HarperSanFrancisco, 2004).

28. For the most recent discussion, see Bradley S. Billings, '"At the Age of 12": The Boy Jesus in the Temple (Luke 2:41-52), the Emperor Augustus, and the Social Setting of the Third Gospel', *JTS* 60 (2009), pp. 70-89; James Howell, 'The Imperial Authority and Benefaction of Centurions and Acts 10.34-43', *JSNT* 31 (2008), pp. 25-51; C. Kavin Rowe, 'Luke–Acts and the Imperial Cult: A Way through the Conundrum?', *JSNT* 27 (2005), pp. 279-300; Seyoon Kim, *Christ and Caesar: The Gospel and the Roman Empire in the Writings of Paul and Luke* (Grand Rapids: Eerdmans, 2008); and Kazuhiko Yamazaki-Ransom, *The Roman Empire in Luke's Narrative* (LNTS, 421; New York: T&T Clark International, 2010).

29. See Raymond E. Brown, *The Birth of the Messiah*, p. 394.

30. See, e.g., U. Becker, 'Gospel', in *NIDNTT*, II, pp. 107-15 (107-108).

the heavenly host to ascribe glory (δόξα, 2.14) to God and to celebrate the arrival of peace on earth (γῆς εἰρήνη, 2.14). Nearly all of the key terms here (κυρίου, δόξα, σωτήρ, εἰρήνη) were shared by both the LXX and the Imperial cult.[31]

No doubt, many readers will now suspect that I am seeking to extend the anti-empire interpretative trend within contemporary New Testament scholarship even deeper into Luke–Acts. However, my concern is more nuanced than that. Elsewhere I have argued that the theology in Paul's letters certainly competed with many of the empire's claims of ultimacy and that Paul himself probably viewed many of the empire's claims as blasphemous. However, Paul's letters probably were not shaped in conscious opposition to the Roman Empire. Paul's rejection of the empire is more implicit than explicit in his letters; Paul's theology—it seems to me—was shaped with its own theological and ideological agendas in mind and should not be read primarily as a reaction to some external force or influence (neither the Roman Empire nor any other supposed opponent). Paul probably saw his gospel as a force of its own and not merely as a reaction to some other set of ideals.[32] I would now suggest that essentially the same thing is also true for Luke–Acts. When Luke–Acts appropriates the language of imperial soteriology, the author could not possibly be unaware of the imperial use of such language. But this awareness alone does not necessarily imply an anti-imperial agenda. After all, this soteriological language was not only deeply rooted in the ideology of the empire; much of it was also deeply rooted in the LXX!

As I imagine it, Luke's agenda was explicitly Christian. As such, Luke's agenda could be interpreted in anti-imperial—and even anti-Jewish—ways, but his agenda was not really 'anti-' anything.[33] Instead, Luke borrowed the soteriological language and symbols of his day and proclaimed his Christian message in the accepted soteriological language of the day. It is in this manner that I understand the sign of the swaddling clothes in Luke's Gospel. Luke undoubtedly knew the stories of deities and the symbolic significance of their swaddling clothes. So, when Luke told the story of Jesus as the Son of God, Luke appropriated

31. On the political implications of these terms, see, for example, Dieter Georgi, 'God Turned Upside Down', in Horsley (ed.), *Paul and Empire*, pp. 148-57.

32. Phillips, *Paul, His Letters, and Acts*, pp. 97-104.

33. On the supposed anti-Judaism in Luke–Acts, see Thomas E. Phillips, 'Subtlety as a Literary Technique in Luke's Characterization of Jews and Judaism', in Richard P. Thompson and Thomas E. Phillips (eds.), *Literary Studies in Luke–Acts* (Macon, GA: Mercer University Press, 1998), pp. 314-26, and Thomas E. Phillips, 'The Mission of the Church in Acts: Inclusive or Exclusive?', in his *Acts in Diverse Frames of Reference* (Macon, GA: Mercer University Press, 2009), pp. 118-29.

this symbol for his own purposes. Luke was probably aware that his references to swaddling clothes interacted with the symbol of a swaddled infant on the level of a broad cultural symbol even if Luke did not have any particular non-LXX textual referent in mind when he penned his text. Luke was probably cloaking his Christian theology in the generic cultural garb of the first century and was not countering any specific ancient text or tradition. Rather, Luke was probably inter-acting—consciously, unconsciously, or more likely, semi-consciously—with a widely recognized cultural sign.

III. *Conclusion*

Neither the characters in Luke–Acts nor the narrator of Luke–Acts make many explicit references to non-LXX Greco-Roman literature (Paul's speech on Mars Hill in Athens is the one notable exception). However, this scarcity of direct citations from non-LXX literature hardly justifies the conclusion that Luke was either unfamiliar with, or even disinterested in, the literary traditions of the broader Greco-Roman world. Luke may have often adopted such commonly used symbols as 'swaddling clothes' and adapted them for his own purposes without leaving any direct evidence of his borrowing from those early traditions. Detecting such less-than-overt Lukan engagement with non-LXX literary traditions will require a far more deliberative and intensive immersion in the Greco-Roman literature than most contemporary New Testament scholars have typi-cally experienced. I would conclude by saying that New Testament scholarship offers no better example of this deliberate and intensive immersion in Greco-Roman literature than the extensive body of work produced by our friend and colleague, Loveday Alexander.

Luke's Use of Papias for Narrating the Death of Judas

Dennis R. MacDonald

It is a privilege to contribute to this volume honoring Loveday C.A. Alexander, from whom I and other students of the Acts of the Apostles have learned so much. Her magisterial *Acts in its Ancient Literary Context* does not discuss Luke's narration of the death of Judas (Acts 1.16-26), nor does she mention Papias of Hierapolis as a possible source for Luke's information. This contribution begins with an assessment of Matthew's account of Judas' demise, then argues that the version known to Papias was a polemic against that Gospel, and finally shows that Luke sided with Papias against Matthew, which he knew and redacted. To demonstrate this literary nexus, I also will reinvestigate Luke's famous prologue, a passage to which Professor Alexander devoted an insightful monograph.[1]

I. *The Q+/Papias Solution to the Synoptic Problem*

Most Gospel scholars hold that the anonymous author of the Gospel of Matthew composed a hybrid account about Jesus from two sources, the Gospel of Mark and a lost Synoptic source, conventionally known as Q. My reconstruction of this source differs from others insofar as I hold to the Q+/Papias Hypothesis, a variant of the dominant Two-Document solution the Synoptic Problem. My preferred view holds that Luke knew not two but at least four antecedent writings about Jesus: Q, Mark, Matthew, and Papias' *Exposition of Logia about the Lord*. Furthermore, it insists that Mark knew Q.

---

1. Loveday C.A. Alexander, *The Preface to Luke's Gospel: Literary Convention and Social Context in Luke 1:1-4 and Acts 1:1* (SNTSMS, 78; Cambridge: Cambridge University Press, 1993).

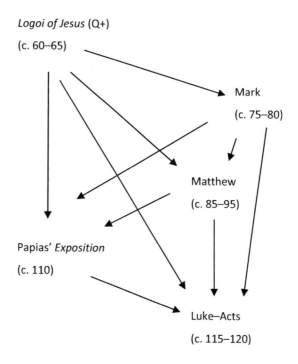

Figure 1. *The Q+/Papias Solution to the Synoptic Problem*

If this intertextual model is correct, one cannot reconstruct Q simply by comparing Matthew and Luke and expunging Markan contamination. Instead, I apply a criterion of inverted priority: the identification of information in Matthew or Luke that is more primitive than similar content in their sources. This essay clearly is not the occasion to defend this reassessment of the Synoptic Problem, but is important to clarify at the outset the intertextual model that informs it.

II. *The Death of Judas in the Gospel of Matthew*

In Q/Q+ Jesus' twelve disciples always appear in a positive light, and in the last recoverable pericope Jesus promises each a throne in his kingdom. Here is my reconstruction of the passage in question, which differs somewhat from *The Critical Edition of Q*:[2] 'Truly I tell you that you are the ones who followed me; my Father will give you the kingdom,

2. James M. Robinson, Paul Hoffmann, and John S. Kloppenborg (eds.), *The Critical Edition of Q* (Hermeneia; Minneapolis: Fortress Press, 2000).

and when the Son of Man sits on the throne of his glory, you too will sit on twelve thrones judging the twelve tribes of Israel'.[3] Mark has no equivalent to this promise; in fact, his Jesus explicitly denies that he has the authority to determine who will sit on his right and left in glory (10.40). Matthew retains his own version of this saying in 19.28 with modestly different wording: 'Truly I tell you that you who have followed me, in the regeneration, when the Son of Man sits on the throne of his glory, you, too, will sit on twelve thrones judging the twelve tribes of Israel'.

But he apparently found it difficult to square this promise with Mark's portrayal of Judas' betrayal, which would seem to disqualify him from sitting on a throne of judgment. To resolve this conflict the Matthean evangelist created an account of Judas' suicide that shifted culpability to the Jewish authorities. Presumably his readers were to conclude that his eventual remorse was sufficient to reinstate him as a legitimate recipient of his promised throne:[4]

> Then, when Judas, the one who delivered him up, saw that Jesus had been condemned, he changed his mind, returned the thirty pieces of silver to the chief priests and elders, saying, 'I have sinned by delivering up innocent blood'. But they said, 'What do we care? You see to it'. He threw the silver into the sanctuary, left, went off, and hanged himself. The chief priests took the silver and said, 'It is not permitted to put these into the sacred treasury, since they are a blood price'. After holding council, they used some of the money to buy the potter's field for the burial of foreigners. Thus that field was called a Field of Blood even to this day. Then what was said by Jeremiah the prophet was fulfilled: 'And they took the thirty pieces of silver, the purchase price set by some of the people of Israel, and they gave them for the potter's field, as the Lord had commanded me'. (Mt. 27.3-10)

Although virtually all of the wording of this passage is typically Matthean, the Field of Blood surely was a real place somewhere near Jerusalem, for Luke independently knew its Aramaic name, *Hakeldamach* (Acts 1.19). This may well be the only traditional element of the logion.

The evangelist's model for the betrayer's suicide surely came from 2 Samuel:

---

3. Compare Mt. 19.28 and Lk. 22.28-30.

4. Arie W. Zwiep concludes his book on Acts 1 by making the harmonization of the promise of thrones in Q and the depiction of Judas the betrayer in Mark his motivation for the selection of Matthias in Acts 1, yet he fails to see that Matthew's presentation of Judas' suicide was a different answer to the same problem (*Judas and the Choice of Matthias: A Story on the Context and Concern of Acts 1:15-26* [WUNT, II/187; Tübingen: Mohr Siebeck, 2004], pp. 181-82).

2 Samuel 17.23	*Matthew 27.3, 5, 7b*
And when Ahithophel saw that (εἶδε ὅτι)	Then, when Judas...saw that (ἰδὼν...ὅτι)
his advice did not come about, he saddled	Jesus had been condemned, he changed
his ass, and went off (ἀπῆλθεν) to his house,	his mind... He threw the silver into the sanctuary, left, went off (ἀπελθών),
and hanged himself (ἀπήγξατο),	and hanged himself (ἀπήγξατο)...
and died, and was buried in the tomb (ἐτάφη ἐν τῷ τάφῳ] of his father.	for the burial (ταφήν) of foreigners.

Also from 2 Samuel came his model for his etiology for the Field of Blood (ἀγρὸς αἵματος), namely, that it was purchased with blood money (τιμὴ αἵματος):

2 Samuel 6.8 (cf. Genesis 26.33)	*Matthew 27.8*
And that place was called (ἐκλήθη ὁ τόπος ἐκεῖνος)	Thus that field was called (ἐκλήθη ὁ ἀγρὸς ἐκεῖνος)
Uzza's Breach even to this day (ἕως τῆς σήμερον ἡμέρας).	a Field of Blood even to this day (ἕως τῆς σήμερον)

Such etiological formulae are common in ancient literature, but in addition to the verbal similarities are contextual ones, including the use of 2 Samuel in Mt. 27.3-7 that immediately precedes Judas' death. Uzza angered God by touching the ark of the covenant, and his death created fear among David and others. Uzza and Judas thus both were sinners whose violations stigmatized a particular location.

The evangelist then found in Jer. 39.6-15 (MT 32.6-15) a text that might show that *mutatis mutandis* the death of Judas was according to Scripture: Jeremiah's narration of purchasing a field (ἀγρός) as 'the Lord' had directed him (vv. 6, 8, 14, and 15). But Jeremiah 39 (MT 32) could not implicate the Jewish authorities, so Matthew awkwardly conflated it with Zech. 11.13. Maarten J.J. Menken presents a compelling reconstruction of the Greek text of Zech. 11.13 that the evangelist most likely used:[5]

a	καὶ εἶπε κύριος πρός με·	And the Lord said to me,
b	κάθες αὐτοὺς (i.e. τριάκοντα ἀγρυροῦς [11.12]) εἰς τὸν κεραμέα.	'Deposit them [the thirty pieces of silver] with the potter,
c	καὶ σκέψομαι εἰ δόκιμόν ἐστιν, ὃν τρόπον ἐδοκιμάσθην ὑπὲρ αὐτῶν,	and I will find out if it is assayed the way I assayed for them'.

---

5. *Matthew's Bible: The Old Testament Text of the Evangelist* (BETL, 173; Leuven: Leuven University Press, 2004), pp. 179-92.

d	καὶ ἔλαβον τοὺς τριάκοντα ἀγρυροῦ,		And I took the thirty pieces of silver
e	καὶ ἔδωκα αὐτοὺς εἰς τὸν κεραμέα.		and gave them to the potter.

The verb ἔλαβον in line d must be a first person singular, but Matthew required it to be the third person plural to make it refer to the Jewish authorities, even though doing so created an absurd change of subject to the first person singular in line e: '*They* took the thirty pieces of silver, and *I* gave them to the potter.' Matthew thus rearranged the sequence of the last three lines to d, c, and e and offered his alternative version of c: he replaced σκέψομαι with the third person plural ἐτιμήσαντο and altered the reference to the assessed value of the prophet's wages to create a wordplay: 'the price of the precious one on whom a price had been set'. At the end of the same line he also clarified the antecedent of the αὐτῶν by adding ἀπὸ υἱῶν Ἰσραήλ. He then changed the first person ἔδωκα in line e to the third-person ἔδωκαν to make the Jewish authorities the buyers of the field. Matthew gave Jeremiah full credit for the citation because, of the two texts, Jeremiah's was the more relevant to the Field of Blood.

It thus would appear that the evangelist created the entire logion to harmonize the traditional promise of thrones with Mark's depiction of Judas as a betrayer. All that is traditional in Matthew's account is a location near Jerusalem called the Field of Blood.

III. *The Death of Judas in Papias'* Exposition of Logia about the Lord

The disappearance of Papias' (c. 110) five-volume commentary is one of the great textual catastrophes of early Christianity, so the recent edition of the surviving fragments by Enrico Norelli is all the more welcome.[6] Papias' book seems to have begun as follows.

- The title: 'Writings by Papias, five in number, are extant, which also bear the title [books] of an *Exposition of Logia about the Lord*' (Frg. 5 [Eusebius, *Hist. eccl.* 3.39.1]). (For Papias a logion was not a saying but a unit of text, similar to what scholars now call pericope.)
- Name of the author: Papias.
- Name of the recipient: unknown (see Frg. 5 [*Hist. eccl.* 3.39.3-4]).

---

6. *Papia di Hierapolis, Esposizione degli oracoli del Signore. I frammenti* (Letture cristiane del primo millennio, 36; Milan: Paoline, 2005).

- Identification of at least three earlier writings about Jesus that presented logia in incompatible sequences.
- Introduction of the elder John and perhaps another elder named Aristion, whose 'expositions of the sayings of the Lord' probably was a written text (Frg. 5 [*Hist. eccl.* 3.39.7, 14]).

Frg. 5 (*Hist. eccl.* 3.39.15); cf. Frg. 5 (*Hist. eccl.* 2.15.1-2):

> The elder used to say this too: 'Mark became Peter's translator; whatever Peter recalled of what was said or done by the Lord Mark wrote down accurately, though not in proper sequence. For Mark himself neither heard the Lord nor followed him, but as I said, he later followed Peter, who used to craft teachings for the needs [of the occasion], not as though he were crafting a sequential arrangement of the logia about the Lord; thus Mark was not in error by thus writing a few things as he remembered them, for he made it his one purpose to omit nothing that he had heard or falsely present anything pertaining to them.'

Frg. 5 (*Hist. eccl.* 3.39.16):

> [Again 'the elder':] 'Matthew, for his part, set in order the logia in the Hebrew language, but each translated them as he was able'.

- Papias then apparently identified the texts that the elder John considered to be translations of Matthew.

Frg. 5 (*Hist. eccl.* 3.39.3-4):

> But I will not hesitate to set in order also for you whatever I learned well and remembered well from the elders with interpretations to confirm their reliability; for I would not take joy, as many would, in those who had much to say, but in those who taught the truth; not in those who remembered the commandments of others, but in those who remembered the commandments given by the Lord for faith and derived from the truth itself. If ever someone who had followed the elders should come by, I would investigate the sayings of the elders, what Andrew or Peter said, or Philip, Thomas, James, John, Matthew, or any other of the Lord's disciples had said, or what Aristion and the elder John, disciples of the Lord, say. For I did not consider things derived from books to benefit me as much as things derived from a living and surviving voice.

Later in this essay I will compare this preface with Lk. 1.1-4, but at this point I would simply point out that Papias not only was familiar with a book that presumably resembled our Gospel of Matthew but also knew of at least one other flawed Greek translation of Matthew's Hebrew original.

A fragment from the writings of Apollinaris of Laodicea (c. 390) reveals what Papias said about Judas' demise:

> Judas did not die by hanging, but he survived for a while because he was taken down before he choked. And the Acts of the Apostles makes this clear: 'falling face down, he burst in the middle, and all his guts poured out'. Papias, John's disciple, records this even more clearly when he speaks as follows in his fourth volume of *Exposition of the Logoi of the Lord*. (Frg. 6)

Apollinaris here tries to harmonize Matthew's account of Judas' hanging, Acts' account of his bursting, and Papias', which read as follows:

> Judas conducted himself in this world as a great paradigm of impiety. His flesh became so bloated that he was unable to pass through an opening large enough for a chariot easily to pass. Not even the massiveness of his head could get through! They say that his eyelids were so swollen that he was entirely unable to see the light, and even physicians with magnifying glasses could not see his eyes, so deeply had they sunk beyond sight. His penis appeared to be more repulsive and larger than any such disgraceful member, and bloody discharge and maggots poured from all over his body, which caused injury whenever he attended to his bodily needs.
>
> They say that after many tortures and punishments, he died in his own plot, which became deserted and uninhabited even to this day due to its stench. Still today no one can pass by that place without pinching his nostrils, such was the efflux that seeped from his flesh to the ground. (Frg. 6)

As we have seen, Matthew apparently created 27.3-10 from biblical texts to solve a problem presented by his two sources, and traces of Matthew's redaction reappear in Papias' account of Judas' death—but only to be refuted! According to the Bishop of Hierapolis, Judas 'did not die by hanging (τῇ ἀγχόνῃ)', a possible correction of Matthew, whose author had created his account from 2 Sam. 17.23, where Ahithophel 'hanged himself (ἀπήγξατο)'. Papias insisted that Judas 'died in his own plot', apparently not in a field purchased by the chief priests after he repented. Matthew crafted from Zech. 11.13 the notion of purchasing a field, which he adapted to read 'they gave them for the potter's field' (Mt. 27.10a). Jewish opposition is entirely missing in Papias' version. Papias' account agrees with Matthew that the field where Judas fell was notorious 'to this very day', but not because Papias knew an independent tradition. Instead, he apparently was aware of objections to Matthew's account and its etiology for the Field of Blood from 2 Sam. 6.8: 'And that place was called Uzza's Breach even to this day'.

Matthew 27	Papias Frg. 6 (apud Apollinaris)
Judas 'hung (ἀπήγξατο) himself' (cf. 2 Sam 17.23).	Judas 'did not die by hanging (τῇ ἀγχόνῃ)'.
The chief priests 'used some of the money to buy the potter's field (ἀγρόν)' (cf. Zech 11.13).	Judas died 'in his own plot (χωρίῳ)'.
'That field was called the Field of Blood	Judas' plot 'became deserted and uninhabited
even to this day (ἕως τῆς σήμερον)' (cf. 2 Sam. 6.8).	even to this day (μέχρι τῆς νῦν) due to its stench.
	Still today (μέχρι τῆς σήμερον) no one can pass by that place without pinching his nostrils'.
Jesus' blood stigmatized the field.	Judas' bodily discharge stigmatized the field.

It therefore would appear that Papias not only was aware of the Gospel of Matthew, he also was aware of a tradition that was critical of its attempt to vindicate Judas through suicide; instead, he continued to conduct 'himself in this world as a great paradigm of impiety'.

IV. *The Death of Judas in Acts 1.16-26*

Even in antiquity readers recognized distinctive connections between Papias' *Exposition* and Luke–Acts. Both present Jesus forgiving a sinful woman (*Expos.* Frg. 5; Lk. 7.36-50); both refer to the martyrdom of James, the brother of John (*Expos.* Frg. 10; Acts 12.1-2); both narrate the death of Judas not as a suicide, as in Matthew, but as divine punishment in his own field (*Expos.* Frg. 6; Acts 1.18-19); both mention Satan's fall from heaven (*Expos.* Frg. 12a; Lk. 10.19); both name Barsabbas Justus (*Expos.* Frgs. 5, 10; Acts 1.23); and both refer to the daughters of Philip (*Expos.* Frgs. 5, 10; Acts 21.8-9). Particularly impressive are similarities between their prefaces. It also is worth noting that both were multi-volume works whose authors intended to arrange the life of Jesus in chronological order; the last volume of each narrated events after Jesus' death.

Insofar as we have precious few fragments of Papias' *Exposition*, this density of overlapping content with Luke–Acts begs for a solution, and scholars have argued for three competing proposals: (1) Papias' *Exposition* and Luke–Acts were independent works; (2) Papias knew the Gospel of Luke; and (3) the author of Luke–Acts knew Papias' *Exposition*.

Option 1: Papias' *Exposition* and Luke–Acts were independent works. Ulrich H.J. Körtner and Norelli, for example, attribute the overlapping names and episodes to shared oral traditions.[7] This is the dominant position.

Option 2: Papias knew the Gospel of Luke. Several scholars have insisted, in my view rightly, that the parallels between the two works are too extensive to attribute merely to common conventions.[8]

But two arguments tell against this direction of dependence. First, Eusebius made a point of listing the books known to Papias, which included the Gospels of Mark and Matthew, 1 John, and 1 Peter. Had he seen evidence that Papias also knew Luke–Acts, he would have said so.[9] Second, Luke probably wrote later than Papias. After an extensive discussion, Norelli concludes that the bishop wrote the *Exposition* around 110–120.[10] Körtner's dating to about 110 is somewhat more realistic insofar as it shortens the interval between Papias' collection of traditions when the elders were still alive and his recording of them. Richard Pervo has argued at length that Luke composed Acts around 115–120 and his Gospel not much earlier.[11] Even though I am persuaded by Norelli's relatively early date for the *Exposition* and Pervo's dating of Luke–Acts, it is safest to assume that Papias and Luke were contemporaries; what tilts the direction of priority to Papias is the derivative nature of Luke's parallels to it.

7. Ulrich H.J. Körtner, *Papias von Hierapolis: Ein Beitrag zur Geschichte des früher Christentums* (FRLANT, 133; Göttingen: Vandenhoeck & Ruprecht, 1983), pp. 173-76, and Norelli, *Papia*, pp. 105-12, 294.

8. Erhardt Güttgemanns argued that shared rhetorical strategies in their prefaces require a literary connection; see his 'In welchen Sinne ist Lukas Historiker? Die Beziehung von Luk 1:1-4 und Papias zur antiken Rhetorik', *LB* 54 (1983), pp. 9-26 (23). Other scholars who hold that Papias knew Luke include J.B. Lightfoot, *Essays on the Work Entitled Supernatural Religion* (London: Macmillan, 1889), pp. 150, 178-86, Charles E. Hill, 'What Papias Said about John [and Luke]: A "New" Papian Fragment', *JTS* NS 49 (1998), pp. 582-629, and Richard Bauckham, *Jesus and the Eyewitnesses: The Gospels as Eyewitness Testimony* (Grand Rapids: Eerdmans, 2006), esp. pp. 412-37.

9. See especially Johannes Munck, 'Die Tradition über das Matthäusevangelium bei Papias', in Willem C. Van Unnik (ed.), *Neotestamentica et Patristica. Eine Freundesgabe H. Prof. Dr. O. Cullmann zu seinem 60. Geburtstag überreicht* (NovTSup, 6; Leiden: Brill, 1962), pp. 250-51.

10. *Papia*, 54. For advocates of an even earlier dating, see J. Vernon Bartlet, 'Papias' "Exposition": Its Date and Contents', in H.G. Wood (ed.), *Amicitiae Corolla* (London: University of London Press, 1933), pp. 15-44; E. Gutwenger, 'Papias: Eine chronologische Studie', *ZKT* 69 (1947), pp. 385-416; Körtner, *Papias*, pp. 88-94; Robert W. Yarbrough, 'The Date of Papias: A Reassessment', *JETS* 26 (1983), pp. 181-91; and Bauckham, *Eyewitnesses*, pp. 13-14, 17-20.

11. Richard I. Pervo, *Dating Acts: Between the Evangelists and the Apologists* (Santa Rosa: Polebridge, 2006), p. 343.

Option 3: The author of Luke–Acts knew Papias' *Exposition*. To my knowledge, only two scholars have proposed this option, and neither did so systematically. In 1956 Rupert Annand argued that Papias wrote around 80–90 and that Luke modeled his preface after the *Exposition*.[12] A few years later, Johannes Munck intimated that this indeed might have been the case.[13]

As we have seen, Apollinaris of Laodicea saw similarities between the accounts of Judas' death in Papias and Acts, similarities that most likely issue from Luke's creative redaction of the *Exposition of Logia about the Lord*:

> This one [Judas] then purchased a plot from the reward of his injustice and, falling face down, burst in the middle, and all his guts poured out. And it became known to all the residents of Jerusalem so that plot was called in their own dialect Hakeldamach, that is, 'Plot of Blood'. For it was written in the Book of Psalms, 'Let his farm become deserted, let there be no inhabitant in it, and let another receive his responsibility'. (Acts 1.18-21)

The *Exposition* and Acts agree in the following respects:

- Papias and Luke concur that Judas never repented.
- According to the bishop of Hierapolis, Judas 'died in his own plot' (ἐν τῷ ἰδίῳ...χωρίῳ); according to the evangelist, 'This one then purchased a plot (χωρίον)'.[14]
- According to Papias, God punished Judas with an 'efflux' of bloody discharge and maggots 'that seeped to the ground'. Similarly in Luke: 'he burst in the middle, and all his guts poured out'.
- Papias stated that Judas' plot 'became deserted and uninhabited'. According to Luke, 'For it was written in the Book of Psalms, "Let his farm become deserted; let there be no inhabitant in it"'.

By far the most popular explanation of these parallels assumes that both authors knew a tradition or a source that they used independently. For example, Hans-Josef Klauck argued that Luke inherited from this tradition his less vivid version of Judas' death, which Papias, or more likely his informants' tradition, graphically embellished.[15] This assessment is problematic.

---

12. Rupert Annand, 'Papias and the Four Gospels', *SJT* 9 (1956), pp. 46-62.
13. Munck, 'Tradition', pp. 249-60.
14. In Acts 1.25 Peter refers to Judas as the one who forsook his place among the Twelve 'to go to his own place' (εἰς τὸν τόπον ἴδιον).
15. Hans-Josef Klauck, *Judas: Un disciple de Jésus: Exégèse et répercussions historiques* (trans. Joseph Hoffmann; LD; Paris: Editions du Cerf, 2006), pp. 127-28.

Apparently it was Luke himself, not a source, who created this vivid description: 'falling face down, he burst in the middle, and all his guts poured out'. Because the adjective πρηνής, 'face down', was rare in Luke's day, readers ancient and modern have been unsure how to take it.[16] The word is common in Homeric epic. When combatants in the *Iliad* died bravely, they received their wounds facing their enemies and thus fell backwards (ὕπτιος), but Homeric cowards, who turned from their enemies, were struck from behind and fell πρηνής. The weapon, usually a spear, struck the man in the back, drove him face down to the earth, and spilled his bowels. For example, Patroclus's spear slew a Trojan as he turned to flee, 'and he fell πρηνής on the ground' (16.310-11).[17]

Luke then states that Judas 'burst (ἐλάκησεν) in the middle', using a verb that appears nowhere else in the New Testament or the Septuagint. The *Iliad* uses it for the cracking of bones in warfare, as when Menelaus struck Peisander in the head with a spear, 'the bones cracked (λάκε), and his bloody eyeballs / fell at his feet in the dust. / He doubled over when he fell' (13.616-18).

Luke ends his depiction of Judas' death by saying 'all his guts poured out'. This revolting expression, too, finds parallels in Homer, who described the death of Polydorus like this:

> Swift-footed noble Achilles struck him square on the back with a cast of his spear as he darted past;...clean through went the spear point beside the navel, and he fell to his knees with a groan, and a cloud of darkness enfolded him, and as he slumped, he clasped his intestines to him with his hands. (20.413-14, 416-18)

Two passages in the epic use an identical formula for disgorging that is similar to Acts 1.18: 'and then all / his guts poured to the ground' (ἐκ δ' ἄρα πᾶσαι/χύντο χαμαὶ χολάδες).[18] The word πᾶσαι with the tmesis ἐκ...χύντο resembles Luke's ἐκεχύθη πάντα. Readers familiar with Homer thus would have taken Judas' falling πρηνής to suggest that he was killed in flight like a coward. His bursting in the middle with his insides spilling to the earth implies impaling by an invisible shaft from behind. In *Does the New Testament Imitate Homer?*, I argued that Luke modeled the entire apostolic lottery after the lottery in the *Iliad* that selected Ajax to stand up to Hector. For example, compare the following:

16. See my *Does the New Testament Imitate Homer? Four Cases from the Acts of the Apostles* (New Haven: Yale University Press, 2003), pp. 107-109.

17. The word πρηνής is used of warriors falling to their deaths also in Homer, *Il.* 5.58; 12.396; 15.543; 16.413, 579; 21.118.

18. Homer, *Il.* 4.525-526 and 21.180-181.

Iliad 7.175-83	*Acts 1.24-26*
And each man marked his lot (κλῆρον) / and cast it into the helmet of Atreides Agamemnon,	[Peter's statement in 1.17 anticipates the casting of lots: Judas won his ministry with the Twelve in a lottery of sorts (ἔλαχεν τὸν κλῆρον).]
and the people prayed and lifted their hands to the gods, looking up to broad heaven, one	They prayed
would speak (εἴπεσκεν) like this: 'Father Zeus,	and said (εἶπαν): 'Lord, knower of hearts,
[I pray that] Ajax may win the lot (λαχεῖν), or the son of Tydeus,	indicate which of these two men you select to take (λαβεῖν) the place of this service and
or the king of gold-rich Mycenae himself'.	apostleship that Judas forsook to go to his own
So they spoke, and the horseman, Nestor of Gerenia, shook them, and out from the helmet popped the lot (κλῆρος) that they had wanted: that of Ajax.	place'. And they gave them lots (κλήρους), and the lot (κλῆρος) fell for Matthias. And he was enlisted with the eleven apostles.

Luke apparently saw the grotesquerie of Judas' death in the *Exposition* and replaced it with a stereotypical punishment of a Homeric coward and an imitation of the selection of a hero by lot. This direction of dependence might explain Luke's subtle alteration of Psalm 68 (MT 69), where Acts uses the adjective ἔρημος, in agreement with Papias (ἔρημον καὶ ἀοίκητον), instead of the participle ἠρημωμένη as in the LXX:

Psalm 68.26 (MT 69.26; cit. [A])	*Acts 1.20*
Let their farm be deserted (ἠρημωμένη);	'Let his farm become deserted (ἔρημος);
let there be no inhabitant (μὴ ἔστω ὁ κατοικῶν) in their tents.	let there be no inhabitant (μὴ ἔστω ὁ κατοικῶν) in it'.

Eusebius claimed that the daughters of Philip told of a

> marvelous event about Justus surnamed Barsabbas—how he drank a fatal poison and, by the grace of the Lord, suffered nothing out of the ordinary. The writing of the Acts [of the Apostles] narrates as here that, after the ascension of the Savior, the holy apostles put forward this Justus along with Matthias and prayed over the lottery for the completion of their number in place of Judas: 'They presented two men: Joseph, the one called (τὸν καλούμενον) Barsabbas, (ἐπεκλήθη) Justus, and Matthias'. (*Expos.* Frgs. 5, 10)

This citation from Acts 1.23 gives the first character three names: the first is Hebrew, the second Aramaic, and the third Latin. Eusebius's reference to Papias, however, speaks of 'Justus surnamed (τὸν ἐπικληθέντα) Barsabbas' and explicitly identifies him with Joseph Barsabbas Justus in

Acts. Philip of Side gives his name as 'Barsabbas, also (ὁ καί) Justus', probably from the influence of Acts. But which version of the name—Luke's Joseph Barsabbas Justus or Papias' Justus Barsabbas—is more primitive?

Papias implies that the man was known primarily as Justus, but also was known as son of Sabbas in Aramaic. He says nothing about the Hebrew name Joseph. Luke, on the other hand, probably added the name Joseph, to give the man purer Jewish pedigree. 'Justus' in Acts appears to be less a name than a sobriquet indicating that Joseph was righteous. This pattern of giving characters bearing Latin names Hebrew ones appears elsewhere in Acts, most famously in Luke's providing Paul with a Hebrew approximation: Saul. To Mark he gave the Hebrew birth name John. In light of Luke's preference for Semitic to Latin names, one might argue that Papias' Justus Barsabbas was the earlier version.

Unfortunately, it is impossible to determine if Papias knew a tradition about a replacement of Judas among the Twelve, but this much is certain: for Papias Judas' betrayal forever disqualified him from being an eschatological judge as promised in Mt. 19.28, which Papias surely had read. Either this promise would be unfulfilled or someone had to replace Judas, which is more likely.

Luke not only knew of Papias' version of Judas' death, he apparently knew Matthew's as well! The Matthean evangelist fabricated from Zech. 11.13 and Jeremiah 39 (MT 32) the purchase of the potter's field; therefore, the parallels in Acts to his buying the plot with 'the reward of his injustice' should not be attributed to independent tradition but to awareness of Matthew. Luke agreed with the account in Papias that Judas died in his own field but used Matthew's reference to the blood money to explain how Judas came to be a property owner. Although Matthew and Acts both cite Scripture to interpret the connection of Judas to his field, the citation in Acts seems to have been informed by the account in Papias about the field being 'deserted and uninhabited'.

Matthew created the etiology for the Field of Blood from 2 Samuel, elements of which suspiciously appear also in Acts:

2 Samuel 6.8	Matthew 27.8	Acts 1.19b
And that place was called (ἐκλήθη ὁ τόπος ἐκεῖνος)	That field was called (ἐκλήθη ὁ ἀγρὸς ἐκεῖνος)	That plot was called (κληθῆναι τὸ χωρίον ἐκεῖνο)
Uzza's Breach	a Field of Blood (ἀγρὸς αἵματος)	in their own dialect *Hakeldamach*, that is, 'Plot of Blood' (χωρίου αἵματος).
even to this day.	even to this day.	

Whereas the blood at issue in Matthew was that of Jesus, in Luke it is the blood of Judas.

From Matthew Luke borrowed the etiology for the Field of Blood, whose Aramaic name, Ἀκελδαμάχ, he also knew. Instead of Matthew's hybrid quotation from Zech. 11.13 and Jeremiah 39 (MT 32), Luke created a hybrid quotation of his own from Pss. 68.26 and 108.8 (MT 69.26 and 109.8). From Papias he derived the tradition that Judas did not die by suicide but was punished by God in a death that included the discharge of bodily fluids in his own field and that this plot became deserted. Peter determined Judas' place among the Twelve by having Matthias and Joseph Barsabbas Justus cast lots.

Were this the only instance of Luke's knowledge of Matthew and Papias, one might search for an alternative explanation, but my commentary on the *Exposition* argues that whenever it and Luke–Acts contain overlapping content, Luke is secondary. The same is true of the prefaces to the two works, to which we now turn.

V. *Luke 1.1-4 as an Imitation of Papias' Preface*

The title of Luke's original, unified work no longer survives, due, no doubt, to its later division into two distinct books.[19] Like Papias, the author of Luke–Acts wrote in the first person singular in the prefaces to both volumes: 'it seemed good to me' (Lk. 1.3), and 'I composed my first account' (Acts 1.1). Furthermore, beginning with Acts 16.10 and several times thereafter the author employed the first person plural voice for narrating the voyages of Paul that take him ultimately to Rome.[20] Surely the reader was to assume that the author accompanied Paul at these points, but the dating of Luke–Acts to 115–120 makes this claim historically impossible. Most scholars view the two-volume work as originally anonymous and seek alternative explanations of the we-voyages.[21]

---

19.   The first volume circulated independently, usually under the title εὐαγγέλιον κατὰ Λουκᾶν. For example, P[75], the earliest textual witness (late second century), contains this title at the end of the Gospel. Other manuscripts read simply κατὰ Λουκᾶν. The second volume was known by several variations of Πράξεις ἀποστό-λων, sometimes with the addition of Λουκᾶ εὐαγγελίστου. The earliest external attribution of the Gospel to Luke appears in Irenaeus, around 180 CE (*Adv. haer.* 3.1.1 (cf. 3.14.1-3 and the Muratorian Canon).

20.   Acts 16.10-17; 20.5-15; 21.1-18; 27.1–28.16.

21.   William Sanger Campbell provides a useful treatment of these proposals; see his *The 'We' Passages in the Acts of the Apostles: The Narrator as Narrative Character* (StBL, 14; Atlanta: SBL, 2007), pp. 1-13, and 'The Narrator as "He", "Me", and "We": Grammatical Person in Ancient Histories and in the Acts of the Apostles', *JBL* 129

It is more likely, however, that the author wrote under the pseudonym Luke. As the Papian fragments show, by Luke's day originally anonymous Gospels had been attributed to Mark and Matthew. Furthermore, most Gospels written in the second century bore the name of an associate of Jesus, such as the Gospels of John, *Thomas, Peter, Judas, Mary*, and the *Protogospel of James*.[22]

Even without the name Luke in the title, readers of the two volumes would have speculated concerning the identity of the author among characters from the Pauline circle. In Philemon 23-24 Paul lists people who were with him; they include Mark and Luke. This list seems to have informed the author of the Deutero-Pauline epistle Colossians, which includes 'Luke, the beloved physician, greets you' (4.14). The salutations at the end of 2 Timothy imitate those at the end of Colossians, and here again one finds Mark and Luke, now in Rome: 'Luke alone is with me. Bring Mark along with you' (2 Tim. 4.11). Ancient subscriptions to these books—Philemon, Colossians, and 2 Timothy—state that each was written from Rome. Even though post-Pauline tradition thus gave increasing prominence to Luke as Paul's associate, his name is conspicuously missing in Acts. But the first person narrator implies that he was with Paul until his imprisonment: 'When we entered Rome' (27.16). In this regard, one also might cite the martyrdom section of the *Acts of Paul* (11.1), which begins with two of Paul's associates awaiting his arrival in Rome, Titus and Luke, two characters entirely missing in action in Acts!

The original title of Luke–Acts likely contained the pseudonym Luke as a strategic literary ploy to announce from the outset that this story about Christian origins would have a Pauline slant. The name Theophilus, 'One-who-loves-God', probably is fictive as well, a symbol for Luke's readers (Lk. 1.3). It is difficult to imagine that a historical Theophilus around 115 would have been duped by the anachronistic pseudonym. Luke–Acts thus is a case of double pseudonymity: the work of a fictive author to an imaginary recipient for the benefit of actual θεόφιλοι.

(2010), pp. 385-407. See also my 'The Shipwrecks of Odysseus and Paul', *NTS* 45 (1999), pp. 88-89. Here is Campbell's sage conclusion: 'The first-person narrator character in Acts reflects the ancient grammatical practice and effects noted in the histories of Thucydides, Polybius, and Josephus. The first-person singular and plural passages in the Acts narrative defend and project the narrator's personal knowledge as eyewitness or researcher' (p. 90). Campbell assumes that Luke wrote anonymously, even though his analogies from ancient literature come from books that bore the names of authors.

22. Exceptions would include the *Gospel of the Hebrews* and the *Gospel of the Egyptians*, but it is by no means certain that these titles were original to these works.

After introducing himself and addressing his unnamed recipient ('you'), Papias discussed at least three Gospels that presented logia about Jesus in differing order: one of these had been attributed to Mark, and two or more of them were considered translations of a Semitic Matthew. Similarly, Luke's preface begins with an acknowledgment of previous attempts to compose expositions about the life of Jesus: 'Since many have attempted to set in order an exposition of the matters that have come to fruition among us, as those who became from the beginning firsthand observers and assistants of the message handed on (παρέδοσαν) to us [their expositions]' (Lk. 1.1-2). These famous verses require careful exegesis.

'*Since many*' (1.1a). Professor Alexander devotes a brilliant book to Luke's two prefaces and rightly refers to 'the tendency of critics to think exclusively in terms of the documents we know: Mark and Matthew/ Q are two, not "many"'.[23] Papias knew of at least four antecedent documents about Jesus, and the elder John informed him about speculations of a fifth. As we have seen, the four were the Gospels of Mark and Matthew, at least one other text with affinities to Matthew, and Aristion's *Expositions*; the hypothetical text was the Hebrew original of the Gospel of Matthew.

'*have attempted to set in order an exposition* (ἀνατάξασθαι διήγησιν) *of the matters that have come to fruition among us*' (1.1b). Here Luke uses a synonym to Papias' συγκατατάξαι, 'to set in order'.[24] As Alexander notes: 'compounds of -τάσσειν' stress 'the ordering of pre-existent material rather than creation *de novo*'.[25] Although the verb ἐπεχείρησαν, translated here as 'attempted', need not be derogatory, v. 3 indicates that Luke considered the earlier attempts to have been deficient.

'*as those who became from the beginning firsthand observers and assistants of the message handed on to us [their expositions]*' (1.2). Alexander translates this verse differently: 'just as the tradition was handed down to us by the original eyewitnesses and ministers of the word'.[26] Her translation and interpretation are inadmissible. The subject of the verb in Greek is not 'the tradition' but the tradents. In fact, the word 'tradition' does not appear at all; she understands the verb παρέδοσαν to imply that what was 'handed down' was 'anonymous oral tradition'.[27] Luke uses this

---

23. Alexander, *Preface*, p. 115. Unfortunately, Alexander mentions Papias' preface only en passant.

24. Alexander, *Preface*, p. 110, states: 'ἀνατάξασθαι is not so much a choice or a recondite word as a newly coined variant on the standard συντάξασθαι'.

25. Alexander, *Preface*, p. 110.

26. Alexander, *Preface*, p. 116.

27. Alexander, *Preface*, p. 120.

verb thirty times elsewhere, and in every case the grammar or the context clarifies what was 'handed on'; there is no analogy to the verb meaning 'to hand on tradition' without a clearly identified object. Surely it is wiser to take the implied object to be the multiple expositions ventured by Luke's predecessors.

Alexander insists that αὐτόπται and ὑπηρέται form a hendiadys and refer to a single category of people; the individuals in this group were both 'original eyewitnesses' and 'ministers'.[28] But the phrase 'from the beginning' seems to modify the observers, and 'of the message' probably modifies only their assistants.[29] Luke thus forged a chain of tradents. The first link, the 'firsthand observers' who handed down their expositions of the life of Jesus, resembles Papias' appeals to Peter, Matthew, and probably Aristion and the elder John, whom he called 'disciples of the Lord'. The second link, the 'assistants of the message', resembles Papias' statements about Mark, the putative translators of the Hebrew Matthew, and the bishop's informants who had personally heard Aristion and John.

After discussing Mark and Matthew's two translations, Papias stated his goal to put the logia again into proper order, 'with interpretations to confirm their reliability' (*Expos.* Frg. 5). Similarly, after discussing the shortcomings of his predecessors, Luke states his goal: '…it seemed good to me, too, having followed them all thoroughly, to write precisely in sequence also for you, most excellent Theophilus, so that you may recognize the certainty of sayings about which you have been instructed' (1.3-4). These verses, too, demand a careful reading.

'*it seemed good to me, too, having followed (παρηκολουθηκότι) them all (πᾶσιν) thoroughly*' (1.3a). Alexander provides compelling parallels where cognates of ἀκολουθεῖν were used to describe investigations into various matters.[30] Luke thus seems to be saying that he carefully consulted all the writings of the eyewitnesses and the assistants before composing his own. Papias gained his information from those 'who had followed (παρηκολουθηκώς) the elders'. He employed the same verb as Luke and in the same gender, number, tense, voice, and mood; only the case is different as dictated by the grammar. Although one might argue that Luke, like Papias, used the verb for following people with personal connections with the past, it would appear that 'them all' refers instead to the written expositions of the 'firsthand observers' and their subsequent 'assistants'.

---

28. Alexander, *Preface*, p. 119.

29. See Acts 26.16, where Paul is called a ὑπηρέτης and μάρτυς.

30. Alexander, *Preface*, pp. 128-30.

'*to write [an exposition] precisely in sequence for you (σοί), most excellent Theophilus*' (1.3b). The infinitive γράψαι, 'to write', has no expressed object, but the meaning is clear: the first clause in the sentence spoke of many who 'attempted to set in order an exposition', a task that Luke, too (κἀμοί), now will attempt. Similarly, Papias spoke of his task as setting in order (συγκατατάξαι) things that he had learned from the elders apparently by rearranging them into the same sequence that Matthew set forth (συνετάξατο) in his Hebrew Gospel, a sequence that the translators skewed. One may take the adverb ἀκριβῶς, 'precisely', either with the participial phrase that precedes it ('having followed all thoroughly') or with what follows it, which is how I understand it.

'*so that you may recognize the certainty of sayings about which you have been instructed*' (1.4). Although Alexander legitimately translates the word λόγων as 'things', I think that 'sayings' comes closer to what Luke had in mind. Similarly, Papias wanted 'to confirm the reliability' of the traditions he received from those 'who taught the truth…who remembered the commandments given by the Lord for faith and derived from the truth itself…I would investigate the sayings (τοὺς…λόγους) of the elders'.

The parallels between the prefaces of Papias' *Exposition* and Luke–Acts are striking:

Beginning of the Exposition	Luke 1.1-4
Title: Λογίων κυριακῶν ἐξήγησις	Title: διήγησις of… (?)
The name of the author: Papias	The name of the author: Luke (?)
The name of the recipient: unknown	The name of the recipient: Theophilus (1.3)
Papias knew a book about Jesus ascribed to Mark and had heard from the elder John that Matthew wrote his arrangement of logia in Hebrew, which 'each translated' the best he could.	'Since many have attempted
'I will not hesitate to set in order (συγκατατάξαι) whatever I learned well.' Matthew 'set in order (συνετάξατο) the logia'.	to set in order (ἀνατάξασθαι) an exposition of the matters that have come to fruition among us,
Mark translated the teachings of Peter; Matthew wrote his own arrangement in Hebrew, and at least two others translated it into Greek. For Papias the value of the elders was their transmission to posterity of traditions (παραδόσεις) about Jesus and the disciples.	as those who became from the beginning firsthand observers and assistants of the message handed on (παρέδοσαν) to us [their expositions],

Papias learned about the teachings of the disciples by inquiring of anyone who had 'followed (παρηκολουθηκώς) the elders'.	it seemed good to me, too, having followed (παρηκολουθηκότι) them all thoroughly
Mark 'wrote accurately (ἀκριβῶς ἔγραψεν)' but not in sequence. 'I [Papias] will not hesitate to set in order also for you (σοι)…'	to write [an exposition] precisely in sequence (ἀκριβῶς καθεξῆς σοι γράψαι) for you, most excellent Theophilus,
Papias wanted 'to confirm the reliability' of the information that he had gathered from those 'who taught the truth…who remembered the commandments given by the Lord for faith and derived from the truth itself… I would investigate the sayings (λόγους) of the elders.'	so that you may recognize the certainty of sayings (λόγων) about which you have been instructed'.

Surely these parallels are too extensive, distinctive, and sequential to be merely generic; they seem to be genetically connected.

It is more reasonable to think that Luke created his fictive authorial name and imaginary recipient in imitation of the names of Papias and his actual recipient than to think that Papias replaced Luke's pseudonyms with real names. Papias, who gathered information from those who had 'followed the elders', surely represents an earlier stage of tradition than pseudo-Luke, who 'followed' only written documents. Whereas Papias rejoiced in learning from 'a living and surviving voice', Luke, writing somewhat later, could appeal only to the written expositions of the 'first-hand observers' and 'assistants of the message'.[31] Furthermore, Luke seems to contrast his exposition with Mark's: 'whatever Peter recalled of what was said or done by the Lord Mark wrote down accurately (ἀκριβῶς ἔγραψεν) though not in proper sequence (οὐ μέντοι τάξει)' (*Expos.* Frg. 5). Luke, on the other hand, intended 'to write [an exposition] precisely in sequence' (ἀκριβῶς καθεξῆς…γράψαι).

Readers familiar with contemporary Gospel studies surely will recognize the revolutionary implications of this proposal. The Q+/Papias Hypothesis holds that Papias provides external reference to the existence of the lost synoptic source; it argues that Mark knew that document; it

31. Alexander provides compelling evidence that Papias reference to 'a living… voice' was proverbial among craftsmen and educators to express a preference for learning from an expert in person to learning merely from a book; see her 'The Living Voice: Scepticism towards the Written Word in Early Christian and in Greco-Roman Texts', in D.J.A. Clines, S.E. Fowl and S.E. Porter (eds.), *The Bible in Three Dimensions* (JSOTSup, 87; Sheffield: JSOT Press, 1990), pp. 221-47.

also holds that Luke knew Papias, and thus knew of three Gospels: one attributed to Mark and two to Matthew. My book, *Two Shipwrecked Gospels*,[32] provides a detailed defense of this solution to the Synoptic Problem and alternative reconstructions of Q (the *Logoi of Jesus* [Q+]) and Papias' *Exposition*. My commentary on Mark will argue that *Logoi* was the evangelist's primary source of information about Jesus, and that his Gospel should be considered a valuable third witness to it.

Although this essay challenges Professor Alexander's interpretation of Luke–Acts at several points, it very much stands in her debt. The last sentence of *Acts in its Ancient Literary Context* is this: 'But that—as they say—is another story', a recognition that other stories have yet to be told. What her book brings to the discipline is best expressed in its subtitle: *A Classicist Looks at the Acts of the Apostles*. Her impressive erudition, fairness in dealing with other scholars, attention to detail, and measured judgments make this work an enduring contribution to understanding Acts. This essay will have achieved its *telos* if it has made a modest contribution of its own.

32. *Two Shipwrecked Gospels: The* Logoi of Jesus (Q+) *and Papias's* Exposition of Logia about the Lord (Early Christianity and Its Literature; Atlanta: Society of Biblical Literature, 2011).

Scared to Death:
The Rhetoric of Fear
in the 'Tragedy' of Ananias and Sapphira

F. Scott Spencer

Intrepid interpreters have tried to unlock the mystery of the shocking Ananias and Sapphira episode (Acts 5.1-11) with various intertextual and conceptual keys, notably: the 'fall' of Adam and Eve in Genesis,[1] the 'theft' of Achan in Joshua,[2] the temptation of Jesus and betrayal of Judas in Luke–Acts,[3] community rules for initiation and excommunication at Qumran,[4] Greco-Roman codes of benefaction,[5] and myths of punitive miracles.[6] None of these approaches, however, has paid adequate attention to the *emotional impact* of the event in Luke's narrative. Because Luke's work is not typically given to histrionic display (nothing like Chariton's depiction of Callirhoe as 'seized with every emotion at once:

---

1. D. Marguerat, *The First Christian Historian: Writing the 'Acts of the Apostles'* (SNTSMS, 121; Cambridge: Cambridge University Press, 2002), pp. 172-78; *idem*, 'La Mort d'Ananias et Saphira (Ac 5.1-11) dans la Stratégie Narrative de Luc', *NTS* 39 (1993), pp. 222-26; T.E. Phillips, *Acts Within Diverse Frames of Reference* (Macon: Mercer University Press, 2009), pp. 141-43.

2. T.G. Crawford, 'The Promised Land: Luke's Use of Joshua as a Christian Foundation Story', *RevExp* 95 (1998), pp. 261–61 (255-57).

3. R.F. O'Toole, '"You Did Not Lie to Us (Human Beings) but to God" (Acts 5,4c)', *Bib* 76 (1995), pp. 182-209 (202-209).

4. B.J. Capper, 'The Interpretation of Acts 5.4', *JSNT* 19 (1983), pp. 117-31; *idem*, '"In der Hand des Ananias…": Erwägungen zu 1 QS VI,20 und der urchristlichen Gütergemeinschaft', *RevQ* 12 (1986), pp. 223-36.

5. R.S. Ascough, 'Benefaction Gone Wrong: The "Sin" of Ananias and Sapphira in Context', in S.G. Wilson and M. Desjardins (eds.), *Text and Artifact in the Religions of Mediterranean Antiquity: Essays in Honour of Peter Richardson* (Studies in Christianity and Judaism, 9; Waterloo: Wilfrid Laurier University Press, 2000), pp. 91-110.

6. H. Havelaar, 'Hellenistic Parallels to Acts 5.1-11 and the Problem of Conflicting Interpretations', *JSNT* 67 (1997), pp. 63-82.

fear, joy, misery, amazement, hope, disbelief'),[7] I take the double emphasis on '*great fear*' (5.5, 11) generated by the deaths of Ananias and Sapphira as an important interpretive clue.[8]

Not only here, but generally, biblical scholarship has lagged behind other disciplines—notably, moral philosophy, cognitive psychology, neuroscience, political science, rhetoric, literature and history—in a burgeoning renaissance of multi-dimensional explorations of passionate/emotional experience.[9] Revisiting what Philip Fisher identifies as 'one of the longest uninterrupted, most intricate and necessary descriptive problems in the intellectual life of Western culture',[10] contemporary scholars have come to appreciate anew the integral role that emotions play, for good or ill, in human welfare. Mounting evidence from neurological and cognitive sciences has confirmed that emotions, far from being mere isolated sensations or impulses, deeply affect—and are affected by—complex physical, mental, decisional and behavioral processes.[11] Whether emotional 'disturbances of mind' (Cicero)[12] or

---

7. Chariton, *Chaer.* 1.9.3; cited and discussed as part of ancient Greek novelists' penchant for 'this kind of emotional conglomerate...where every emotion in turn runs across the face of the actors, or with individuals who experience all the emotions together', in L.C.A. Alexander, 'The Passions in Galen, Chariton and Xenophon', in J.T. Fitzgerald (ed.), *Passions and Moral Progress in Greco-Roman Thought* (New York: Routledge, 2008), pp. 175-97 (182).

8. Cf. Marguerat, *First Christian Historian*, p. 155: 'The story of...Ananias and Sapphira...is the most tragic episode in the book of Acts. The Lucan art of dramatization reaches the height of *pathos*... The pragmatic effect sought by the narrator is apparent in the text itself: "great fear seized all who heard of it" (5.5, 11). This is a story that is meant to provoke fear'; *contra* O'Toole, '"You Did Not Lie to Us"', p. 196: 'Fear...was not Luke's main purpose in writing the story. In fact, in a number of passages, most of which are unique to him, Luke writes, "Do not fear".'

9. The bibliography in each of these fields of emotional study is massive and increasing; for a remarkably wide-ranging, interdisciplinary investigation, see M.C. Nussbaum, *Upheavals of Thought: The Intelligence of Emotions* (Cambridge: Cambridge University Press, 2001). For recent renewed interest in emotions in the New Testament and its environment, see T.H. Olbricht and J.L. Sumney (eds.), *Paul and Pathos* (SBLSymS, 16; Atlanta: SBL, 2001); Fitzgerald (ed.), *Passions and Moral Progress*; M.A. Elliott, *Faithful Feelings: Rethinking Emotion in the New Testament* (Grand Rapids: Kregel, 2006); K.A. Kuhn, *The Heart of Biblical Narrative: Rediscovering Biblical Appeal to the Emotions* (Minneapolis: Fortress Press, 2009).

10. P. Fisher, *The Vehement Passions* (Princeton: Princeton University Press, 2002), p. 4.

11. See, e.g., A. Damasio, *The Feeling of What Happens: Body and Emotion in the Making of Consciousness* (Orlando: Harcourt, 1999); *idem, Looking for Spinoza: Joy, Sorrow, and the Feeling Brain* (Orlando: Harcourt, 2003); J. LeDoux, *The Emotional*

'upheavals of thought' (Proust)[13] have a positive or negative influence and should be celebrated, regulated or eradicated, accordingly, remains contested; but a growing consensus across the humanities and sciences affirms that emotions should in no case be neglected.

And so we come to contemplate the mega-phobic reactions to the Ananias/Sapphira calamity. A basic fearful response predictably fits this double-death scene, but so what? What does this fear *mean*—ethically, philosophically, theologically, pastorally? What or who is the prime object of the audience's fear? What should they do with their fear, other than shake and shudder? What short- or long-term effects might this fear have on the developing church or on outside observers? Does fear leave any room for pitying or lamenting Ananias and Sapphira's misfortune?

Recognizing that understandings of the self—not least the emotional self—have changed over the centuries, we need a framework for interpreting the early church's response to Ananias and Sapphira's sudden demise grounded in ancient physiology, psychology and philosophy. Explaining negative emotions as heart squeezing or blood boiling is a rather different etiology than neurological networking among the amygdala and cortices of the brain; and fearing the evil eye, magic curses or Roman legions is quite distinct from fearing a surveillance camera's eye, MRI results or nuclear warfare.

Arguably the most formative and provocative reflections on emotions in ancient Western thought come from Aristotle,[14] who will serve as my

Brain: The Mysterious Underpinnings of Emotional Life (New York: Simon & Schuster, 1996); idem, The Synaptic Self: How Our Brains Become Who We Are (London: Penguin, 2002).

12. See, e.g., *perturbatio animi* ('disturbance of mind') in *Tusc.* 3.18; 4.54; M. Graver, *Cicero on the Emotions: Tusculan Disputations 3 and 4* (Chicago: University of Chicago Press, 2002), pp. xxxviii-xxxix.

13. Nussbaum, *Upheavals*, p. vii, draws the title of her work from a passage in M. Proust, *Remembrance of Things Past*: 'Love in this way produces real geological upheavals of thought. In the mind of M. de Charlus…a mountain range had abruptly thrust itself into view…in giant and swollen groupings, Rage, Jealousy, Curiosity, Envy, Hate, Suffering, Pride, Astonishment, and Love'.

14. See E.S. Belfiore, *Tragic Pleasures: Aristotle on Plot and Emotion* (Princeton: Princeton University Press, 1992); as well as the essays by J.M. Cooper, M.C. Nussbaum, G. Striker, S.R. Leighton, and D. Frede in A.O. Rorty (ed.), *Essays on Aristotle's* Rhetoric (Berkeley: University of California Press, 1996); W.W. Fortenbaugh, *Aristotle on Emotion* (London: Duckworth, 2nd edn, 2002); M.K. Sokolon, *Political Emotions: Aristotle and the Symphony of Reason and Emotion* (DeKalb: Northern Illinois University Press, 2006); D.M. Gross, *The Secret History of Emotion: From Aristotle's* Rhetoric *to Modern Brain Science* (Chicago: University of Chicago

primary dialogue partner with Luke in this study. In his *Rhetoric*, Aristotle defines emotions as 'all those affections which cause men to change their opinion in regard to their judgments, and are accompanied by pleasure and pain; such are anger, pity, fear, and all similar emotions and their contraries'.[15] Regarding fear, which registers on the 'pain' scale, Aristotle associates involuntary physical reactions of facial pallor, body chilling, heart pounding, tongue paralysis, voice/hand/lip trembling, bowel loosening, and genital tightening.[16] But he places most emphasis on emotions' cognitive potential to affect 'opinion in regard to…judgments (κρίσεις)'. Fear, in particular, 'makes men deliberate' or 'sets us thinking what can be done'[17] to escape the perilous situation and find 'salvation' (σωτηρία). Though the body might make the 'first move' in a fearful context, the mind soon kicks into gear to assess the particular *objects* and *occasions* that spark fear—which is where we begin with the Ananias/Sapphira 'tragedy'.

I. *Whom/What Shall We Fear?*

Aristotle advised that we must fear 'the right things…for the right purpose…in the right manner…at the right time'.[18] On any reckoning, the sudden drop-deaths of a married couple in the early Jerusalem church are scary, disturbing events. But where should respondents' fear be properly, reasonably, directed? What would Luke regard as 'rightly' focused fear? Potential fearsome candidates in the Ananias/Sapphira incident include: (a) God (and the Holy Spirit); (b) God's apostolic agent, Peter; (c) God's adversary, Satan; (d) humanity's ultimate foe, Death; and (e) honor's antithesis, Shame or Disgrace.

Press, 2006); D. Konstan, *The Emotions of the Ancient Greeks: Studies in Aristotle and Classical Literature* (Toronto: University of Toronto Press, 2006).

15. *Rhet.* 2.1.8, 1378a20-22; cf. *Eth. eud.* 2.2.4-5, 1220b12-14; all Aristotle citations, unless otherwise noted, are from the Loeb Classical Library (LCL).

16. *Prob.* 27, 947b-48a; *Rhet.* 2.13.8, 1389b32; *De an.* 1.1, 403a5-24; Belfiore, *Tragic Pleasures*, p. 184.

17. This translation is by W.R. Roberts in *The Basic Works of Aristotle* (ed. R. McKeon; Modern Library; New York: Random House, 2001), p.1391.

18. *Eth. nic.* 3.7.5, 1115b18-20; cf. *Eth. eud.* 2.3.5-6, 1221a18-19. Aristotle discusses 'right' fear in relation to courage. The truly brave person, he argues, must find the rational, moderating mean between cowardice (δειλία) that excessively fears what ought not to be feared and rashness (θράσος) that recklessly ignores what should be feared.

a. *God*

First, should we fear that God might smite us dead, especially if we fudge on our charitable contributions or otherwise misrepresent ourselves? Stories of divine capital punishment are common enough in ancient religion; and divine involvement is integral to the Ananias/Sapphira story: the fraudulent couple deceive God and test the Holy Spirit (Acts 5.4, 9). Further, God certainly qualifies, in Aristotelian terms, as a source of terrible fear with overwhelming power (δύναμις) to inflict painful punishment fueled by 'outraged virtue (ἀρετή)'.[19] Luke's Jesus warns his followers to 'fear [God] who, after he has killed, has authority to cast into hell' (the same God, eerily enough, who lovingly watches over every sparrow and hair follicle, Lk. 12.4-7), and Luke's Paul reminds all who 'fear God' of God's annihilating 'seven nations' obstructing Israel's conquest of Canaan (Acts 13.16-19). But none of this proves the deaths in Acts 5 are 'divinely instigated',[20] as often assumed.

The only clear case of divine *execution* in Luke and Acts depicts the angel of the Lord 'striking down' the preening Herod Agrippa 'because he had not given glory to God' (Acts 12.20-23); otherwise, punitive miracles result in muting (Zechariah, Lk. 1.19-20) and blinding (Elymas, Acts 13.9-11), but not death. In Ananias/Sapphira's case, the presence of God, though palpable, is entirely *passive*. God and God's Spirit are *objects* of the couple's lying/testing, but do not respond explicitly. Ananias falls down and dies when he hears (from Peter) that he has 'lied *to God*' (5.4), not when God speaks or does anything, retributive or otherwise. No causative agent of Ananias' death is reported beyond Ananias' own behavior and response. Likewise with Sapphira, though she learns (from Peter) that she has tempted the Lord's Spirit (5.9), this same Spirit—though dynamically explosive thus far in Acts—makes no retaliatory move. Sapphira is blown away by no mighty wind and burnt up by no fiery tongues; again, she simply collapses and expires.

b. *Peter*

But where God may be passive, does Peter not act as God's apostolic agent of judgment? Peter represents another δύναμις figure potentially worthy of fear: Luke summarizes that 'signs and wonders' performed by Peter and fellow apostles in fact brought *fear* (φόβος) 'upon everyone' in

---

19. *Rhet.* 2.5.4-6, 1382a34–1382b3.

20. Havellar, 'Hellenistic Parallels', pp. 64, 72, 81; I would now retract my own ill-chosen description of the demise of Ananias and Sapphira as 'suddenly struck dead by the hand of God' (F.S. Spencer, *Journeying through Acts: A Literary-Cultural Reading* [Peabody, MA: Hendrickson, 2004], p. 67).

the early Jerusalem church (2.43; cf. 4.33). Moreover, following Aristotle's tip that 'those who have committed some wrong' are volatile persons to be feared, especially 'when they have the power',[21] we might remain wary of Peter as one himself convicted of perjury—lying about knowing Jesus, no less (Lk. 22.54-62). Still, since he has been forgiven by Jesus, restored to a place of community leadership and thus far used the power of Jesus' name only for beneficent miracles in Acts, we do not readily fear Peter's punitive punch. On the contrary, we might even expect him to show some sympathy toward the truth-denying Ananias and Sapphira. But then again, this very *unexpectedness* of Peter's harsh judgment might help account for the mass fear following the couple's deaths.[22] Aristotle closely connects the emotion of fear with *pity* (ἔλεος): 'for in general...all that men fear in regard to themselves excites their pity when others are the victims';[23] and he views as especially pitiable (or fearful when it happens to someone else) when 'some misfortune comes to pass from a quarter whence one might have reasonably expected something good'[24]—like Peter, in our story, if indeed he were the catalyst of Ananias and Sapphira's deaths.

However, although Peter plays a dominant role—he has almost all the lines—he does not kill the offending couple (no Phinehas-style spearing here) or even pronounce a death sentence as such. He plays grand inquisitor and prescient prophet.[25] He grills the pair with damning, even entrapping (with Sapphira), questions and exposes their fraudulence with supernatural intuition (there's no hint that Peter or the church's 'treasurer' had audited Ananias' books). True, Ananias dies 'as he hears these words [of Peter]' (ἀκούων τοὺς λόγουος τούτους, 5.5), but these are words of revelation and accusation, not retribution and execution. Peter comes closer to pronouncing Sapphira's death (as might anyone after witnessing Ananias' fate), but technically only *predicts* it. He does not levy a death curse, summon an angel of death or direct the vengeful 'hand of the Lord' against Sapphira (as Paul does with Elymas); he simply

---

21. *Rhet.* 2.5.8-9, 1382b12-13.

22. Cf. Fisher, *Vehement Emotions*, p. 9: 'Events in fear-centered stories have an abruptness and unexpectedness'.

23. *Rhet.* 2.8.13, 1386a27-29; cf. 2.5.12, 1382b26-27; see M.C. Nussbaum, 'Tragedy and Self-Sufficiency: Plato and Aristotle on Fear and Pity', and A. Nehamas, 'Pity and Fear in the *Rhetoric* and the *Poetics*', in Rorty (ed.), *Essays on Aristotle's Poetics*, pp. 261-90 and pp. 291-314, respectively.

24. *Rhet.* 2.8.11, 1386a12-13.

25. On Peter's role in this story as God's apostolic agent and prophet like Jesus 'who knows what others are thinking, confronts them and whose prophecies are actualized', see O'Toole, '"You Did Not Lie to Us"', pp. 188-209 (188).

announces that the community bouncers 'will carry you out' as they did her husband three hours earlier (5.9).[26] Certainly no one would mistake Peter for a kind and gentle pastor here; his explosive personality or, better put, his 'boldness' (παρρησία) is on parade here (cf. 2.29; 4.13, 29, 31). He is not terribly comforting and more than a little threatening. But he is not homicidal or tyrannical. He is worth keeping an eye on, but not deserving of 'great fear' or panic. In fact, getting close enough to catch his shadow might still prove beneficial, as the ensuing scene demonstrates (5.14-16).

c. *Satan*

We contend not only with upright, morally outraged authorities (God and God's apostle), but also with powerful and destructive evil forces associated with Satan. But are God's people not protected from such diabolical attacks and thus without reason to fear them? Apparently not—at least not entirely. Peter poses the crucial question to Ananias: 'Why has Satan filled your heart to lie to the Holy Spirit and to keep back part of the proceeds of the land'? (5.3). The question is rhetorical, expecting no answer (which Ananias gets no chance to answer if he wanted to!); but it also intimates a deeper concern. Presumably, Ananias believed in Christ and had been 'filled with the Holy Spirit', either at Pentecost (2.4) or most recently, at a community prayer gathering following Peter and John's release from prison (4.31). *Why* indeed, then, has Satan now 'filled' Ananias' heart to *defraud the Spirit*? How can two antithetical forces 'fill' the same space (cf. Lk. 11.14-23)? Moreover, has Luke's narrative not stressed Jesus and his followers' repeated *overcoming* and *expelling* of Satan and his agents? Jesus certifies Satan's 'fall from heaven like a flash of lightning' and his messengers' authority over demons in his name (10.17-19). True, an exorcised malevolent spirit can return to its host with seven nastier cohorts, but they can only assume residence if the place is vacant, not if it is already occupied, especially by the Holy Spirit (11.24-26). Jesus also acknowledges—to Peter!—Satan's ongoing nefarious plans to put the disciples through the ringer ('sift all of you like wheat'); but Jesus also guarantees his prayerful support which will sustain Peter, who in turn, will 'strengthen [his] brothers' (22.31-32).

So the early Jerusalem church seems faced with a critical theological as much as moral problem regarding the demonic hypocrisy of Ananias, akin to that surrounding the treachery of Judas whom Satan suddenly

---

26. O'Toole, '"You Did Not Lie to Us"', p. 194: 'This prophecy [in 5.9] is much more direct than that spoken to Ananias in v. 4c and surely implies her death; but Peter's statement is more explanatory than condemnatory'.

'entered' and incited to betray Jesus (22.3-6).[27] As with Ananias, nothing in Luke's plot and characterization prepares us for this diabolical turn of events. Both Judas and Ananias fit Aristotle's category of the 'in-between' (μεταξύ) figure, notably neither vile nor virtuous, but suddenly and surprisingly swept up in 'some kind of error (ἁμαρτίαν)'. And such portrayals readily provoke fearful responses, as most people recognize in these figures the fragile sinfulness of 'one like ourselves'.[28] If Satan can enter such typical 'in-between' folk close to Jesus and filled with the Holy Spirit and abruptly lead them to deceptive and destructive behavior, is anyone safe? Who might Satan pick off next? Is it I, Lord?

d. *Death*

Apart from powerful, fearsome agents that inflict death by fiat or force, is the specter of Death itself, whatever its cause. Death potentially marks the most universal and ultimate, painful and harmful evil humanity fears.[29] I say *potentially*, because certain factors can mitigate the fear of death, notably, as Aristotle avers, perceptions of death as *noble* (as in war); *distant* (for most people); *peaceful* (i.e. not 'painful' [λύπη]; 'at least she didn't suffer', we might console ourselves);[30] or, as early Christians

---

27. On the parallels between Judas and Ananias/Sapphira, surrounding money and their own deaths (cf. Lk. 22.5-6; Acts 1.16-20) as well as becoming instruments of Satan, see F.S. Spencer, *The Portrait of Philip in Acts: A Study of Roles and Relations* (JSNTSup, 67; Sheffield: Sheffield Academic Press, 1992), pp. 124-26; O'Toole, '"You Did Not Lie to Us"', pp. 204-05.

28. *Poet.* 13.3-9, 1453a4-9. In the introduction to his translation of Aristotle's *Poetics* (LCL, 199; Cambridge, MA: Harvard University Press, 1995), S. Halliwell stresses Aristotle's broad use of ἁμαρτία to designate 'various sources of fallibility which could activate a tragic calamity' (p. 16) or 'all the ways in which human vulnerability, at its extremes, exposes itself not through sheer, arbitrary misfortune…but through the erring involvement of tragic figures in their own sufferings' (p. 17). Similarly, M.C. Nussbaum, *The Fragility of Goodness: Luck and Ethics in Greek Tragedy and Philosophy* (Cambridge: Cambridge University Press, 1986), p. 383, concludes that Aristotle's 'notion of *hamartia* takes in a variety of important goings-wrong that do not result from settled badness'.

29. Cf. Aristotle, *Eth. nic.* 3.6.6, 115a27: 'Now the most terrible [fearful (φοβερώ-τερον)] thing of all is death; for it is the end…' Corey Robin, *Fear: The History of a Political Idea* (Oxford: Oxford University Press, 2006), p. 36, comments on the thought of Thomas Hobbes: 'The purest form of fear was the fear of death, the ultimate future evil. Focused on the long-term, ultimate evil, the fear of death had an elective affinity with reason. It was the one passion that…offered a perfect coincidence of thought and feeling.'

30. See *Rhet.* 2.5.1-2, 1382a19-31; *Eth. nic.* 3.6.6-12, 1115a27-15b6; *Eth. eud.* 3.1.23-24, 1229b14-20.

like Paul believed, death is a *transitional* state to a glorious resurrection for the righteous (the wicked, of course still have much to fear).[31]

However we judge the seriousness of Ananias and Sapphira's error or its causal connection to their deaths, nothing in the story suggests anything noble or admirable about their final moments in this world; while we might muster some pity for this poor couple, we would be hard pressed to praise them for courage or promote them ahead of Stephen for the 'first Christian martyr' title. Likewise, we take little comfort in the timing of Ananias and Sapphira's deaths; far from living to a ripe old age or having opportunity to put their affairs in order, they epitomize the shock and fear of *sudden* death.[32] But someone else's sudden, unexpected death, while initially confronting us with our own mortality, does not usually produce deep and durative fear that *we* will also die suddenly, much less soon. Experience teaches that sudden death, while tragic, is comparatively rare and not contagious, *unless* extraordinary circumstances prevail (plagues, storms, bombs). As for Ananias and Sapphira, their double sudden deaths in the same place on the same day (three hours apart) pushes toward the extraordinary: two cases do not make an epidemic, but they might start one; and the startled audience in Acts 5 does not yet know what we know—that Ananias and Sapphira are exceptions (thank God!) and not the rule among the developing churches in Acts.

As for how the couple died or felt in their final moments, the story gives us little to go on. Did they die in peace or pain? The ominous tone of the account gives scant cause for assuming a peaceful passing (no cherubic faces or beatific visions, as Stephen has, Acts 6.15; 7.55-56); but neither is any emphasis laid on a painful finale (no stones [Stephen, 7.58] or worms [Herod, 12.23]). Again, the sudden, apparently instantaneous, nature of the deaths argues against their painfulness; but at the same time they could hardly be called pleasant experiences. Although, in Aristotle's framework, 'fear of pain' might not be the primary response to Ananias and Sapphira's deaths, the situation remains ripe for generating fear of unpleasant termination. And neither do beliefs of afterlife offer much therapy against fear in this case. Although Luke does not speculate on the couple's destiny, as hell-bent interpreters are wont to do, it is hard to hear Jesus summoning them to paradise (as with the rebel on the cross, Lk. 23.43) or to see him standing at God's right hand to welcome them home (as with Stephen, Acts 7.55-56). But neither do they wake up in

---

31. E.g. 1 Cor. 15.12-58; 2 Cor. 5.1-10; 1 Thess. 4.13-18; Phil. 3.20-21.

32. '*Immediately* (παραχρῆμα) she fell down at his feet and died' (Acts 5.10); cf. D. Daube, *The Sudden in the Scriptures* (Leiden: Brill, 1964), p. 43.

fiery torment in Hades, as the rich man in the parable, begging for a drop of water (Lk. 16.24). Still, in any case, the eerie uncertainty[33] about Ananias and Sapphira's fate would tend to fuel more fear than comfort. Ultimately, reflection on their sudden collapses more reinforces than relieves the sting of Death.

e. *Shame*

In his *Nicomachean Ethics*, Aristotle ranks shame or disgrace (ἀδοξία) first among all 'evil things' people fear, followed by 'poverty, disease, lack of friends, [and] death'.[34] While granting that poverty and disease are not always worthy of fear (that is, when they occur naturally, so to speak, not from personal vice or self-destructive behavior), Aristotle insists that it is base, brash, and even mad *not to fear* disgrace: 'One who fears disgrace is an honourable man, with a due sense of shame; one who does not fear it is shameless'; further, it is a credit to his virtue if 'a man…fears insult to his wife and children' or any other damage to his good name.[35] Moreover, in the *Rhetoric*, right after discussing fear and confidence, Aristotle further explicates the emotion of shame/disgrace. After defining shame (αἰσχύνη) as 'a kind of pain or uneasiness in respect of misdeeds (κακῶν), past, present, or future, which seem…to bring dishonour (ἀδοξίαν)', he delineates several particularly shameful 'misdeeds' which prove pertinent to the Ananias/Sapphira episode, such as 'boastful' pretentiousness ('mak[ing] all kinds of professions') and various signs of financial 'stinginess'. The latter include: (1) withholding security deposits; (2) profiteering in 'petty or disgraceful' ways; (3) contributing nothing or less than we can afford; (4) accepting aid from those less fortunate than ourselves; and (5) manipulating all sorts of shady loan deals. Bottom line: generous benefaction is honorable; tightwad calculation is shameful.[36]

---

33. On the nexus between uncertainty and fear, see D. Hume, *A Treatise of Human Nature*, 2.3.9, including such statements as, 'Thus all kinds of uncertainty have a strong connexion with fear' (2.3.9.27); 'Thus we still find, that whatever causes any fluctuation or mixture of passions, with any degree of uneasiness, always produces fear' (2.3.9.30); citations from D.F. Norton and M.J. Norton (eds.), *David Hume: A Treatise of Human Nature* (Oxford: Oxford University Press, 2000), pp. 285-86; cf. Fisher, *Vehement Passions*, pp. 17, 111-12.

34. *Eth. nic.* 3.6.3, 1115a10-11; cf. the full discussion of Aristotle's views on the fear of shame/disgrace in Belfiore, *Tragic Pleasures*, pp. 189-215.

35. *Eth. nic.* 3.6.3, 1115a10-11.

36. *Rhet.* 2.5.6, 1383b12-32; cf. Ascough, 'Benefaction Gone Wrong', pp. 96-105; S.S. Bartchy, 'Community of Goods in Acts: Idealization or Social Reality?', in B.A. Pearson (ed.), *The Future of Early Christianity: Essays in Honor of Helmut Koester* (Minneapolis: Fortress Press, 1991), pp. 315-18.

Although Ananias and Sapphira's conduct is not explicitly described as shameful or disgraceful, it hardly enhances their reputation in the Acts narrative or early church. Their good names, ironically meaning 'God is gracious' and 'Beautiful', respectively, are irreparably tainted. Their sudden deaths leave no room for redemption or restoring family honor; pity their children, if they had any. Whatever the amounts of their real estate profits (no figures are given), following Aristotle's catalog of dishonorable 'misdeeds', one can scarcely imagine a more shameful scenario than two community members lying about financial dealings, big or small, in a public setting where community judgments were rendered[37]— before the sacred fellowship of God and the Spirit, Peter and the apostles, and Barnabas and others who laid total proceeds from property sales at the apostles' feet (cf. Acts 4.32-37). And the fearful force of this shame comes crashing down on Ananias, first, and then his wife, when each *hears within this holy assembly* that their error has been found out. As much as anything, exposure effects their expiration. No one, divine or human, lifts a lethal finger. Ananias and Sapphira literally die of shame.[38]

Still, while Ananias and Sapphira's fear of shame might explain their deaths as well as any theory, Luke emphasizes not the couple's emotions, but the great fear gripping 'the whole church (ἐκκλησία) and all who heard (τοὺς ἀκούοντας) these things' (5.11; cf. 5.5). Moreover, Ananias and Sapphira's personal shame is mitigated somewhat by the decent

37. Cf. *Rhet.* 1.14, 1374b24-75a21 for other of types of 'wrong acts' or 'misdeeds', which helpfully inform the Ananias/Sapphira case: (1) the worst wrongs can be the 'most trifling', as in the charge Callistratus levies against Melanopus for defrauding the temple-builders of three half-obols, the rationale being 'that the greater potentially inheres in the less'—if you care and dare enough to withhold three measly half-obols, there is little limit to the calculus of your greed and dishonesty; (2) premeditated wrongs merit heavier penalty than spontaneous missteps; (3) a wrong is intensified if committed against one's benefactors, resulting in extreme public disgrace; (4) a wrong openly committed in a judicial setting—such as perjury—is as reprehensible as it is brazen (the early Christian assembly, though not an official court in Acts, is a place of judgment).

38. Bartchy, 'Community', accentuates the severity of the couple's shameful (and shameless) conduct as a gross betrayal of patron responsibilities within a fictive family of faith: 'By not telling the truth, especially about a matter so central to their relationship with their fictive kin group, Sapphira and Ananias seriously violated the honor of the group... When specific needs arose among the brothers and sisters of the congregation...patrons, such as Barnabas, Ananias, and Sapphira, became especially aware of their expected role as benefactors. Yet how they would respond remained in their control. That is why honor—or shame, or even death—could result from their actions' (pp. 316-17).

burials they receive; their bodies are not publicly displayed for ridicule or discarded in some garbage heap, like crucifixion victims.[39] And the promptness of the burials—a crew of young men immediately scoots in to carry out and bury the bodies—suggests a strong communal sensitivity: we need to clean up this embarrassing mess as soon as possible; can you imagine the fallout if people hear about this?

But of course they do hear, both within and outside the church (5.5, 11). This is not the kind of thing you can sweep under the rug (or ground). People will talk and people will listen; and given the extreme disgrace and severity of the reported tragedy, they will, as Aristotle suggests, become as afraid as if they had witnessed the event themselves.[40] Outsiders will avoid this perilous community like the plague. It comes as no surprise that 'none of the rest dared to join them' in 5.13; nothing puts a damper on evangelism like two parishioners dropping dead after the offering.

As for those *within* the congregation, two additional factors would exacerbate their fear. First, Ananias and Sapphira were not just some nominal church members everyone knew casually, but not closely. In this congregation, 'the whole group of those who believed were of one heart and soul' (4.32). Such intimacy inspired both a reciprocity of goods in which 'no one claimed private ownership of any possessions' (4.32) and a sense of deep corporate identification susceptible to fear in the face of misfortune. Upon learning that two in their tight-knit fellowship had not simply lied about their contribution, but had been exposed as liars and consequently died before God and the assembly, members would have felt as if such a tragic experience not only *could* befall them, but actually *did*. Either way, there would be ample cause for fear of shame and death. How can we survive in a community where everything we do or think might be publicly broadcast at any moment? If Ananias and Sapphira— people like us and united with us—died of shame, so might we all.

Second, however, Ananias and Sapphira were not just like us and part of us; they were the *first* to lie before us and die among us. From Aristotle's perspective, such distinctions would heap heightened blame

---

39. Cf. C.K. Barrett, *A Critical and Exegetical Commentary on the Acts of the Apostles* (ICC; 2 vols.; Edinburgh: T. & T. Clark, 1994), I, p. 269: 'The disgrace of unceremonious burial was not inflicted'.

40. *Poet.* 14.4-7, 1453b3-7: '[E]ven without seeing [the tragedy] performed the person who hears (τὸν ἀκούοντα) the events occur experiences horror and pity at what comes about (as one would feel when hearing [ἀκούων] the plot of Oedipus)'; cf. *Rhet.* 1.14.5, 1375a7-8.

and shame on this couple and, potentially, great fear and foreboding, among those who shared a 'common' (κοινός) identity with them.[41] They were the 'original sinners' in the post-resurrection Jesus community, the church's Adam and Eve, as Marguerat has suggested.[42] Thus far in Acts, nothing has prepared us for Ananias and Sapphira's tragic 'fall'. Judas certainly disappointed and dismayed us, but that nasty business is behind us now. The Lord, who 'knows everyone's heart' (1.24), chooses Matthias to replace Judas, the Spirit is poured out, thousands believe and are baptized and many restorative wonders are performed in Christ's name. The community enjoys 'the goodwill of all the people' (2.47). Peter and John spend a little time in jail but soon are miraculously freed and joyously welcomed by a united, prayerful community (4.23-31). There is nary a hint of internal trouble or evil *until* the Ananias and Sapphira episode shatters the Edenic community. Now, suddenly, supernatural knowledge of everyone's heart turns ominous; death and shame infect the vital and venerable church; and the future becomes frighteningly precarious. Jesus may be the 'first fruits' of resurrection life and hope (cf. Acts 26.23; 1 Cor. 15.20), but Ananias and Sapphira are the 'first fruits' of reprehensible death and shame. And we wonder and worry with great trepidation: Which harvest will we be? Whose pattern will we follow?

II. *What Shall We Do?*

The strong cognitive-moral approach to emotions taken by Aristotle (and confirmed by much modern philosophical reflection and scientific research)[43] stresses the vital nexus between emotional experience and thought-and-action responses. Emotions, however intense, are not—or need not be—tidal waves overwhelming us and sweeping us away, but more like channeled rapids alerting and directing us to critical, 'deliberative' reactions. Fear, in particular, as noted above, 'sets us thinking what can be done'.

Blindsided with great fear about exposing Satan-induced hypocrisy within a Spirit-imbued community, triggering instantaneous and ignominious death, the whole Jerusalem church and any outside who hear about the Ananias/Sapphira tragedy—including we readers—suddenly

---

41. *Rhet.* 1.14.4, 1375a1-2: 'Again a man's crime is worse if he has been the first man, or the only man, or almost the only man, to commit it' (Roberts, *Basic Works of Aristotle*, p. 1373).

42. Marguerat, *First Christian Historian*, pp. 172-78.

43. See the helpful survey in Elliott, *Faithful Feelings*, pp. 16-55.

have a lot to deliberate. What are we going to do now? How did the early church in Acts respond to the terrifying 'upheaval in thought' sparked by the Ananias/Sapphira incident?

Rather than trivializing this episode as an unfortunate hiccup in the church's progress, promptly cured and dismissed, or spiritualizing it as simply reinforcing the community's reverence for God (the 'fear/awe of the Lord'),[44] its pervasive, mega-phobic effects demand that we seriously consider its impact on subsequent events. While it would be worth investigating how such a monumental tragedy casts a shadow over the entire balance of Acts, I briefly sample its interpretive influence through 9.31, which announces the church's renewed experience of peace, growth, and 'the comfort of the Holy Spirit'.

a. Acts 5.12-16

The summary scene immediately following the deaths of Ananias and Sapphira features the apostles' continued performance of 'many signs and wonders...among the people (λαῷ)'. These 'people' include both faithful insiders who remain harmoniously 'all together' and congenial outsiders who hold the apostles 'in high esteem' and eventually join the community 'in great numbers' (5.12-14). Thus, internally, the fearful Ananias/Sapphira crisis brings the church closer together (if ever there were a time for mutual support, this would be it), and, externally—and surprisingly—the same crisis does not impede evangelistic growth as much as we supposed above. True, 'none of the rest (λοιπῶν)'—that is, skeptical outsiders—'dared (ἐτόλμα) to join them' (5.13). The verb connotes courage in the face of a fearful circumstance (cf. 7.32; Phil. 1.14), which 'none' (οὐδείς) could muster in this case. Those already hostile or indifferent to the church would scarcely be softened by the horrible double-death report. But those seekers already sympathetic are not so readily deterred. Despite the risk intensified with Ananias and Sapphira's fiasco, there is potentially still too much to gain from following the powerful Jesus and his apostles.

---

44. Commenting on Acts 5.11, Barrett, *Acts*, I, p. 270, states: 'The effect of the terrible and supernatural events just described...is naturally to induce fear; in this verse φόβος must be more than reverence'. *Contra* R. Thompson, *Keeping the Church in Its Place: The Church as Narrative Character in Acts* (London/New York: T&T Clark International, 2006), p. 84: 'The "great fear" that the text mentions twice...does not describe the beginning of an atmosphere of terror but the recognition of God's presence and activity within the group'. On 'the modern spiritualization of fear in the sublime', see Fisher, *Vehement Emotions*, pp. 146-50.

But a cautious approach seems prudent. Encountering the apostles and company in the open spaces of Solomon's Portico and the city 'streets' (5.12, 15) is a safer bet than attending a home fellowship meeting where anything can happen, like being publicly humiliated and hauled out the door—dead! Even then, they come in desperation, bearing the terribly sick and demon-possessed on their 'cots and mats', many of these already at death's door, and they do not get too near. Even though Peter did not personally kill Ananias and Sapphira, best to remain wary and keep one's distance: a brush of Peter's shadow will do (5.15-16).

b. *Acts 5.17-42*

Following the brief report of the apostles' healing work, the focus shifts back to threatening plots against the church. Now, however, the assault comes from outside the community, targeted primarily at its leaders: 'Then the high priest [and cohorts] took action' and imprisoned the apostles (5.17-18). Now the negative emotions of these priestly officials come to the fore. They are driven by '*jealousy*' (5.17) at the apostles' booming popularity with the people but at the same time must tread lightly out of *fear* of the people's reprisals (the temple police 'were *afraid* of being stoned by the people'[!], 5.26). Moreover, the authorities become murderously '*enraged*' over the apostles' audacious claims to be representing the interests of God and the Holy Spirit (5.33). Fortunately, one respected councilman, Gamaliel, reminds his fellow judges that these men just might be fulfilling God's plan (βουλή) and, if not, God can vindicate his own good name. What they must avoid, in any case, is being 'found fighting against God' (5.34-39)—a futile and fearful proposition, to be sure, as Ananias and Sapphira could well attest from their graves!

Within the strategic flow of the narrative, the tables have quickly turned from the ill-fated couple within the community to the misguided religious rulers outside the fellowship; now the Council members are the ones fearing reprisal and courting disaster. The politics of fear has shifted away from internal self-destruction to a powerful, yet vulnerable, external threat. Rallying together against a common enemy replaces paralyzing fear and self-doubt with renewed boldness and purpose.

c. *Acts 6–7*

'A man full of faith...the Holy Spirit...grace and power' named Stephen distinguishes himself as a dedicated table-servant, sagacious preacher, powerful miracle-worker (6.1-10)—and the first true *martyr* in the early church. Stephen's death stands in marked contrast to that of Ananias/Sapphira. He dies bravely and nobly; they die fearfully and shamefully.

His death results from false witnesses put up by hostile authorities outside the church (6.11-13); their deaths follow their own fallacious testimony before the believing community. His innocent face shines like an angel's (6.15); their tainted hearts reflect Satan's influence. At his last breath, he looks up, sees Jesus standing at God's right hand, and prays for his executioners (7.55-60); they fall down, collapse at Peter's feet, and have no chance to plead for forgiveness. He is buried by 'devout men' who lift a 'loud lamentation' on his behalf (8.2); they are uncere-moniously buried by a squad of efficient 'young men' who say nothing.

Once again, the perplexing, intra-community fear focused upon Ananias and Sapphira's sudden demise is effectively displaced to an external threat. But more than that, against the backdrop of 5.1-11 which set the congregation (and readers) to thinking intently about fearful, dishonorable death, the Stephen case clarifies what is truly worth fear-ing—and *not* fearing—and dying for. Fear of shameful exposure and shocking death within the church should not mushroom into pervasive paranoia about human mortality in a dangerous world. Bold witnesses to God's way, like Stephen and others following the trail blazed by Jesus, can expect virulent opposition from outsiders; and such circumstances call for courage and faithfulness that overcome cowardice and fear. As the Lukan Jesus exhorted (and exemplified): 'Do not fear those who kill the body and after that can do nothing more... [W]henever they bring you before...the authorities, do not worry about how you are to defend yourselves or what you are to say; for the Holy Spirit will teach you at that very hour what you ought to say' (Lk. 12.4, 11). The dynamic Stephen indeed speaks with unassailable 'wisdom and Spirit' (Acts 6.10) and shows no fear throughout his trial and execution, as opposed to Ananias and Sapphira who lie to the Spirit and muster no defense. In Stephen's case, to equivocate and *not risk* further inciting his opponents against him would have been duplicitous and timorous. *Not to die* would have been the truly fearful and shameful outcome, not only for Stephen, but also for the wider church still needing to reclaim its robust identity after the Ananias/Sapphira disaster. Stephen's noble martyrdom—and dramatic vindication by the risen, exalted Christ—helps the community to redeem its tragic loss, in some measure, and surmount its great fear with renewed confidence and hope.

d. *Acts 8.1-4; 9.1-31*

Such renewal does not mean, however, that the church's troubles are coming to an end. Quite the contrary—in one sense, matters get pre-cipitously worse. The Stephen incident sparks an aggressive terrorist campaign against the church spearheaded by a young man named Saul who had witnessed, and perhaps supervised, Stephen's stoning (7.58; 8.1). Saul 'ravages the church', hunting down followers of Jesus, hauling them to prison and 'breathing threats and murder' against them (8.1-3; 9.1-2). Given the classic 'fight or flight' responses to fearful danger, most in the Jerusalem church choose the latter option, scattering throughout Judea and Samaria and eventually into Syria and beyond. The apostles elect to stay behind, but evidently they cannot persuade the congregation to stand with them (8.1). Enough death threats already, inside and outside the community; enough losses, with Ananias/Sapphira and Stephen (however different their situations). With Saul now on the rampage, perhaps best to cut our losses and run.

But the narrative does not portray these exiles so much beating a cowardly retreat as pursuing fresh opportunities for witness, as the risen Jesus envisioned (1.8). For as they disperse 'from place to place', the believers on Saul's hit list 'proclaim the word' everywhere they go and establish new congregations. This message focuses on the good news of Jesus, the risen and exalted Messiah who conquered death and empowers his emissaries to heal the infirm and free the oppressed through his name (8.4-8). The capacity for fear to paralyze action and thwart initiative is well known (deer in the headlights); as Edmund Burke observed, 'No passion so effectually robs the mind of all its powers of acting and reasoning as fear'.[45] But remarkably, early itinerant Christian evangelists like Philip find a way to surmount their fear, turn their flight to advantage and become an agent of restoring, rather than reinforcing, 'the paralyzed' (παραλελυμένοι, 8.7).

Along with those who witness in his name, the living Jesus himself tackles the chief source of fear head on. Spiritually present but passive in the Ananias/Sapphira incident and standing poised for action on heaven's portal during Stephen's ordeal, Jesus comes down now, so to speak, and directly confronts—and transforms—the church's arch-villain, Saul: 'I am Jesus, whom you are persecuting', he tells the befuddled, blinded terrorist. 'Now get up and enter the city, and you will be told what you are to do' (9.5-6). What Saul is now 'to do' is to proclaim and suffer for the very name of Christ he had tried to stamp out! (9.16). Although some disciples, like Ananias in Damascus and the remnant left behind in Jerusalem, initially remain skeptical and afraid of Saul, such doubts and fears are dispelled either by another visionary manifestation of Jesus (to

45. E. Burke, *A Philosophical Inquiry into the Origin of the Ideas of the Sublime and Beautiful* (ed. A. Phillips; Oxford World's Classics; Oxford: Oxford University Press, 1990), p. 53; cf. Fisher, *Vehement Emotions*, p. 115.

Ananias, 9.10-16) or by appeal to Saul's visionary encounter with the risen Lord (9.26-27). In any case, the early church in Acts increasingly finds confidence to overcome its fears and move forward in the power and presence of the crucified-risen Christ who knows their suffering firsthand and overcomes death with life.

Such renewed boldness and progress, however, are not blithely taken for granted. Too much has happened, for ill as well as good, to justify overconfidence. As the summary note in 9.31 makes clear, peace and growth have not so much replaced fear as refocused it in a more honorable direction: 'Living in the *fear of the Lord* and in the *comfort* (παρακλήσις) *of the Spirit*, it increased in numbers'. Given recent events, God-fearing should not be reduced to some bland obligation of religious respect or reverence. There remains a genuinely fearful uncertainty about what the potent Lord God, Jesus Christ, and Holy Spirit might do—or not do—next. Moreover, the Spirit's παρακλήσις carries the active force of 'compulsion' and 'exhortation' as well as the palliative balm of 'comfort' and 'encouragement'.

So, under the Spirit's guidance and empowerment, the developing church in Acts forges its ways through fearful obstacles. But like a wildfire, fear controlled in one place can quickly erupt elsewhere. Mega-phobic traumas are not easily overcome once for all. Through Peter and John's imprisonment, Stephen's stoning, Saul's terror campaign—and beyond —the terrible and terrifying Ananias/Sapphira tragedy hangs like a pall over the otherwise triumphant Acts narrative, never quite fully buried and laid to rest.

DOES THE ROAD TO DAMASCUS RUN THROUGH THE LETTERS OF PAUL?

R. Barry Matlock

Thanks to the portrait drawn in Acts, Paul is the proverbial convert. Whenever we find ourselves 'on the Damascus road', when 'the scales fall from our eyes', when, as Hank Williams sang, we finally 'see the light', we partake in the history of reception of Luke's story of Paul, even if unknowingly. Some, however, know all too well. In the face of such cultural and linguistic riches, the New Testament scholar, armed with a critical awareness of the distinction between Acts and Paul's letters as sources for Paul, is faced with a dilemma. Questions about 'the real Paul' are difficult to suppress at a number of points with this traditional picture; yet this Paul is more real for far more people than any scholarly reconstruction. One *could* attempt a systematic cross-examination of both sources in pursuit of 'what really happened'. But it is not necessary to see the casual and the critical reader as being in competition. For amidst the great variety of readers engaged in 'reading Acts today', this 'critical reader', though a late arrival on the scene, has his or her own legitimate place at the table, to pursue her or his own particular interpretative project.

There are, of course, many such 'critical readers', under which rubric all the readers contributing to the present project would be embraced, along with the one whose work it celebrates. My own particular case is that of a Pauline specialist. How might such a reader, one who assigns a methodological priority to Paul's own letters and who brings to bear a particular set of disciplinary concerns, read Acts? I will focus on one point of common yet disputed ground between Acts and Paul: Paul's 'conversion'. I will take it as read that there is a difference in kind between Paul's letters as our 'primary sources' and Acts as an important early 'secondary source' for Paul (a simple qualitative distinction between what one says about oneself and what another says on one's behalf); and that Acts and Paul each have their own agenda and must be read in light of such, whether separately or in comparison (and so to that extent the source distinction is neutral). The same conventional considerations apply within the Pauline corpus, between undisputed and disputed letters. These two kinds of considerations (source distinctions and an awareness of agenda) are, of course, basic to and indeed definitive of what we mean by a 'critical' reading (and even the act of suspending such considerations, in the interests perhaps of a pre- or post-critical perspective, is itself a critical exercise).

There is not scope here for a systematic comparison and contrast between Acts and Paul.[1] I will primarily consider Paul's 'conversion' from the point of view of his letters and of issues raised in contemporary Pauline studies, drawing such comparisons with Acts as appear relevant from that perspective. Although I give priority to Paul's undisputed letters, I do not assume that they give us immediate and unfiltered access to our subject. What they give us is Paul's own slant as opposed to somebody else's—not the straight story, but a differently crooked one, so to speak. This inquiry concerning Paul's 'conversion' will cast a broader light on the peculiar interpretative perspective a certain kind of reader of Paul might bring to a reading of Acts, and what might happen to Acts when that perspective is brought to bear.

I. *Framing the Inquiry*

I begin with a couple of methodological questions.[2] First, what are we after? There are different ways of being interested in Paul's 'conversion', and we should try to be clear about this from the outset. We might wish to reconstruct what really happened on the proverbial Damascus road. What, exactly, did Paul experience on that fateful day? What did he see or hear? In what religio-historical, sociological, or theological context might we place this experience? Or we could attend rather to Paul's subsequent reckoning with this 'event' (notice that merely to speak thus of a singular 'event' is already to be subtly influenced by Acts). How does Paul narrate and interpret this experience? What effect has it had on

---

1. For such a comparative study of Acts and Paul, see most recently T.E. Phillips, *Paul, his Letters, and Acts* (LPS; Peabody, MA: Hendrickson, 2009).

2. For an overview of research, see L.W. Hurtado, 'Convert, Apostate or Apostle to the Nations: The "Conversion" of Paul in Recent Scholarship', *SR* 22 (1993), pp. 273-84; R.N. Longenecker (ed.), *The Road from Damascus: The Impact of Paul's Conversion on His Life, Thought, and Ministry* (McMaster New Testament Studies; Grand Rapids: Eerdmans, 1997); S.J. Chester, *Conversion at Corinth: Perspectives on Conversion in Paul's Theology and the Corinthian Church* (SNTW; London: T&T Clark International, 2003), pp. 3-42.

him? How does it feature in his theology, in his sense of identity and purpose, or in the argumentative strategies of his letters? This question of what we are after concerns both our own interpretive aims and interests and the nature and character of our sources (Acts and Paul's letters). Are we recovering an originary event or analyzing a mobile construct? Arguably, Acts encourages the first sort of interest, while Paul's letters more readily lend themselves to the latter. In theory either interest may be valid, though in practice they may be seen to compete.

Note that this choice can have an ideological dimension. An interest in the *immediacy* of Paul's conversion (understood both temporally and in terms of the directness of his encounter with God) can easily become a means of *validating* Paul, an effort to maximize what is thought to be 'given' with Paul's experience as opposed to what arose through historical contingency.[3] Alternatively, an emphasis on the *retrospective* character of conversion accounts might imply (whether intentionally or not) an underlying positive event that is inherently distorted in (or completely vanishes behind) the remembering and retelling.[4] However that might be, my interests lie more with Paul's retrospective accounts of his conversion/call, rather than in probing beneath them for some event itself; I would resist assigning an inherent value to either interest, while preferring to approach Paul's 'conversion' as something that lives in the very telling.

Second, whatever it is we are after, what should we call it? This is the now familiar question of terminology, as it was forcefully raised by Krister Stendahl. In classic studies first presented or published in the early 1960s, Stendahl famously posed the alternative 'call rather than conversion', sensitizing a whole generation of New Testament scholars to their use of these terms and persuading most to drop 'conversion' in favour of 'call', or to combine the two ('call/conversion'), or at the very least to place 'conversion' in 'inverted commas' (call them 'Stendahl scare quotes', now sprinkled liberally across Pauline studies, including the preceding paragraphs).[5] The most basic reason Stendahl offered for

3. S. Kim, *The Origin of Paul's Gospel* (Grand Rapids: Eerdmans, 1982), marks this end of the spectrum.

4. See the influential study of P. Fredriksen, 'Paul and Augustine: Conversion Narratives, Orthodox Traditions, and the Retrospective Self', *JTS* NS 37 (1986), pp. 3-34; cf. B.R. Gaventa, *From Darkness to Light: Aspects of Conversion in the New Testament* (OBT; Philadelphia: Fortress Press, 1986); A.F. Segal, *Paul the Convert: The Apostolate and Apostasy of Saul the Pharisee* (New Haven: Yale University Press, 1990).

5. See K. Stendahl, *Paul among Jews and Gentiles and Other Essays* (Philadelphia: Fortress Press, 1976), pp. 7-23, 84-85.

avoiding talk of 'conversion' is that it suggests a change of religions, from Judaism to Christianity, which would be anachronistic from Paul's early first-century standpoint.[6] Simply put, there was no 'Christianity' as distinct from 'Judaism' for Paul to convert *to*.[7] This consideration is certainly correct, so far as it goes. But does this demand the alternative 'call *rather than* conversion'? Why is it not rather an argument for defining more carefully what we mean by 'conversion'? Can talk of Paul's 'call' replace that of his 'conversion' *without remainder*? More recently, Beverly Roberts Gaventa and Alan F. Segal, among others, have argued that it cannot. After all, Paul experienced a dramatic and radical reversal that is hardly captured by the term 'call'—he did a complete about-face, from vigorous persecutor to tireless promoter, which entailed a marked change in religious practice and religious community, if not religions.[8] For such reasons, talk of Paul's 'conversion', suitably qualified, has largely been rehabilitated.

Note that this question of terminology can also have an ideological dimension. In attempting to *replace* 'conversion' with 'call', Stendahl was arguably smuggling in a considerable degree of continuity between Paul and Judaism; granted, 'conversion' might do the same for discontinuity unless properly qualified, but in any case continuity vs. discontinuity is precisely what is at issue and should not simply be built into the descriptive terms employed (even if 'call' is Paul's own term, used precisely as a claim to continuity of some sort).[9] Gaventa opposes Stendahl's terminological reduction, but is equally averse to the term 'conversion' for reasons of her own; her preferred term, 'transformation', demotes (if not devalues) human religious experience in preference to divine action and initiative (this too is arguably in keeping with Paul's preferences, but again he has his reasons).[10] Terminological and conceptual debate continues.[11] Whatever the terms, there are (at least) two phenomena here,

6. Stendahl, *Paul*, p. 11.

7. This is a sustained emphasis of P. Eisenbaum, *Paul Was Not a Christian: The Original Message of a Misunderstood Apostle* (New York: HarperCollins, 2009), in conscious continuity with Stendahl.

8. Gaventa, *Darkness*, pp. 28, 40; Segal, *Paul*, pp. 5-7.

9. On continuity vs. discontinuity, compare J.D.G. Dunn, *The Epistle to the Galatians* (BNTC; London: A. & C. Black; Peabody, MA: Hendrickson, 1993), pp. 51-71, and J.L. Martyn, *Galatians: A New Translation with Introduction and Commentary* (AB, 33A; New York: Doubleday, 1997), pp. 136-68.

10. Gaventa, *Darkness*, pp. 8-13, 39-40, 41-46.

11. See Chester, *Conversion*, pp. 149-64; P.T. O'Brien, 'Was Paul Converted?', in D.A. Carson, P.T. O'Brien and M.A. Seifrid (eds.), *Justification and Variegated Nomism*. II. *The Paradoxes of Paul* (WUNT, II/181; Tübingen: Mohr Siebeck/Grand

not one; and for want of better ones, I will use both terms, 'conversion' and 'call', or sometimes 'conversion/call', to indicate Paul's dramatic reversal and his sense of being appointed to a special task, respectively.

II. *The Pauline Texts: Overview*

Turning from these preliminaries to Paul's letters, I will give a brief overview of the principal texts, Gal. 1.11-17; Phil. 3.2-11; and 1 Cor. 15.1-11, followed by even briefer mention of other, possibly relevant texts.

First, then, we will consider *Gal. 1.11-17*. Notice first that the lead-in to the subject of Paul's conversion/call is a statement regarding the source of the 'gospel' (εὐαγγέλιον) that Paul 'proclaims' (εὐαγγελίζεσθαι). Its origin is divine, not human (vv. 11-12): it is not 'of human origin' (κατὰ ἄνθρωπον), he has neither received nor been taught it 'from a human source' (παρὰ ἀνθρώπου), but 'through a revelation of Jesus Christ' (δι' ἀποκαλύψεως 'Ιησοῦ Χριστοῦ; cf. the double denial of 1.1: Paul is an 'apostle' 'sent neither by human commission nor from human authorities', οὐκ ἀπ' ἀνθρώπων οὐδὲ δι' ἀνθρώπου); while this does not preclude an interest on Paul's part in his own status and authority, it does show the terms that Paul prefers to place to the fore (it is not about him, it is about the gospel—*or so he says*).[12]

As Paul turns directly to the conversion/call account proper (v. 13), he offers an intriguing incidental detail: he begins 'you have heard (ἠκούσατε), no doubt, of my earlier life...' He does not specify the Galatians' source of information, whether himself or someone else.[13] In any case, v. 23 ('they [the Judean churches] heard it said, "The one who formerly was persecuting us is now proclaiming the faith he once tried to destroy"') suggests that Paul's reputation preceded him, that in his own time he had already achieved a certain notoriety for his *volte-face* (the beginnings of a trajectory that may be traced through Acts 7–9 and 1 Tim. 1.12-17). Paul gives a name, 'Judaism', to the 'way of life' he left behind (τὴν ἐμὴν ἀναστροφήν ποτε ἐν τῷ 'Ιουδαϊσμῷ—as is often and rightly

---

Rapids: Baker Academic, 2004), pp. 361-91; Z.A. Crook, *Reconceptualizing Conversion: Patronage, Loyalty, and Conversion in the Religions of the Ancient Mediterranean* (BZNW, 130; Berlin: W. de Gruyter, 2004); P. Fredriksen, 'Mandatory Retirement: Ideas in the Study of Christian Origins Whose Time Has Come to Go', *SR* 35.2 (2006), pp. 231-46 (232-37); *eadem*, 'Judaizing the Nations: The Ritual Demands of Paul's Gospel', *NTS* 56 (2010), pp. 232-52.

12. Translation NRSV, here and throughout.

13. Paul himself: Kim, *Origin*, pp. 28-29; others, i.e. 'the Teachers'?: Martyn, *Galatians*, p. 153 (suggested, perhaps, by the NRSV's addition of 'no doubt').

pointed out, here we are to think not of a 'religion' as distinct from 'Christianity', but simply of Jewish practice of the law, of 'ancestral tradition', v. 14). And he includes several details by way of characterizing both that way of life and his approach to it: he 'was violently persecuting the church of God and was trying to destroy it' (καθ' ὑπερβολὴν ἐδίωκον τὴν ἐκκλησίαν τοῦ θεοῦ καὶ ἐπόρθουν αὐτήν) (v. 13); he tells us that he sailed through the ranks of 'Judaism' among his peers (προέκοπτον ἐν τῷ Ἰουδαϊσμῷ ὑπὲρ πολλοὺς συνηλικιώτας ἐν τῷ γένει μου); and he describes himself as having been 'zealous' (ζηλωτής), exceedingly so (περισσοτέρως), specifying the object of his zeal as 'the traditions of my ancestors' (τῶν πατρικῶν μου παραδόσεων) (v. 14).

But, he says, God had other plans for him! Employing the language of 'appointing' (ἀφορίζειν), 'calling' (καλεῖν) and 'grace' (χάρις), and with an echo of 'prophetic call' (Jer. 1.5) and 'Servant' (Isa. 49.1) texts (variously emphasized by, e.g., Stendahl, Seyoon Kim, and James Dunn), Paul returns in vv. 15-17 to the language and thought of vv. 11-12: God 'reveal[ed] his Son' to Paul, with the intent that he 'proclaim him among the Gentiles' (ἀποκαλύψαι τὸν υἱὸν αὐτοῦ ἐν ἐμοί, ἵνα εὐαγγελίζωμαι αὐτὸν ἐν τοῖς ἔθνεσιν), and Paul did not 'at once' (εὐθέως) 'confer with any human being' (οὐ προσανεθέμην σαρκὶ καὶ αἵματι) or go up to Jerusalem 'to those who were already apostles before [him]' (πρὸς τοὺς πρὸ ἐμοῦ ἀποστόλους), but rather he went to Arabia. Notice the placement of εὐθέως, 'immediately'. While the NRSV is not incorrect to place it according to sense with the positive statement about Paul's departure to 'Arabia', Paul's word order must be significant: it is attached to his double denial that he consulted 'flesh and blood' generally or reported to the Jerusalem apostles specifically; compare again the laboured denials of 1.1 and 1.11-12, and contrast this with Jesus' words to Paul, as reported in Acts 9.6 and 22.10, that he should go into Damascus and wait to be told what to do. Finally, Paul says he returned later to Damascus (καὶ πάλιν ὑπέστρεψα εἰς Δαμασκόν). Somewhat oddly, this first mention of Damascus speaks of a 'return' without telling us how that city may have featured earlier in the story—does Paul assume knowledge of this as part of what the Galatians have 'heard', whether from others or from himself (cf. 2 Cor. 11.32-33; Acts 9.19b-25)?

We turn next to *Phil. 3.2-11*. In this text, we are recognizably within the same world of thought as Galatians 1. The roaring success that was Paul's 'former life' of Jewish practice is here given enumeration in a list of items of which Paul could boast (καυχᾶσθαι)—were he of a mind to put 'confidence in the flesh', that is (πεποιθέναι/πεποίθησις ἐν σαρκί) (vv. 3-4). Again Paul speaks of his former glowing record as (he now specifies) a Pharisee, 'blameless' (ἄμεμπτος) in his pursuit of the law and 'zealous' to the extent of 'persecuting the church' (κατὰ ζῆλος διώκων τὴν ἐκκλησίαν) (v. 6).

Paul's reversal is now strikingly stated three times over in terms of counting every erstwhile 'gain' (κέρδος) as 'loss' (ζημία), indeed as 'rubbish' (σκύβαλον), in view, he says, of 'knowing Christ Jesus my Lord' (διὰ τὸ ὑπερέχον τῆς γνώσεως Χριστοῦ Ἰησοῦ τοῦ κυρίου μου), both in 'power' (δύναμις) and in 'sufferings' (παθήματα), of 'gaining' and 'being found in him, not having a righteousness of my own that comes from the law, but one that comes through faith in Christ, the righteousness from God based on faith' (ἵνα Χριστὸν κερδήσω καὶ εὑρεθῶ ἐν αὐτῷ, μὴ ἔχων ἐμὴν δικαιοσύνην τὴν ἐκ νόμου ἀλλὰ τὴν διὰ πίστεως Χριστοῦ, τὴν ἐκ θεοῦ δικαιοσύνην ἐπὶ τῇ πίστει) (vv. 7-9).

On a more general level, the polemical context of these verses—with their talk of 'dogs' and 'evil workers', of 'mutilation of the flesh' (κατα-τομή) vs. (true? [cf. Rom. 2.28-29]) 'circumcision' (περιτομή), of those who 'place confidence in the flesh' (οἱ ἐν σαρκὶ πεποιθότες) vs. those who 'boast in Christ Jesus' (οἱ καυχώμενοι ἐν Χριστῷ Ἰησοῦ) (vv. 2-4)—bears obvious comparison to the polemical setting of Galatians as a whole (to note but one striking correspondence, cf. Gal. 6.12-13).

Finally, we consider *1 Cor. 15.1-11*. This text is anticipated in 9.1, where Paul asks: 'Am I not an apostle? Have I not seen Jesus our Lord?' (οὐκ εἰμὶ ἀπόστολος; οὐχὶ Ἰησοῦν τὸν κύριον ἡμῶν ἑόρακα;). Here in 1 Cor. 15.1-11, we are equally at home in the world of Gal. 1.11-17 as we found to be the case with Phil. 3.2-11, but yet in a quite different way. There is again the emphasis on the 'gospel' (εὐαγγέλιον) that Paul 'proclaims' (εὐαγγελίζεσθαι) (vv. 1-2). Much has been made of the contrast between Paul's denial of a human source for his gospel in Gal. 1.11-12 ('for I did not receive it from a human source, nor was I taught it', οὐδὲ ἐγὼ παρὰ ἀνθρώπου παρέλαβον αὐτὸ οὔτε ἐδιδάχθην) and his use here in 1 Cor. 15.1, 3 of quasi-technical terms for transmitting traditions ('hand on', παραδιδόναι; 'receive', παραλαμβάνειν). There is indeed a certain tension here—but I think it has been overplayed. In Galatians 1, Paul speaks alternatively of the 'gospel' and of 'God's Son' having been 'revealed' to him (vv. 11-12, 16); here in 1 Corinthians 15, he speaks of his having 'received' (παρέλαβον) the 'gospel' and of Christ having 'appeared' (ὤφθη) to him (vv. 3, 8). While there is no polemic here against relying on human tradents, neither is there any *explicit* mention of such (and note 1 Cor. 11.23, 'I received *from the Lord*', παρέλαβον ἀπὸ τοῦ κυρίου [emphasis added]); and any implicit admission on Paul's part of his reliance on such tradition may be a matter for him particularly of the accounts of resurrection appearances to others. (That is, I think Paul could have stated the affirmations and denials of 1 Corinthians 15 and Galatians 1 side by side without embarrassment.)

In both Galatians 1 and 1 Corinthians 15, Paul speaks of the founding revelation of his apostleship; in neither case does he elaborate in terms of any specific vision or audition, nor relate this revelation to other occasions of learning about or reflecting on his gospel and mission, or indeed on the life and teachings of Christ, though we know there must have been such. On Paul's telling (v. 8), Christ's resurrection appearance to him is of a piece with that to Peter, James and the Twelve (just as he had spoken earlier of those who were 'apostles before [him]', οἱ πρὸ ἐμοῦ ἀπόστολοι, whom he had no need to consult [Gal. 1.17], here he is 'last of all', ἔσχατον πάντων)—even if Paul is something of an anomaly in having been an opponent rather than a follower of Christ on the occasion of his resurrection experience (an ἔκτρωμα, 'one untimely born'[14]). Notice that, while Paul pointedly numbers his own experience with Christ's *resurrection appearances* to the original *apostles*, Luke, who is as big a fan of Paul as any, defines both categories to Paul's disadvantage (Acts 1.21-26); Paul is an 'apostle' in the same sense as Barnabas (Acts 14.4, 14), but not apparently the Twelve. (Such indirect points of comparison can perhaps be more telling than direct comparison between Paul's 'conversion' accounts and those of Acts.)

Once again we find reference to Paul's having 'persecuted the church of God' (ἐδίωξα τὴν ἐκκλησίαν τοῦ θεοῦ), on account of which, he now says, he is the 'least' of the apostles (ὁ ἐλάχιστος τῶν ἀποστόλων), 'unfit' even to be 'called' an apostle (οὐκ εἰμὶ ἱκανὸς καλεῖσθαι ἀπόστολος) (v. 9). And here again is the language of 'calling' (an apparent play on the more mundane and the more exalted sense of καλεῖν; see also 9.16-17), and an even greater emphasis on the 'grace' (χάρις) manifest in Paul's apostleship (see v. 10, where Paul comes close to congratulating God on his choice of him, before turning the matter back onto God's doing).

And there you have it: these are the three texts in which Paul focuses explicitly on that turning point in his life which we call his conversion. We could expand on these three, perhaps, drawing a few more texts into the discussion—though these are all either more general or more ambiguous. On a few occasions, Paul uses the verb ἐπιστρέφειν, 'turn', in a sense something like our English term 'conversion': in 1 Thess. 1.9, he

---

14. See G.W. Nickelsburg, 'An Ἔκτρωμα, though Appointed from the Womb: Paul's Apostolic Self-Description in 1 Corinthians 15 and Galatians 1', *HTR* 79 (1986), pp. 198-205.

speaks of the those who have 'turned to God from idols, to serve a living and true God'; compare the reverse movement in Gal. 4.9, 'turning back again' (πάλιν) from God to the 'elemental spirits' (στοιχεῖα); and in 2 Cor. 3.16, he says that 'when one turns to the Lord, the veil [between one's mind and the law, vv. 14-15] is removed'. In the latter text, one may well catch a (highly refracted) glimmer of Paul's own conversion experience—and some would argue more than just a glimmer in light of the several possible references in this same context to Christophanic visions of the 'glory' (δόξα) and 'image' (εἰκών) of God (2 Cor. 3.18; 4.4-6; cf. Phil. 3.21).[15] Some would bring Rom. 10.2-4 into the picture, in part because of the links between these verses and Phil. 3.6, 9.[16] Paul's language of 'calling' (καλεῖν, κλῆσις, κλῆτος) and 'believing' (πίστις, πιστεύειν) could extend our account of 'conversion' in the Pauline letters still further.[17] Among the many contributions of Stephen Chester's *Conversion at Corinth* to our understanding of conversion in Paul are the way that he mines the incidental details of 1 Cor. 14.20-25 for insights into Gentile conversion as according to Paul and the original and stimulating way in which he brings Rom. 7.7-25 back into the discussion of Paul's conversion.[18]

III. *The Pauline Texts: Analysis*

Having made this (all too) brief overview of the texts, a few comments may be ventured by way of analysis. The first thing to observe here has already begun to emerge above, namely the way in which these three texts form two different pairings, Gal. 1.11-17 first with Phil. 3.2-11, then with 1 Cor. 15.1-11. Juxtaposing them in this way casts light on all three, and reinforces the point that there are two phenomena to be kept in view ('conversion' and 'call'), not one. A sense of 'calling' is most explicit in Gal. 1.15-16; it is more muted in 1 Cor. 15.9, where Paul states his unworthiness to be 'called an apostle', but he is that all the same; in Philippians 3, Paul's calling or commissioning is implicit, not explicit.

---

15. See, e.g., Kim, *Origin; idem, Paul and the New Perspective: Second Thoughts on the Origin of Paul's Gospel* (Grand Rapids: Eerdmans, 2002); Segal, *Paul;* C.C. Newman, *Paul's Glory-Christology: Tradition and Rhetoric* (NovTSup, 69; Leiden: Brill, 1992).

16. See, e.g., Kim, *Origin*, pp. 3-4 and n. 4.

17. For a recent overview, see Chester, *Conversion*, pp. 59-112.

18. Chester, *Conversion*, pp. 114-25, 183-95; cf. Gaventa, *Darkness*, pp. 43, 33-36; see further R.B. Matlock, Review of S. Chester, *Conversion at Corinth* and S. Gathercole, *Where is Boasting?*, *JSNT* 26 (2003), pp. 251-55.

The sense of discontinuity and dramatic reversal we call 'conversion' is clearly, though differently, expressed in each text. In Galatians 1, a promising career 'in Judaism' is abruptly abandoned, and Paul changes from persecutor and would-be destroyer of 'the church of God'/'the faith' to apostle to the Gentiles and proclaimer of the gospel; in Philippians 3, former privileges and achievements, even the rigour of a Pharisee and the zeal of a persecutor, count for nothing, and now Paul 'boasts' only 'in Christ Jesus', in 'knowing' and 'gaining' him and 'being found in him'; in 1 Corinthians 15, Paul, again, changes from persecutor to apostle, and in the later capacity he more than makes up for the former (or rather God working in him, he corrects himself to say).

While each of these three texts relates to what must surely be regarded as an intimate and significant facet of Paul's life, in no case does Paul write simply out of some autobiographical urge; moreover, he never focuses squarely on some conversion 'event' itself. Quite telling in this latter regard is Gal. 1.15-16, where the detail about God 'revealing his Son' to Paul is part of a long temporal and purposive build-up to Paul's response to this revelation—about which he is equally unrevealing: *when the God who set him apart and called him was pleased to reveal his Son to Paul so that he would proclaim him to the Gentiles*, Paul *did not* straightaway consult with flesh and blood nor report to the Jerusalem apostles but (at last we reach the main verb) he *departed to Arabia* (exactly where and why and for how long he does not say). In 1 Cor. 15.8, the report of the revelatory event itself is reduced to two words: ὤφθη κἀμοί, 'he appeared also to me'—the elision of καὶ ἐμοί to κἀμοί resulting in the most compact statement possible! In Phil. 3.2-11, there is clearly a before and an after, but no narrative at all of any turning point itself. And while 2 Cor. 3.7–4.6 may well reflect Paul's conversion experience, it does not narrate it. Spare a thought for someone like Luke who would fill out these narrative gaps—Paul's own 'conversion narrative' is almost all gap!

In each of the three principal texts Paul draws upon his own story according to some agenda. Galatians as a whole is marked by explicit polemic and apologetic, including Galatians 1–2 (an apologetic and a paradigmatic rationale for these chapters are not mutually exclusive[19]); here Paul's radical reversal is both a dramatic testimony to the divine hand at work in his mission and a means of legitimating himself and scoring points against his rivals. Philippians 3 suggests a similar polemic (though perhaps directed more against a potential than an actual threat); here Paul draws more pointedly on his own experience, now with an

19. Cf. B.R. Gaventa, 'Galatians 1 and 2: Autobiography as Paradigm', *NovT* 28 (1986), pp. 309-26.

explicitly paradigmatic intent (Phil. 3.17). In 1 Corinthians 15, Paul's apostleship is hardly itself the focus (though on this subject polemic or apologetic may never be far below the surface); rather, it is incidental to Paul's attempt to move from what he regards everyone in the community as having accepted (Christ's resurrection) to what is at issue (resurrection generally).

Another feature of these texts, deserving of more attention than is possible here, is the Christological focus: in both Galatians 1 and 1 Corinthians 15, it is Christ who is revealed to Paul, and in Philippians 3 it is Christ in whom Paul 'boasts', whom he desires to 'know' and 'gain', and 'in' whom he wishes to be 'found'.

The one item that features most conspicuously on each occasion when Paul recounts this turning point in his life is his 'persecution' of the church: Gal. 1.13 (cf. v. 23); Phil. 3.6; 1 Cor. 15.9. How exactly does this relate to Paul's conversion/call? Gaventa plays it down, both in terms of its severity and its bearing on Paul's conversion.[20] It is true that the terms Paul uses—διώκειν, 'pursue, persecute'; καθ' ὑπερβολήν, 'to the utmost'; πόρθειν, 'destroy'—do not of themselves settle the question of the precise nature of Paul's activity; that the narratives of Acts may have coloured our perception of this; and that 'it is extremely difficult to explain how Paul could have legally carried out a violent persecution' (Gaventa argues, following D.R.A. Hare, that 'Jewish persecution of Christians' mostly 'took the form of informal social ostracism and economic boycott', with 'little evidence for execution, flogging, or imprisonment').[21] Yet her conclusion that Paul's 'persecution' was probably 'verbal rather than violent' seems too cautious.[22] The truth may lie somewhere between 'threats and murder' (Acts 9.1) and mere tongue-lashings. The relative severity of Paul's 'persecution' is reflected not just in the terms noted above, but in their combination (which has an intensifying effect), in the associations of the added term 'zeal', in the reaction of others (Gal. 1.23), and in Paul's own retrospective judgment (1 Cor. 15.9).[23] And however scarce the

20. Gaventa, *Darkness*, pp. 25-26, 39.

21. Gaventa, *Darkness*, pp. 26, 47 n. 24.

22. Gaventa, *Darkness*, pp. 26, 39; similarly, L. Lietaert Peerbolte, *Paul the Missionary* (CBET, 34; Leuven: Peeters, 2003): Paul directed his opposition against the views, not the persons of early Christ-followers (pp. 143-45, 160, 176).

23. On 'zeal', see, e.g., M. Hengel (in collaboration with R. Deines), *The Pre-Christian Paul* (trans. J. Bowden; London: SCM Press; Philadelphia: Trinity Press International, 1991), pp. 70-71; T.L. Donaldson, 'Zealot and Convert: The Origin of Paul's Christ-Torah Antithesis', *CBQ* 51 (1989), pp. 655-82; Dunn, *Galatians*, pp. 60-62; N.T. Wright, 'Paul, Arabia, and Elijah (Galatians 1:17)', *JBL* 115 (1996), pp. 683-92.

evidence for violent persecution, Paul is one way or another implicated in much of it (2 Cor. 11.23-25; cf. Rom. 15.31; 1 Thess. 2.14-16). Given the ideologically fraught nature of the question of 'Jewish persecution of Christians', it is well to remind ourselves that in this period we are talking about intra-Jewish strife. Moreover, 'persecution' is subject to perspective: what to the persecutor may be a legitimate exercise of internal discipline, to the victim may be an act of violent repression.[24] And in between the legal exercise of due process and an outbreak of mob violence, both of which Paul experienced on the receiving end (again, 2 Cor. 11.23-25), there is the potential for legal process to be used as a pretext for violence. The question remains what bearing this has on Paul's conversion—again, an association created by Paul himself. Why did Paul persecute Christ-followers, and how does this relate to his conversion/call, and to the later contexts in which he harks back to it?

Strictly speaking, the one item relating to Paul's conversion/call with the least *explicit* emphasis in Paul's letters is the single mention of 'the Gentiles' in Gal. 1.16. This is the opposite of what both Stendahl and Acts might lead us to expect (Acts 9.15; 22.21; 26.17; cf. Col. 1.24-29; Eph. 3.1-13). This is not to take away from the fact that this is a significant point of correspondence between Acts and Paul or to diminish the importance of Paul's sense of being 'Apostle to the Gentiles' (Gal. 2.7-9; Rom. 1.5, 13-15; 11.13; 15.15-16, 18-20, 23-24), just to note this Pauline reserve in terms of associating his mission to the Gentiles explicitly with some singular revelatory event or experience ('conversion', 'call', or what have you). For that matter, there is on closer inspection a certain ambivalence to the Acts accounts: in the direct narrative of Paul's conversion in Acts 9, the detail about Paul being sent to the Gentiles is revealed after the Damascus road experience to Ananias and not to Paul (9.10-16); in Paul's first retelling of the story in Acts 22, he himself learns that he is to be sent to the Gentiles in yet a third revelatory experience, a vision (ἔκστασις) of Jesus that occurs while he is praying in the temple in Jerusalem (22.17-21); in Paul's second retelling of the story in Acts 26, the content of these subsequent revelations to Ananias and to Paul, including the part about his being sent to the Gentiles, is poured back into the original conversion experience as part of Jesus' first words to Paul (26.12-18). Finally, this point may be joined to the previous: how do Paul's persecution, his conversion/call, and the origin of a Gentile mission relate to one another?

24. See A.J. Hultgren, 'Paul's Pre-Christian Persecutions of the Church: Their Purpose, Locale, and Nature', *JBL* 95 (1976), pp. 97-111; cf. P. Fredriksen, 'Judaism, the Circumcision of Gentiles, and Apocalyptic Hope: Another Look at Galatians 1 and 2', *JTS* NS 42 (1991), pp. 532-64 (548-58).

IV. *The 'New Perspective' and Paul's 'Conversion'*

In relation to that complex question, a few comments about the 'new perspective on Paul' in connection with Paul's conversion must suffice. The 'new perspective' has two aspects: it is a correction both of an older Christian caricature of Judaism as a 'legalistic' religion and of the individualism and interiority of traditional Protestant readings of Paul. Both aspects necessitate a re-evaluation of Paul's 'conversion'. Stendahl's contrast between Paul's 'robust conscience' and the 'introspective conscience of the West' is directed toward the latter aspect.[25] Stendahl's negative point has prevailed, and so it is now customary to point out, quite rightly, that the conversion texts surveyed above betray no trace of the soul-strivings of Luther.[26] His positive point about Paul's 'robust conscience' has been overplayed, I think; that is, these texts do not offer us a transparent window into Paul's 'subjective conscience' as either 'troubled' or 'robust', but rather they purport, at least, to reflect an objective public record about Paul's former life. At any rate, Stendahl regards his 'salvation historical' reading of Paul as 'open[ing] up a new perspective' for our contemporary understanding of Paul.[27] E.P. Sanders' *Paul and Palestinian Judaism* is directed more toward the first aspect of the 'new perspective'. Sanders' Paul famously experienced a complete revolution in 'patterns of religion', in the wake of which Paul could only fault 'Judaism' for not being 'Christianity'.[28] When Sanders argues that 'Paul did not so much misunderstand the role of the law in Judaism as gain a new perspective which led him to declare the law abolished', he gestures toward Paul's 'conversion' or 'call', but makes no attempt to penetrate any further into this experience or process.[29]

To James Dunn such a supposed leap on Paul's part seems arbitrary, and in reaction to this his long-running attempt to systematize a 'new perspective on Paul' includes an impressively sustained series of studies on Paul's 'conversion'.[30] According to Dunn, Paul's earlier persecuting

25. Stendahl, *Paul*, pp. 7-23, 78-96.

26. See, e.g., Gaventa, *Darkness*, pp. 26, 28, 31-33, 35-37.

27. Stendahl, *Paul*, p. 95.

28. E.P. Sanders, *Paul and Palestinian Judaism: A Comparison of Patterns of Religion* (Philadelphia: Fortress Press, 1977), pp. 548-52.

29. Sanders, *Paul and Palestinian Judaism*, p. 496.

30. J.D.G. Dunn, *Jesus, Paul and the Law: Studies in Mark and Galatians* (Louisville, KY: Westminster John Knox, 1990), pp. 89-107; *idem*, *The Partings of the Ways between Christianity and Judaism and their Significance for the Character of Christianity* (London: SCM Press; Philadelphia: Trinity Press International, 1991), pp. 119-27; *idem*, *Galatians*, pp. 51-71; *idem*, 'Paul and Justification by Faith', in Longenecker

zeal was a violent policing of the boundaries of Judaism directed against a law-free Jewish Christian mission to Gentiles already underway, of which Paul the 'convert' then became a chief proponent. Dunn emphatically dates Paul's awareness of this mission to the very moment of the conversion/call itself, which he takes to be the significance of the ἵνα of Gal. 1.16: 'God reveal[ed] his Son to me, *so that* I might proclaim him among the Gentiles'.[31] This offers a straightforward alignment of persecution, conversion/call and Gentile mission ('Paul was converted to what he had persecuted', i.e. Gentile inclusion[32]), but assumes a very early date for the origins of such a mission and the controversy surrounding it.[33]

Terrence Donaldson argues that the 'new perspective' bears a much greater explanatory burden than the 'old' in terms of accounting specifically for Paul's concern for Gentiles, and his own reconstruction (relying particularly on Gal. 5.11) pushes the origins back further still, positing a law-observant Pauline mission to Gentiles *already in Paul's pre-conversion life 'in Judaism'*.[34] On Francis Watson's impressive critical sifting of the evidence both of Paul's letters and of Acts, Paul's Gentile mission, both in practice and in theory, is a later development arising out of Paul's earlier mission experience, in fact a failed mission to Israel.[35] In contrast to Dunn, Watson argues that Gal. 1.16 'cannot be safely used as evidence for [Paul's] self-understanding at the time of his conversion', since 'Paul here is reflecting on his conversion as he now understands it, in a highly charged polemical context, perhaps twenty years after the event' (an appeal to the retrospective character of Paul's account); and 'even here, Paul does not actually claim that his vocation to preach to Gentiles was part of the initial disclosure', but rather the ἵνα expresses 'the fundamental divine *intention* in a revelation that embraced [Paul's] existence in its entirely, "from my mother's womb" (v. 15)', as Paul says.[36]

(ed.), *The Road from Damascus*, pp. 85-101; *idem*, *The Theology of Paul the Apostle* (Grand Rapids: Eerdmans, 1998), pp. 346-54; *idem*, *The New Perspective on Paul: Collected Essays* (WUNT, 185; Tübingen: Mohr Siebeck, 2005), pp. 341-59, 463-84.

31.   Dunn, *Jesus, Paul and the Law*, pp. 89, 98, 100; *idem*, *Galatians*, p. 66; *idem*, *New Perspective*, pp. 356-57.

32.   Dunn, *New Perspective*, p. 357.

33.   Cf. Fredriksen, 'Judaism, Gentiles', pp. 552-58.

34.   At length, T.L. Donaldson, *Paul and the Gentiles: Remapping the Apostle's Convictional World* (Minneapolis: Fortress Press, 1997); in brief, *idem*, 'Israelite, Convert, Apostle to the Gentiles: The Origin of Paul's Gentile Mission', in Longenecker (ed.), *The Road from Damascus*, pp. 62-84.

35.   See F. Watson, *Paul, Judaism, and the Gentiles: Beyond the New Perspective* (Grand Rapids: Eerdmans, rev. and expanded edn, 2007), pp. 59-86.

36.   Watson, *Paul, Judaism, and the Gentiles*, pp. 70-71.

Stendahl and Sanders provoked a re-evaluation of Paul's 'conversion' that is still ongoing. (For what it is worth, I lean toward Watson here, though he does not attempt a systematic account of persecution and conversion/call.) As Dunn, Donaldson and Watson testify, fundamental questions surrounding Paul's persecution, the origins of his Gentile mission and the retrospective character of his conversion/call accounts are live and unresolved.

V. *Conclusion*

We have it on no less authority than that of C.K. Barrett that a historical approach to New Testament theology is particularly facilitated by reading Acts in light of Paul's letters.[37] Few have made a more distinguished contribution to the study of both Acts and Paul than Barrett, and one could hardly ask for better precedent for my own modest effort here. Returning to the matter of the peculiar perspective a certain kind of reader of Paul might bring to a reading of Acts, and of what might happen to Acts when that perspective is brought to bear, I now briefly draw together some of the observations made above, and add a few more.

The need to keep in view both a sense of Paul's dramatic reversal and of his being called to a special task is confirmed by Luke's treatment of Paul's conversion/call, where both aspects figure (particularly in the emphasis on 'persecution' and on 'the Gentiles').[38] Here Acts and Paul's undisputed letters cohere well enough. However, in implicating Paul in *deadly* violence (Acts 7.58; 8.1; 9.1; 22.4, 20; 26.10), Luke goes beyond what Paul says of himself (again, cf. 1 Tim. 1.12-17). And the tendency since Stendahl to elevate above all else Paul's singular experience of a 'call' to mission to 'the Gentiles' may actually have been subtly influenced by Acts over against Paul's letters (though, as we noted above, Acts is not univocal in terms of relating this 'call' specifically to an original revelatory experience: again, see Acts 9.15; 22.21; 26.17).

We noted above in passing two other points of tension between Paul and Acts: Paul's assertion of his independence contrasts somewhat with the role Acts gives to Ananias (Gal. 1.1, 11-12; Acts 9.6, 10-19a; 22.10, 12-16). And Paul's claim to apostleship based on Christ's resurrection

---

37. C.K. Barrett, *A Critical and Exegetical Commentary on The Acts of the Apostles* (ICC; 2 vols.; Edinburgh: T. & T. Clark, 1994, 1998), I, p. ix.

38. All three accounts in Acts narrate, with slight variations, both Paul's campaign of persecution of 'the disciples of the Lord', 'the Way', 'the saints' (Acts 9.1-2; 22.4-5; 26.9-11) and Jesus' question 'why are you persecuting me?' and answer 'I am Jesus, whom you are persecuting' (9.4-5; 22.7-8; 26.14-15).

appearance to him as to the earlier apostles contrasts more pointedly with Luke's perspective on the same matters (1 Cor. 15.8; Gal. 1.17; Acts 1.21-26). Neither tension need be regarded as intolerable; nevertheless, these represent important differences of perspective between Acts and Paul.[39]

Finally, I suggested at the outset that Acts might tend to encourage the effort to reconstruct Paul's original experience, while Paul's letters lend themselves more to an emphasis on the retrospective character of conversion narratives. This was stated particularly in view of the focus in Acts on auditory and visual features of Paul's Damascus road encounter. But I am now in a position to juxtapose the opposite suggestion: Luke in Acts is also the first to take an interest in Paul's retrospective recounting of his conversion/call. For the second and third conversion/call accounts in Acts 22 and 26 are presented as Paul's own self-narration before adversarial audiences. And one who comes to these from the Pauline texts cannot help but be struck by their pointedly 'apologetic' character (Acts 22.1, ἀπολογία; 26.1, ἀπολογεῖσθαι; cf. Gal. 1–2; Phil. 3); by the precise terms in which Paul emphasizes his Jewish *bona fides* (Acts 22.3, 'educated strictly according to our ancestral law', 'zealous'; 26.4-5, 'the strictest sect of our religion…a Pharisee'; cf. Gal. 1.13-14; Phil. 3.4-6); and even by the fact that the subject of 'resurrection' comes (differently) into the picture in each (Acts 23.6; 24.21; 26.6-8, 23; cf. 1 Cor. 15). Here, Luke displays quite a Pauline sense both of the kinds of context that call for a recounting of Paul's conversion/call, and even of the particular rhetoric of such recounting.

Turning finally to the question posed by my title: does the Damascus road run through Paul's letters? Strictly speaking, no. But this may in large part be simply a matter of genre. The very phrase 'road to Damascus' is a narrative fragment invoking a larger whole of the kind offered by a narrative work like Acts but not Paul's discursive letters. And although Galatians 1–2 offers a rare instance of extended Pauline narrative, even here he largely declines the opportunity it affords him to elaborate on the story of his conversion. Nevertheless, Gal. 1.17 (Paul's incidental reference to his 'return to Damascus') might conceivably represent a single, visible paving stone of a road now running beneath the surface of his letters. As Paul himself seems to suggest ('you have heard', Gal. 1.11; cf. 1.23), perhaps word had already got round about his conversion experience, and perhaps Paul himself was involved in the process of apostolic tradition-making that made its way ultimately to Luke, and beyond.

---

39. Cf. Barrett, *Acts*, I, pp. 443-44.

To close with a personal word, this last suggestion was reinforced by my friend and colleague Loveday Alexander in her response to an earlier version of this paper (a joint session of the Paul and the Book of Acts Seminars at the British New Testament Conference, Durham, 5 September 2008). Although we worked side by side at the University of Sheffield over a number of years—a great privilege in my life—this was the only occasion, shortly after Loveday's retirement, when our respective research focuses placed us on the same conference panel. And after all, the interests of Pauline and of Lukan studies do overlap and ought not be kept forever apart. As my small contribution to this volume celebrating Loveday's work suggests, even when we approach the question of Paul's conversion/call according to the priorities of Pauline studies, we are led back to broader questions of early Christian history that are her own particular province. On the earlier occasion of Loveday's retirement, I had the honour and pleasure of saying a few words, toward the end of which I mentioned her forthcoming work:

> Her time away from us will be spent not just pining for Sheffield but will be devoted to the completion of much-anticipated academic works. To mention but two: she is writing the commentary on the Book of Acts, the first history of early Christianity, in the prestigious Black's New Testament Commentary series…; and she is writing her own history of early Christianity in the equally prestigious New Testament Library series. In both cases, I ask you, to whom else could these distinguished series better have turned to fill these important gaps?[40]

To whom else indeed. I close, then, with something of a 'Macedonian call', to Loveday and perhaps even to Luke, to come over and help in untangling some of the tightly knotted historical questions into which we have found our brief inquiry into Paul's 'conversion' leading us!

---

40. Unpublished address, 17 December 2007.

Part II

READING THEMES IN ACTS

LUKE–ACTS, OR LUKE AND ACTS?
A REAFFIRMATION OF NARRATIVE UNITY

Joel B. Green

Almost two decades have passed since the publication of *Rethinking the Unity of Luke and Acts*.[1] In the pages of this slim volume, Mikeal Parsons and Richard Pervo set off a fireworks show, the afterglow of which has proven to be surprisingly long-lived. I say 'fireworks' because this book is characterized more by question-raising and thought experiments than by thoroughgoing argumentation, with the result that it is surprising that it has achieved the landmark status it now enjoys among some New Testament scholars.

Responses to Parsons and Pervo have been legion, and these have been amply summarized in recent analytical surveys of the ensuing conversation.[2] In a certain sense, then, their call for serious attention to issues of unity served well to press Lukan scholars to make explicit the working knowledge many had shared since Cadbury fixed the hyphen between 'Luke' and 'Acts' in the 1920s.[3] Although the bulk of their discussion centered on generic, narrative, and theological unity, contemporary discussion has reintroduced the issue of common authorship, which they took for granted, and the closely related questions of canonical placement and reception history. In this essay, I want to discuss these present issues as a precursor to commenting on the narrative unity of Luke–Acts.

---

1. Mikeal C. Parsons and Richard I. Pervo, *Rethinking the Unity of Luke and Acts* (Minneapolis: Fortress Press, 1993).

2. See Patrick E. Spencer, 'The Unity of Luke–Acts: A Four-Bolted Hermeneutical Hinge', *CBR* 5 (2007), pp. 341-66; Michael F. Bird, 'The Unity of Luke–Acts in Recent Discussion', *JSNT* 29 (2007), pp. 425-48.

3. 'They are not merely two independent writings from the same pen; they are a single continuous work' (Henry J. Cadbury, *The Making of Luke–Acts* [with a new introduction by Paul N. Anderson; Peabody, MA: Hendrickson, 2nd edn, 1958 (1st edn, 1927)], pp. 8-9).

I. *Rethinking the Unity of Luke and Acts:*
Canon, Reception History, and Authorship

Each in their own way, Robert Wall, C. Kavin Rowe, and Patricia Walters have reanimated interest in the relationship of Luke's Gospel and the book of Acts and, in some circles at least, begun to reinvigorate a negative assessment of the unity of Luke–Acts.

a. *Robert Wall and the Canonical Placement of Acts*
In the twentieth century, study of Luke's Gospel, for the most part, focused on the Gospel itself or on the Gospel in its relationship to Acts, without primary reference to its canonical location. Redaction criticism located Luke's Gospel in relation to the other Synoptic Gospels but pressed backward, behind the text, to presumed literary relations between or among the Gospels of Matthew, Mark, and Luke; or to their purported sources, whether literary (Q? L? A Lukan passion source?) or oral; and not to their canonical juxtaposition. Luke's Gospel has also been read in relation to the book of Acts, an approach that allocated little if any significance to the plain fact that Luke and Acts do not appear side-by-side in the biblical canon. Not without good reason, then, Parsons and Pervo spoke of 'canonical disunity' in their complaint regarding scholarly imprecision in claims to the unity of Luke and Acts, and Robert Wall has urged that, from a canonical perspective, Acts must be read in relation to the Fourfold Gospel (Matthew, Mark, Luke, and John) on the one hand, the epistolary collections on the other.[4]

The 2002 publication of Robert Wall's commentary on Acts in *The New Interpreter's Bible* was a welcome achievement, not least because of Wall's well-known and longstanding commitment to a canonical approach to engaging biblical texts. Reflecting on this commentary, though, I am puzzled at the status Wall grants to the work of Parsons and Pervo's book, a status that allows Wall to proceed along his own canon-critical course, having set aside without additional comment the narrative, generic, or theological unity of Luke's two volumes. As I have already suggested, Parsons and Pervo fired a warning shot across the bow of scholarship which presumed the unity of Luke and Acts, but they hardly

---

4. E.g. Robert W. Wall, 'The Acts of the Apostles in Canonical Context', in Robert W. Wall and Eugene E. Lemcio (eds.), *The New Testament as Canon: A Reader in Canonical Criticism* (JSNTSup, 76; Sheffield: JSOT Press, 1992), pp. 110-28; *idem*, 'The Acts of the Apostles: Introduction, Commentary, and Reflections', in Leander E. Keck *et al.* (eds.), *The New Interpreter's Bible* (12 vols.; Nashville: Abingdon Press, 2002), X, pp. 1-368.

sunk the ship. Nevertheless, referring to their work as 'a fresh intro-duction to a vexing issue of Lukan scholarship',[5] Wall operates as though Parsons and Pervo had fully cleared the way for his own undertaking. True, Wall seems to affirm 'the narrative unity between the Gospel and Acts',[6] but, like Parsons and Pervo, he never defines 'narrative' and so charts a course for reading Acts quite apart from the contribution which the Third Gospel might make to that enterprise. The possibility of theological unity is not really considered. Nor does the issue of genre come in for nuanced consideration. This is unfortunate, since these three—theology, narrative, and genre—are closely related in a text like the one under consideration. After all, if, following Aristotle, 'narrative' is characterized by its *telos*, and if narrative is further characterized by its orientation around a single narrative aim, then one might wonder how Wall can simply claim that Luke's Gospel concerns 'the life story of the Savior from conception to ascension' whereas Acts 'sketches the origins of a religious movement'.[7] (This is especially true since the origins of this particular 'religious movement' are, according to Acts, explicitly tied to the particularly Lukan account of Jesus' life and mission; see below.) If Luke and Acts comprise the ongoing narration of the actualization of God's βουλή among his people, then the narrative aim of Luke's Gospel is really a *divine* aim—and 'the story of the Savior' must account for the reality that, for Luke, the identification of Jesus as Savior must somehow be correlated with the identification of God as Savior (Lk. 1.47; 2.11; Acts 5.31; 13.23; cf. Lk. 1.69); the theology of Luke and Acts read together, as Luke–Acts, must be examined for its coherence and development; and the easy segregation of Luke and Acts on generic grounds is problem-atized.[8]

Of course, it may be that Wall would prefer simply to adopt a reading strategy focused on the canonical placement of the book of Acts between the Fourfold Gospel Canon and the Epistolary Collection. This would be a useful move, but I would have hoped he would do so by naming and pursuing relentlessly his own reading strategy, rather than by dismissing other reading strategies on the basis of otherwise unwarranted claims.

---

5. Wall, 'The Acts of the Apostles', p. 34.
6. Wall, 'The Acts of the Apostles', p. 8.
7. Wall, 'The Acts of the Apostles', p. 12.
8. Despite the title of his essay ('The Genre of Acts: Moving Toward a Con-sensus?' *CBR* 4 [2006], pp. 365-96), Thomas E. Phillips documents ways in which scholars have navigated the generic unity of Luke–Acts, especially in terms of history/writing.

The interpretive issues at stake here should not be minimized. Let me give two examples. First, forty years ago, James D.G. Dunn complained that Pentecostals based their presumption of a second experience of the Spirit, subsequent to and distinct from the new birth, on a problematic hermeneutic when they read Acts 2 as the 'second experience' subsequent to the 'first experience' in Jn 20.22. 'This appeal to John's Gospel raises a basic methodological issue: Are we to approach the New Testament material as systematic theologians or as biblical theologians and exegetes?'[9] One might take issue with Dunn's characterization of systematic theologians, but the point is clear enough. Can we simply flatten these narratives so as to allow us to move easily from John to Acts as though the one were self-evidently the continuation of the other? Note, however, Wall's apparent claim that Acts provides a sequel better suited to John's Gospel than to Luke's:

> [T]he importance of retaining the final shape of the New Testament rather than combining Luke and Acts as a single narrative is indicated by the significant roles performed by Peter and the Holy Spirit in Acts where Jesus is absent—roles for which Luke's Gospel does not adequately prepare the reader of Acts. Peter's rehabilitation at the end of John (John 21:15-17) as well as the teaching about the Spirit's post-Easter role by John's Jesus (John 14–16) signify the important role that John's Gospel performs in preparing the reader for the story of Acts.[10]

In response to this line of thinking, we might inquire on what basis Luke's own preparation for Peter's status in Acts (see Lk. 22.28-32) and the coming of the Spirit (Lk. 3.16; 11.13; 24.49) are pronounced unsatisfactory.

To take another example, what are we to make of the way Wall's canonical perspective leads him to a reading of Acts that establishes the authority and divine legitimization of the apostles? This is necessary, we discover, because Acts *authorizes* these early church 'pillars' (Gal. 2.9) so as to pave the way for canonical readers to heed their voices in the New Testament epistolary collections. Accordingly, this canonical perspective leads to a reading of Acts according to an interpretive frame in league with the self-legitimation of the church *qua* institution. A canonical reading thus seems necessarily tied to an authorizing of ecclesial leadership. It is worth recalling, though, that 'legitimacy' cuts two ways. It authorizes the status of an institution, leader, or position, *but it also sets limits on the*

---

9.   James D.G. Dunn, *Baptism in the Holy Spirit: A Re-examination of the New Testament Teaching on the Gift of the Spirit in Relation to Pentecostalism Today* (Philadelphia: Westminster Press, 1970), p. 39.

10.   Wall, 'The Acts of the Apostles', p. 30.

exercise of that authority. Without denying the importance of canon, I wonder what would happen if we were to read the narrative of Acts in these terms, in that other sense of *canon*—that is, as a narrative that takes the measure of the church that sees itself in continuity with the ancient purpose of God as this is recounted in Luke–Acts. What if Acts were read first not as an authorization of Peter, Paul, and the rest, but more basically, and essentially, so as to underscore the legitimating role of God's word? In this case, the apostolic 'pillars' would enjoy divine authorization insofar as their words and practices were congruent with the gospel. In fact, it is arguable that the repetition of a key phrase in the narrative of Acts—namely, 'God's word grew'—provides Acts with a structure and focus that give definition to the gospel that the church and its authorized persons and structures serve. This phrase appears in Acts 6.7; 12.24; 19.20, each time marking the cessation of opposition, signaling the advance of the missionary movement in the midst of persecution, and anticipating the next major development in the narrative. Taking the reiteration of the word's progress seriously with reference to the book's structure brings focus to key phases of the narrative—the mission in Jerusalem (1.15–6.7), expansion from Jerusalem to Antioch (6.8–12.25), expansion from Antioch to Asia and Europe (13.1–19.20), and finally the journeys of Paul the missionary prisoner (19.21–28.31)—and underscores Luke's thematic development of the 'word of salvation'. Not coincidently, it also takes seriously Luke's fundamental concern with the effects of the word—that is, its germinal role in the production and growth of God's people, a status grounded in Jesus' message in Luke's Gospel (8.4-15).

If this other, *canon*ical perspective were taken seriously, then we would see that the resolution of conflict within the community of goods, as Wall describes Acts 6.1-7, was not focused on 'the problem of supply and demand that growth has created';[11] nor does the successful resolution of the problem signal 'the next triumph of [the apostles'] leadership'.[12] Recalling that those who were being neglected in the daily distribution of the food were widows, recalling the place of widows both in Israel's Scriptures and in Luke's Gospel, and recalling that, everything else being equal, the law of probability would have it that both Hellenistic Jewish Christian widows and Hebraic Jewish Christian widows would have suffered neglect, it seems reductionistic to suggest that the problem here is practical. It is, rather, profoundly theological. Or, to turn Peter's words against him, is it possible to serve the word *and* neglect widows? Far from

11. Wall, 'The Acts of the Apostles', p. 110.
12. Wall, 'The Acts of the Apostles', p. 115.

celebrating apostolic leadership, this scene dismantles their authority with the result that the pioneers of the mission 'to the end of the earth' are not the Jerusalem apostles but The Seven.[13]

Wall has succeeded in identifying canonical placement as an important interpretive context, but the terms of the discussion should not be narrowed too quickly. Other factors merit consideration in a decision whether Luke and Acts ought to be read, as Christian Scripture, as Luke and Acts or as Luke–Acts. If, as I shall demonstrate below, Acts itself invites a reading strategy that ties the narrative of Acts back into Luke's Gospel, with Acts as a deliberate narratival continuation of Luke, then does this not suggest an important interpretive constraint for making sense of Acts?

b. *C. Kavin Rowe and the Reception History of Luke*
In two recent essays, C. Kavin Rowe calls into question the view that contemporary interpretation of Luke and Acts as a continuous work, Luke–Acts, is modeled on the way Luke and Acts were read historically.[14] Earlier, Andrew Gregory had demonstrated that the unity of Luke–Acts is a modern construct, that there is very little evidence to suggest that these two books were read together.[15] Rowe takes this argument further, denying that we have any evidence whatsoever that Luke and Acts were read early on as a single, unified literary whole. He summarizes the situation as follows:

> No ancient author exhibits a hermeneutical practice that is founded upon the reading of Luke–Acts as one work in two volumes; no ancient author argues that Luke and Acts should be read together as one work in two volumes; and, there is not a single New Testament manuscript that contains the unity of Luke–Acts or even hints at this unity by placing Acts directly next to the Gospel of Luke.[16]

13. See, more fully, Joel B. Green, 'Neglecting Widows and Serving the Word? Acts 6:1-7 as a Test Case for a Missional Hermeneutic', in Jon Laansma, Grant Osborne and Ray Van Neste (eds.), *Jesus Christ, Lord and Savior* (Carlisle: Paternoster; Eugene, OR: Wipf & Stock, in press).

14. C. Kavin Rowe, 'History, Hermeneutics and the Unity of Luke–Acts', *JSNT* 28 (2005), pp. 131-57; *idem*, 'Literary Unity and Reception History: Reading Luke–Acts as Luke and Acts', *JSNT* 29 (2007), pp. 449-57.

15. Andrew Gregory, *The Reception of Luke and Acts in the Period before Irenaeus: Looking for Luke in the Second Century* (WUNT, II/169; Tübingen: Mohr Siebeck, 2003); cf. *idem*, 'Looking for Luke in the Second Century: A Dialogue with François Bovon', in Craig G. Bartholomew, Joel B. Green, and Anthony C. Thiselton (eds.), *Reading Luke: Interpretation, Reflection, Formation* (Scripture and Hermeneutics, 6; Grand Rapids: Zondervan, 2005), pp. 401-13.

16. Rowe, 'Literary Unity', p. 451.

Although Rowe's argument is not without its problems, even if we were to take it at face value, its ramifications for our interest in the unity of Luke–Acts would be far from clear. As Rowe himself admits, how these two books were received in the early church in no way constrains the range of ways in which they might now be read.

We can push further. For example, Rowe insists that the guild of New Testament studies shares an almost unquestioned assumption, that to read Luke–Acts together is to interpret this literary unity historically. I offer two observations here. First, surprisingly, he provides no grounds for this claim. Second, such a claim would not at all be representative of persons who read Luke–Acts as a unity on narratological grounds. Moreover, as Luke Timothy Johnson has observed, we have no evidence of how Luke and Acts were received by their first audiences, and only minimal evidence of how they were read in the second century—facts that mitigate the significance of reception history for addressing the question of the literary unity of Luke–Acts.[17] Johnson voices the additional concern that the question put to the evidence is problematic due to its anachronism. On what basis might one query whether Luke and Acts were read as a single literary composition when we have little evidence that *any* New Testament writings were read early on as 'literary compositions'? Rather than depend on reception history, then, Johnson advises that we account for the composition's own 'rhetorical intentionality':

> To put it simply, the way the composition itself is put together suggests readers with certain characteristics and capabilities. Analysis of the composition's rhetorical or narrative logic also reveals not only the writing's argument but also something about the direction in which that argument wishes to turn its intended readers.[18]

This does not signal Johnson's interest in the failed experiment of reconstructing an alleged 'Lukan community',[19] but seems more akin to Rabinowitz's notion of an 'authorial audience'—that is, the readers who can be discovered by looking at the text in terms of the literary-historical context within which it arose.[20] How the early church might have

17. Luke Timothy Johnson, 'Literary Criticism of Luke–Acts: Is Reception-History Pertinent?', *JSNT* 28 (2005), pp. 159-62.

18. Johnson, 'Literary Criticism', p. 160.

19. See Luke Timothy Johnson, 'On Finding the Lukan Community', in *SBLSP* (1979), pp. 87-100; cf. Stephen C. Barton, 'Can We Identify the Gospel Audiences?', in Richard J. Bauckham (ed.), *The Gospels for All Christians: Rethinking the Gospel Audiences* (Grand Rapids: Eerdmans, 1998), pp. 173-94 (esp. 186-93).

20. Peter J. Rabinowitz, *Before Reading: Narrative Conventions and the Politics of Interpretation* (Ithaca, NY: Cornell University Press, 1987).

received Luke and Acts, then, is not necessarily a reliable barometer of the narrative's own intentionality.

In point of fact, this problem with reception history is not limited to the second century, at least not in the case of Luke–Acts, since what indications we have suggest that, for centuries, Luke was read less as a literary composition and more as a library of episodes from which favorites might be borrowed. Luke's stories of the birth of Jesus or the Emmaus encounter are cases in point, but one could also point to the parables of the Good Samaritan or the Prodigal Son—all texts typically sundered from their narrative service within the Third Gospel. If we search for early commentaries on Luke's Gospel, we find only four collections of homilies—those of Origen, Ambrose of Milan, Cyril of Alexandria, and the Venerable Bede—a small number when compared to commentary on Matthew and John.[21] Early tendencies toward harmonization blossomed in Tatian's *Diatessaron*, an effort that remained influential into the fifth century. And they have continued to blossom. In the early eighth century, for example, Bede participated in this enterprise, producing homilies on Gospel texts, working as though each narrative was cut from the same cloth as the other, without attending to the particular perspective of any single Evangelist.[22] In the sixteenth century, Calvin departed from his own practice of commenting on each of the biblical books when he produced a *Commentary on a Harmony of the Evangelists, Matthew, Mark, and Luke*. Whether in the nineteenth century or the twenty-first, those engaged in the quest for the historical Jesus bypass the narrative character of the individual Gospels in order to provide their own accounts of what they take to be true of Jesus. In short, the history of interpretation of Luke's Gospel serves to underscore Johnson's concern that the nature of Luke–Acts as a literary composition might be assessed on the basis of interpretive practices that generally do not account for its literary nature.

It will be clear that I have little confidence in the potential contribution of reception history for informing us how Luke and Acts were intended to be read, how they were received by their first readers, or how they might faithfully be read. Reception history does give us a sense of how Luke and Acts, or Luke–Acts, has been and might still be read, but is only minimally relevant to the question of the unity of Luke's work.

---

21.   Arthur A. Just Jr., ed., *Luke* (Ancient Christian Commentary on Scripture, 3; Downers Grove, IL: InterVarsity Press, 2003), pp. xvii-xxvi.

22.   The Venerable Bede, *Homilies on the Gospels* (2 vols.; Cistercian Studies Series, 110-111; Kalamazoo, MI: Cistercian, 1991).

c. *Patricia Walters and Authorial Unity*

Challenges to the common authorship of Luke and Acts have surfaced before, but Lukan scholarship has moved forward with hardly a side glance at the issue. Questions have centered on the identity of the historical author, not on whether Luke and Acts were authored by the same person. Indeed, Parsons and Pervo devoted no more than two sentences to the question.[23] Scholarly nonchalance on this issue is likely to change as a result of the 2009 publication of Patricia Walters' dissertation, *The Assumed Authorial Unity of Luke and Acts.*[24]

In a remarkably well-structured study, Walters urges on statistical grounds that we no longer attribute Luke and Acts to a common author. Her research design is as follows: (1) Avoiding texts that might be attributed to the sources of Luke and Acts, she identifies material within both books that scholars have identified as deriving from the hand of the author, namely, the seams and summaries of the two books. (2) Assuming that the author(s) of Luke and Acts would have been influenced stylistically by the prose compositional conventions familiar to those who learned to write Hellenistic Greek, she surveys the works of ancient literary critics (Aristotle, Demetrius, Dionysius of Halicarnassus, and Longinus) to identify compositional elements whose patterns might be analyzed in the seams and summaries of Luke and Acts. These include euphony (i.e. hiatus and dissonance patterns), rhythm, and sentence structure. (3) She investigates the presence or absence of these conventions in the seams and summaries of Luke and Acts, determines the characteristic style of the seams and summaries of each book, then evaluates whether the differences in the style between the two books are statistically significant. She concludes:

> Because the patterns in one book's seams and summaries do not repeat the compositional preferences found in the other book—a set of circumstances one reasonably expects in the case of single authorship—it is confirmed with a high degree of confidence and beyond reasonable doubt that the compositional elements analyzed herein actually differentiate Luke and Acts.[25]

23. Parsons and Pervo, *Rethinking the Unity of Luke and Acts*, pp. 7-8.

24. Patricia Walters, *The Assumed Authorial Unity of Luke and Acts: A Reassessment of the Evidence* (SNTSMS, 145; Cambridge: Cambridge University Press, 2009). Walters ably surveys previous discussion related to authorial unity on pp. 24-35. For what follows, see Joel B. Green, review of Patricia Walters, *The Assumed Authorial Unity of Luke and Acts: A Reassessment of the Evidence*, *Review of Biblical Literature* [http://www.bookreviews.org] (2009), <http://www.bookreviews.org/pdf/7084_7695.pdf>, accessed September 2010.

25. Walters, *Unity*, p. 191.

From here, Walters goes on to argue that the theory that makes the best sense of the evidence she has garnered is that Luke and Acts did not share a common author.

Although her research design seems straightforward, a number of questions linger:

(1) Walters' dependence on seams and summaries is based on the assumption that we find here an author's hand unbound by source considerations. It should not escape our notice that this assumption is grounded in early-twentieth-century form-critical views about the growth of the Synoptic tradition—views that were then carried over into study of Acts. For the form critics, the evangelists worked with units of tradition that they wove together, so that their particular contributions were to be found in the seams and transitions between traditional units, and in summaries. To proceed on the basis of this assumption is problematic both because our understanding of the growth of the Synoptic tradition has repeatedly been reevaluated and rewritten over the past seven decades, and because one cannot take for granted that Luke would (or could) have executed his narrative craft while writing Acts on the analogy of what he has done in his Gospel. If it is true that New Testament scholarship has repeatedly found itself questioning form-critical assumptions about the tendencies of the Synoptic tradition, and if it is true that New Testament scholarship has in the last two decades opened itself to consider again a variety of theories for making sense of Synoptic relationships, then it is even more true that identifying putative sources behind the narrative of Acts has become, if anything, a more vexing problem than it already was. In theory—and on this issue we have little else on which to stand other than theory—there is no reason that Luke might have had less access to traditional material when formulating the summaries of Acts than when formulating other parts of his narrative. The question surfaces, then, whether Walters has built her house on a base of sand.

(2) Walters' study assumes a level of rhetorical education not generally granted the author of Luke and/or Acts among New Testament scholars and does not account for other stylistic influence (e.g. from the LXX) on the Lukan narrative(s). This raises the question how pervasively Luke might have been influenced stylistically by the prose compositional conventions developed among ancient literary critics—and, thus, the degree to which issues of authorship can be adjudicated in these terms.

(3) Walters moves forward under the assumption that the sort of analysis she has undertaken will provide reliable conclusions. Her analysis would have been more convincing, however, had she been able to demonstrate the success of this kind of analysis with 'control' studies. I

wonder whether, using this form of analysis, we would find that Josephus' *Antiquities* was written by multiple authors—likewise, Polybius, Dionysius, and so on. To turn in a different direction, I wonder whether the author of Luke's Gospel was consistent with himself, style-wise; in other words, might this sort of study demonstrate the need to posit different authors for different segments within a single book? I wonder if some seams and summaries in Acts are stylistically congruent with some seams and summaries in Luke's Gospel, even if taken as aggregates (per Walters' study) these books display significant differences.

(4) To what degree can the elements of style Walters has identified be trusted to provide the unique fingerprint of an author? Is there widespread evidence that hiatus and dissonance patterns, syntax at the end of a clause or sentence, and clause or sentence segues were in fact markers of the distinctive compositional style of authors of first-century C.E. narratives? To say that these elements are discussed by ancient 'literary critics' is not the same thing as saying that they are the identity markers this study requires them to be.

(5) This last point is especially worrisome when we recognize that the stylistic fingerprint unique to the author of Acts (for example) is constructed from a database of only 31 verses and four partial verses, with some two-thirds of the data deriving from Acts 1–5. Although one might appreciate the predicament Walters finds herself in with respect to the problem of determining which material comes from the author's sources versus what comes from his unfettered hand, it is nevertheless troublesome to imagine that the authorship of Acts would be determined from so tiny a data pool.

(6) Although less pressing in importance, I should also mention the need for more rigor in the way Walters draws conclusions from her data. At several points when discussing possible reasons why the issues of style she addresses might differ between Luke's Gospel and Acts, she concludes against options consistent with stylistic variation and common authorship when the path of agnosticism seems the more prudent one. For example, her discussion of the possibility that the same author writing in two different genres might adopt different compositional styles is equivocal and, actually, not altogether on point.[26] As a result, Walters' decision firmly to exclude this possibility seems ill-advised. Similarly, she asserts but does not demonstrate her claim that an ancient author's style remains consistent across that author's writing career.

---

26. The force of this question rests with the internal consistency of Walters' argument, since she imagines that Luke's Gospel and Acts represent different genres—a position I do not share.

Another, more general, question nags. This is whether decisions about the authorship of these two books can be made on the basis of so small an evidence pool, with all other data off the table. I refer to the intratextual connections between Luke and Acts, to the way Acts develops narrative-theological interests first broached in Luke's Gospel, for example, or the patterns of representation by which characters and events in Acts recall Luke's presentation of Jesus and his career in the Third Gospel, or even the overall narrative pattern of Luke that is recapitulated in Acts; to the patterns of LXX usage in Acts, already familiar to readers of Luke's Gospel; to theological patterns, such as Lukan pneumatology, his theology of conversion, his perspective on suffering and persecution, or his understanding of the divine plan; to his character-building, and on the list might go—that is, to the kinds of observations that have been the bread and butter of so much Lukan study in recent decades and that have no place in Walters' study. Of course, in the face of this evidence, Walters might reply that all of these observations, even if they were valid, are nonetheless explicable under the assumption of authorial disunity if we simply admit that the author of Acts purposefully tied his narrative patterns and theology so tightly into the narrative of Luke's Gospel. But if the author of Acts can so fully take on the persona of the narrator of Luke, then it is hard to know what purpose discussions of authorship might serve. After all, in this instance the author of Acts would be little more than an epiphenomenal curiosity.

II. *Rethinking the Unity of Luke–Acts*

Parsons and Pervo identified a range of ways to think about the unity of Luke and Acts—canonical, authorial, theological, narratival, and generic. My comments thus far have been moving toward a proposal that, of these, the most important for interpreting Luke and Acts *as literary compositions* and, more pointedly, as a narrative representation of historical events (that is, as historiography), is narrative unity. The issue of *genre* is less pivotal since (1) biography was a recent outgrowth of historiography and shared many of its essential features and (2) narratology does not distinguish meaningfully among various narrative genres for interpretive purposes.[27] I have already suggested that *canonical* unity holds no trump cards for how Luke and Acts must be read as a narrative

---

27. Despite obvious differences among narrative genres, narrators face the same problems and employ the same literary conventions, and their readers employ the same interpretive protocols—cf. Wallace Martin, *Recent Theories of Narrative* (Ithaca, NY: Cornell University Press, 1986), pp. 72-75.

representation of historical events, and that a case for *authorial* unity or disunity cannot be made apart from the question of *narrative* unity. *Theological* unity is predicated on a prior decision regarding narrative unity, since how one construes theological positions depends on the body of work one considers. This is not a naive denial of the possibility—indeed, the actuality—of theological tensions within the Lukan corpus. It is, rather, a recognition that human beings have a characteristic ability to find coherence in discourse and, once confronted with the boundaries of a discourse, find themselves able to abstract thematic (we might say, theological) coherence.[28] For this reason, we might theorize a 'theology' of Lk. 4.16-30, or of Lk. 4.14–9.50, or of Luke's Gospel, or of Luke–Acts, or of the New Testament, or of the Old and New Testaments. That is, once a 'text' is placed before us—whether it is a single pericope or even a set of biblical books—we are able to discern and discourse intelligibly about its internal coherence. The pivotal question, then, concerns the narrative unity of Luke–Acts, and in what follows I will refer to 'Luke' as narrator (and not as the historical author).

a. *What Is a Narrative?*
Any attempt to attribute narrative unity to Luke's two volumes (or to deny that unity) requires, first, an understanding of 'narrative'.[29]

(1) *Narrative is a defining feature of the human family by which we make sense of our lives.* Scientist-theologian Anne Foeret refers to humans as '*Homo Narrans Narrandus*—the storytelling person whose story has to be told', who tells stories to make sense of the world and to form personal identity and community.[30] Embodied human life performs like a cultural, neuro-hermeneutic system, locating (and, thus, making sense of) current realities in relation to our grasp of the past and expectations of the future,

---

28. It is a staple of discourse analysis that 'the natural effort of hearers and readers alike is to attribute relevance and coherence to the text they encounter until they are forced not to' (Gillian Brown and George Yule, *Discourse Analysis* [Cambridge Textbooks in Linguistics; Cambridge: Cambridge University Press, 1983], p. 66). On the working of 'theming' in narratology, see, e.g., Gerald Prince, *Narrative as Theme* (Lincoln: University of Nebraska Press, 1992).

29. See, e.g., Gerald Prince, *Dictionary of Narratology* (Lincoln: University of Nebraska Press, 1987), pp. 58-60; Michael J. Toolan, *Narrative: A Critical Linguistic Introduction* (London: Routledge, 1988), pp. 1-11; H. Porter Abbott, *The Cambridge Introduction to Narrative* (Cambridge: Cambridge University Press, 2002), pp. 12-24.

30. Reported in S. Jennifer Leat, 'Artificial Intelligence Researcher Seeks Silicon Soul', *Research News and Opportunities in Science and Theology* 3, no. 4 (2002), pp. 7, 26 (7). Cf. Kay Young and Jeffrey L. Saver, 'The Neurology of Narrative', *SubStance* 30 (2001), pp. 72-84.

and to speak thus of past, present, and future is already to frame meaning in narrative terms. This is not so much a statement about genre or
interpretive method, but rather about narrativity as an essential aspect
of our grasp of the nature of the world and of human identity and
comportment in it. 'To raise the question of narrative', observed Hayden
White, 'is to invite reflection on the very nature of culture and, possibly,
even on the nature of humanity itself.'[31] Although our recognition that
humans are basically hard-wired to render events meaningful within a
narrative frame does not yet provide for us a definition of 'narrative', it
does point toward important ingredients of such a definition.

(2) *Narrative locates events in a temporal frame characterized by cause-
and-effect relations.* Aristotle wrote of a narrative 'whole' as possessing a
beginning, middle, and end. At one level, this assumes narrative progress
from one point to the next, organizing the progression of events through
time. At another, though, this narrative progression transcends the passing of time in order to claim some sort of meaningful, even necessary, set
of relationships among the events that, in narrative, order time. The
'beginning' is not simply the first thing to be narrated, but the thing
before which nothing is necessary and after which something naturally
follows. The 'end' is not simply the last thing to be recounted, but
something that is naturally after something else (generally as its necessary
consequence) and that requires nothing after itself (*Poetics* 1450b).

(3) *Narrative is a particular performance of a story.* It follows, then,
that integral to 'narrative' is the particular ordering of events by which
significance accrues to those events. This is the classic distinction made
by Seymour Chatman between 'story' and 'discourse'—that is, between
the 'what' (events, characters, settings) and the 'how' (the organization of
those events, characters, and settings in a particular telling).[32]

(4) *Narrative progression serves a (single) narrative aim.* Finally, a
narrative *telos* guides the selection and organization of the elements of
story. The identification of a beginning, middle, and end and the structuring of settings, actors, and events in a web of causal relations are
teleologically determined. They serve an overall purpose that presses the
narrative forward toward its resolution (or denouement). We may
discern within a narrative various currents and countercurrents—and
these bear witness to the elasticity of narrative, the hospitality of narrative

31. Hayden White, *The Content of the Form: Narrative Discourse and Historical
Representation* (Baltimore: The Johns Hopkins University Press, 1987), p. 1.
32. Seymour Chatman, *Story and Discourse: Narrative Structure in Fiction and
Film* (Ithaca, NY: Cornell University Press, 1980).

to multiple agenda—but, in narrative study, these are tamed in relation to the overall purpose of the narrative. Accordingly, a more thoroughgoing discussion of the unity of Luke–Acts would need to account for the overarching purpose at work in and through the narrative, and the division within the text of those characters who embrace (or help) this purpose versus those hostile to (or who oppose) that purpose.

Key to the question of narrative unity, then, is the initial introduction of a deficit that presses the narrative forward in a more-or-less typical series of movements, a narrative cycle, by which this state of deficiency is addressed (or not). A typical healing story carries us through the entire cycle: a person presents with an illness, Jesus restores the person to health, people respond. Sometimes additional elements are introduced, perhaps heightening the need or developing the motif of resistance, but we nonetheless recognize in the span of only a few verses a complete narrative account—a beginning, middle, and end. If a text such as Lk. 13.10-17, the account of the restoration of the woman-bent-over, can thus be characterized as a complete narrative account, we should not be surprised to discover that Luke's Gospel itself can be understood as a complete narrative account, with its own beginning, middle, and end. Read from this perspective, the Third Gospel follows a plot line whose denouement must be discerned in Jesus' post-resurrection appearances in Luke 24. In other words, to embrace the unity of Luke–Acts as a narrative is not to deny that this 52-chapter account is itself comprised of constituent narrative accounts. The question, rather, is whether the narrative of Acts invites a reading in which it is seen as a self-conscious continuation of Luke's Gospel—and, then, whether the whole of Luke and Acts comprises a single narrative cycle.

b. *Mining Acts 1.1-14*

One may formulate multiple possibilities for testing the unity of Luke–Acts. For example, in a complementary proposal, Daniel Marguerat has urged that the text of Luke–Acts guides a certain way of reading, so that its inclusions, prolepsis, narrative chains, and *syncrisis* lead to a unitary reading of Acts as the 'effect' of Luke's Gospel.[33] Another way to address this question is to examine the opening verses of Acts, 1.1-14, where we encounter 'the problem of a beginning' ubiquitous among all narratives. How does a narrator indicate the logic whereby the initial events are shown to be the product of forces within the discourse itself rather than a

---

33. Daniel Marguerat, *The First Christian Historian: Writing the 'Acts of the Apostles'* (SNTSMS, 121; Cambridge: Cambridge University Press, 2002), pp. 43-64.

given reported by the narrative.[34] Acts locates its beginning in the story of Jesus, particularly as this is represented in Luke's Gospel; that is, Acts presents itself as the continuation of a narrative cycle begun elsewhere, in the Third Gospel. For Acts, then, the problem of a beginning is less pressing, since Luke has already demonstrated that 'the beginning' of his account is to be found in the story of Jesus, the story of Jesus in the story of Israel, and the story of Israel in the purpose of God.[35]

Note, for example, the points of contact between the respective openings of the Third Gospel and of Acts—including, for example, the presence of a Hellenistic preface in Lk. 1.1-4 partnered with the secondary preface in Acts 1.1-14; the fact that both volumes refer to Theophilus as Luke's literary patron; the analogous geographical focus on Jerusalem; and such parallels as the following:

Luke 1–2	*Acts 1.1-14*
In the Gospel, 'Mary' appears only in chs. 1–2.	In Acts, 'Mary' appears only in v. 14.
Simeon is 'looking forward to the consolation of Israel' (2.25); Anna speaks 'about the child to all who were looking for the redemption of Jerusalem' (2.38).	The apostles ask, 'Lord, is it at this time that you are restoring to Israel its sovereignty?' (v. 6).
Anna serves as a witness (2.38).	'You will be my witnesses…' (v. 8).
The Holy Spirit figures prominently in chs. 1–2; Gabriel promises, 'The Holy Spirit will come upon you, and the power of the Most High…' (1.35).	The Holy Spirit figures prominently (vv. 2, 4, 5, 8); Jesus promises, 'You will receive power when the Holy Spirit comes upon you…' (v. 8).
Angels have a prominent role (1.11-20, 26-38; 2.9-14).	Angels have a prominent role (v. 11).
Anna prays 'day and night' (2.37; cf. 1.10, 14).	Those gathered 'were all persevering in prayer together' (v. 14).

34. See Aristotle, *Poetics* 23.1 §1459a.17-29; Edward W. Said, *Beginnings: Intention and Method* (New York: Basic Books, 1975). More generally, cf. Dennis E. Smith, 'Narrative Beginnings in Ancient Literature and Theory', *Semeia* 22 (1991), pp. 1-9; Mikeal C. Parsons, 'Reading a Beginning/Beginning a Reading: Tracing Literary Theory on Narrative Openings', *Semeia* 22 (1991), pp. 11-31.

35. See Joel B. Green, 'Internal Repetition in Luke–Acts: Contemporary Narratology and Lucan Historiography', in Ben Witherington III (ed.), *History, Literature, and Society in the Book of Acts* (Cambridge: Cambridge University Press, 1996), pp. 283-99; *idem*, 'The Problem of a Beginning: Israel's Scriptures in Luke 1–2', *BBR* 4 (1994), pp. 61-85.

Even more impressive are the parallels between the closing of Luke and the opening of Acts. Both record:

- appearances of Jesus to his followers
- Jesus eating in front of/with his followers
- demonstrations that Jesus is really alive
- the directive to remain in Jerusalem
- reference to the fulfillment of the Father's promise (of the Holy Spirit)
- the designation of the disciples as 'witnesses'
- reference to the universal scope of the impending mission
- the ascension
- the disciples' obedience as they remain in Jerusalem

That is, almost every detail in Acts 1.1-14 finds its antecedent in Luke 24. This degree of repetition internal to the narrative indicates two things. First, for Luke, there is only one story to tell—namely, the story of God's gracious activity on behalf of Israel, grounded in God's ancient plan, fulfilled in God's gracious visitation in the Spirit-anointed mission of Jesus, and continued by means of the empowerment of the Spirit in the church's life and mission. Second, Acts 1.1-14 is transitional. It recapitulates the closing of Luke's Gospel and establishes the need within the narrative for a Spirit-empowered mission 'to the end of the earth'—a 'state of deficit' rooted not only in Lk. 24.47, but more fundamentally in the opening chapters of Luke (e.g. 2.30-32). These opening verses of Acts constitute an invitation to Luke's audience to re-enter the already-begun narrative and to follow the progress of God's gracious initiative in Jesus.

If in Acts Luke did not face 'the problem of a beginning', he did need to chart for his audience a course that would carry them from Book One to Book Two. Luke invites his readers to adopt again a point of view from within the narrative by the subtle shifts in his opening: from first-person narration (vv. 1-3) to third-person (beginning in v. 4), and from indirect discourse (v. 4a) to direct (vv. 4b-8); he also appeals directly to his audience to visualize with the disciples the presence of the heavenly visitors ('Look!', v. 10).

Four motifs are intertwined in these opening verses of Acts:

(1) The *ascension* (Acts 1.2, 9-11), anticipated since the scene of transfiguration and onset of Jesus' journey to Jerusalem (Lk. 9.28-36, 51), marks Jesus' departure, but not his absence. Accounts of ascension in Second Temple Judaism and the Greco-Roman world generally functioned to mitigate the sense of divine–human separation, and Luke's is no exception, even if it does so in the unusual way of tying the ascension

of Jesus into the promise of Jesus' return, the powerful utility of 'his name', and the outpouring of the Holy Spirit.

(2) The importance of *God's kingdom* is signaled not only in Luke's notation that it constitutes the center of Jesus' instruction to his disciples (Acts 1.3), but also by the fact that the Acts narrative opens and closes (28.23, 31) with reference to God's redemptive plan configured in kingdom-language.[36] Jesus' message raises immediate questions about the relation of God's kingdom to Israel's sovereignty (1.6). What is the relationship between Israel's hope, imperial Rome, and God's sovereign presence? This collocation of issues has been on the table since Luke 1 (e.g. 1.67-79).

(3) The *Holy Spirit* (Acts 1.2, 4, 5, 8) had anointed Jesus at the onset of his ministry (Lk. 3.21-22; 4.18-19), so his mission proceeded in the power of the Spirit; now Jesus promises his followers that he will fulfill John's prediction and actualize the Father's promise by baptizing them with the Spirit for the continuation of that ministry. Luke thus sets the stage by anticipating the actualization of John's prophecy of a messianic Spirit-baptism (Lk. 3.15-17; cf. 11.13).[37]

(4) Jesus' *followers* are increasingly in focus as Acts begins. Throughout the Gospel, the disciples were known mostly for their presence 'with' Jesus and, as the Gospel progressed, they were more and more characterized by an acute lack of understanding rooted in their unreconstructed notions of what God might do.[38] At the end of the Third Gospel, however, Jesus 'opened their minds to understand the Scriptures' (Lk. 24.45), and now they are portrayed as those whom Jesus had commissioned and taught, who witness his resurrected life and his departure, and who obey his instructions to wait in Jerusalem. What is more, they do so in persevering prayer—potentially an echo of Jesus' earlier instruction regarding

---

36. For discussion see Alexander Prieur, *Die Verkündigung der Gottesherrschaft: Exegetische Studien zum lukanischen Verständnis von βασιλεία τοῦ θεοῦ* (WUNT, II/89; Tübingen: Mohr Siebeck, 1996), pp. 20-117; also Constantito Antoinio Ziccardi, *The Relationship of Jesus and the Kingdom of God according to Luke–Acts* (Tesi Gregoriana Serie Teologia, 165; Rome: Editrice Pontificia Università Gregoriana, 2008).

37. See Hee-Seong Kim, *Die Geisttaufe des Messias: Eine compositionsgeschichtliche Untersuchung zu einem Leitmotiv des lukanische Doppelwerks: Ein Beitrag zur Theologie und Intention des Lukas* (Studien zur klassischen Philologie, 81; Frankfurt: Peter Lang, 1993), pp. 94-131.

38. On the characterization of discipleship in Luke's Gospel as being 'with' Jesus, see Lk. 6.17; 7.11; 8.1, 22; etc.; Joel B. Green, *The Theology of Gospel of Luke* (New Testament Theology; Cambridge: Cambridge University Press, 1995), pp. 108-109. On the problem of perception, see, e.g., Lk. 9.37-50; 18.31-34.

faithfulness in prayer to a God who was ready to give graciously and quickly even the gift of the Holy Spirit to those who ask (see Lk. 11.1-13). The disciples, commissioned to participate in and carry on the mission of Jesus, have yet to perform in ways that signal their competence for the mission; although the closing of the Third Gospel portends transformation in their character, we await the evidence that will now begin to unfold.

These motifs share a commonality that is integral to the opening of Acts—a gathering up of the past that anticipates a future well-grounded in that past. That is, Acts 1.1-14 is concerned with continuity between the progress of Jesus' life and ministry (Luke) and that of the church (Acts), set within the plotline of God's faithfulness to his saving promise. Continuity is guaranteed through the commission of Jesus' witnesses and the promised baptism with the Holy Spirit.[39]

III. *Conclusion*

Various approaches to Luke and Acts call for different ways of construing the relationship between these two books. A canonical approach will of necessity concern itself with how Acts provides a bridge between the fourfold Gospel and the letters of Paul, while diminishing the claims Acts makes regarding Luke's 'first book'. A canonical approach has neither need nor basis for denying other interpretive strategies. Historical approaches might want to examine more closely issues of genre or authorship, and these may lead some interpreters to side against the unity of Luke–Acts. Interpretation of Luke and Acts as narratives, and particularly as narrative representations of history, however, can scarcely escape the text's own intention to be read not as two discrete accounts, one focused on Jesus and the other on the church, but as a single narrative of the coming of salvation in all its fullness to all people.

---

39. Cf. Manfred Korn, *Die Geschichte Jesu in Veränderter Zeit: Studien zur bleibenden Bedeutung Jesu im lukanischen Doppelwerk* (WUNT, II/51; Tübingen: Mohr Siebeck, 1993), pp. 175-92.

Luke's Jerusalem Perspective

James D.G. Dunn

Sixty years ago Olof Linton[1] noted that there are some points in common between the account of Paul contested by the apostle himself and Luke's representation of him, notably in Paul's relations with Jerusalem. Particularly worthy of note were the observations that the qualifications for an 'apostle' in Acts 1.21-22 would exclude Paul (14.4, 14 notwithstanding), something Paul vigorously disputes (Gal. 1.1). Again, Luke seems to be suggesting in Acts 9.23-27 what Paul so vehemently denied in Gal. 1.18-20. And a report such as Luke records in Acts 16.3 may have provoked Paul's protest in Gal. 5.11. Linton concluded that Luke deliberately painted a more conciliatory picture of Paul: he 'wanted to correct Paul slightly in order to make him better'.[2] Linton's article has been sadly neglected, but in my recent intensive study of Acts[3] I found myself repeatedly harking back to Linton's thesis to help explain the tensions between Luke's Acts and Paul's letters. So much so that it now seems to me very probable that Luke drew much of his presentation of Paul from the version of the relationship between Paul and Jerusalem which he heard in Jerusalem itself or from the representatives of the Jerusalem church whom he encountered when gathering the material for his second volume.

Such a thesis does not ignore or play down the more obvious thesis that Luke saw Paul as the great hero of the second half of Acts, or even that he wrote the book in part at least as an apologia for Paul. Indeed, Linton may have detected the way in which Luke's apologia for Paul was intended to be effective. That is, conscious of Paul's controversial reputation among Jewish Christians generally and particularly among

---

1. Olof Linton, 'The Third Aspect: A Neglected Point of View', *ST* 3 (1949), pp. 79-95.

2. Linton, 'The Third Aspect', p. 95.

3. J.D.G. Dunn, *Beginning from Jerusalem* (Grand Rapids: Eerdmans, 2009). I draw on this volume extensively in what follows.

those stemming from Jerusalem (Acts 21.21) or who looked back to the Jerusalem community as the mother church, Luke deliberately chose to rub off the jagged edges of Paul's relationship with Jerusalem and to present a more harmonious relationship than had actually been the case. In this he would presumably have been helped by the awareness that there were two sides to such a relationship, and that Paul's own attitude on the matter was not dispassionate and was perhaps more intemperate than Luke wished to record. Linton's thesis, in effect, is that in order to present a more harmonious picture of the relationship Luke chose to follow the Jerusalem version of controversial issues and events rather than Paul's version, if he also knew that.

The thesis does help explain the tensions between Acts and Paul's letters, and provides a more sympathetic interpretation of Luke's intention and methods. If true, it means that we do not need to ascribe to Luke a willingness to twist information arbitrarily to serve his purpose, or to invent episodes in a way that historians ancient and modern would find highly questionable. On the contrary, the thesis suggests that Luke was able to present accounts of Paul which he had derived from reputable sources, versions of events different from those maintained by Paul, perhaps, but nevertheless maintained in good faith by those who differed from Paul on the subject.

As with all such theses, however, its plausibility rests on the explanatory power it has in regard to the data available. So I turn to that task, as my humble offering to one who belongs to that select band who have done so much to illuminate Acts in the past two decades.

I. *The Resurrection Appearances of Christ and Paul's Apostleship*

It is worth beginning with the notable facts that Luke confines the Jerusalem appearances of the risen Christ to Jerusalem and limits the appearances to a forty-day period which effectively excludes Paul's claim to have been granted such an appearance.

(1) The limitation of the appearances of Jesus to Jerusalem is not so explicit in the Acts account. Yet it was already made clear in the closing paragraphs of the preceding Gospel, where the disciples on the evening of the first day of resurrection appearances (in Jerusalem) are explicitly told to 'stay in Jerusalem until you have been clothed with power from on high (Pentecost)' (Lk. 24.49). The Acts account echoes the explicit instruction: 'while he was in their company he (Jesus) ordered then not to leave Jerusalem, but to wait for the promise of the Father (Pentecost)' (Acts 1.4). For anyone aware of the recollections of appearances in

Galilee, appearances attested by the other three Evangelists,[4] Luke's repeated emphasis on this point must have come across oddly.

The inference (that Luke has ignored other appearance traditions) is strengthened by the further fact that Luke seems to have gone out of his way to exclude any tradition of appearances in Galilee. Noteworthy is what appears to be Luke's editing of Mark's account of the young man at the tomb commanding the women to 'Go, tell his disciples and Peter that *he is going ahead of you to Galilee*; there you will see him, *just as he told you*' (Mk 16.7, referring back to 14.28). In this he is followed by Matthew (Mt. 28.7). But Luke has instead: 'Remember *how he told you, while he was still in Galilee*, that the Son of Man must be handed over...' (Lk. 24.6-8). Since Luke has simply omitted the earlier Markan promise ('After I am raised up, I will go before you to Galilee', Mk 14.28), it is hard to avoid the conclusion that Luke has deliberately edited Mark at this point.[5] In which case the implication clearly is that Luke wanted to focus the events of these forty days around Jerusalem[6] and took steps deliberately to exclude accounts of appearances elsewhere.

The motivation will hardly have been simply a concern for tidiness. There is evidently a theological intention at work here. It is evident also in the way the narrative of the first five chapters of Acts focuses exclusively on Jerusalem, and in the way the Jerusalem leadership of the young church monitors and approves the first three great breakthroughs in Christian mission.[7] We can guess already that Luke wanted to maintain the theological and ecclesiastical point that Jerusalem was the centre and fountainhead of Christian mission, thus probably reflecting the Jerusalem church's own perspective, but also maintaining the continuity of the new movement with the Israel of old.[8] At this point, of course, Paul is not in view. But it is not hard to see here a presentation which reflects the perspective of the mother church itself.

(2) The limitation of the resurrection appearances of Jesus to forty days[9] would seem at first to be less controversial. The accounts of other

---

4. Details in my *Jesus Remembered* (Grand Rapids: Eerdmans, 2003), §18.3.

5. E.g. I.H. Marshall, *The Gospel of Luke* (NIGTC; Exeter: Paternoster Press, 1978), p. 886; J.A. Fitzmyer, *The Gospel according to Luke* (AB, 28; 2 vols.; New York: Doubleday, 1981, 1985), II, p. 1545.

6. Since Emmaus was only about seven miles from Jerusalem—that is, about three hours on foot from Jerusalem—the account of Lk. 24.13-32 does not weaken the focus on Jerusalem, especially since the sequel was an immediate return of the two concerned to Jerusalem (24.33).

7. Acts 8.14-25; 11.1-18, 25-26.

8. See further Fitzmyer, *Luke*, I, pp. 164-68.

9. Acts 1.3: 'during forty days'; cf. 13.31: 'for many days'.

appearances in the Gospels could be fitted into that time frame, even though several of them are located in Galilee. The problem arises with the fuller list of appearances that Paul reports in 1 Cor. 15.5-8, which seem to envisage a chronological sequence[10] of appearances stretching well beyond forty days. The appearance to 'more than five hundred brothers at once' (1 Cor. 15.6) presupposes a larger number of disciples than ever is envisaged in the forty-day period;[11] presumably it took place after the initial expansion of the new movement was under way—on Luke's timetable, post-Pentecost. The appearance to James is indeterminable (cf. Acts 1.14),[12] but the appearance to 'all the apostles' (1 Cor. 15.7) seems to presuppose the emergence of a larger group who believed themselves to be called to mission ('apostles'), and whose commissioning probably marked and helps explain the first major outreach beyond Jerusalem.[13]

The appearance to Paul himself (15.8) is generally reckoned to have taken place roughly between eighteen months and three years following the resurrection.[14] A little thought indicates the unlikelihood of Paul's claim to such an appearance being accepted (by deeply suspicious disciples)[15] after such a lengthy interval, had the only other recognized appearances ceased long before, after forty days. The issue, however, was crucial for Paul himself. His vehement claim, indicative of his suppressed anger on the point, is clearly expressed in the opening words of his letter to the Galatians: 'Paul, apostle, not from human beings nor through a human being, but through Jesus Christ and God the Father' (Gal. 1.1; similarly 1.12). But the wording of the agreement made later in Jerusalem raises the possibility, even likelihood, that though Paul's commission to take the gospel to Gentiles was acknowledged by the Jerusalem leadership (Gal. 2.7-9), there was some hesitation about recognizing his mission as

---

10. The sequence of εἶτα...ἔπειτα...ἔπειτα...εἶτα ('then...then...then...then'), followed by ἔσχατον δὲ πάντων ('last of all'), is most naturally read as a chronological sequence (BDAG, p. 361).

11. Acts 1.15 speaks of only 120 as the crowd of believers.

12. See my *Jesus Remembered*, pp. 862-64.

13. The circle of 'apostles' was more extensive than the twelve, and included Andronicus and Junia (Rom. 16.7), and possibly Apollos (1 Cor. 4.9), Barnabas (Gal. 2.8-9) and Silvanus (1 Thess. 2.6-7). For bibliography on 'apostle', see, among others, the reviews by H.D. Betz, 'Apostle', *ABD*, I, pp. 309-11; J.A. Bühner, 'ἀπόστολος', *EDNT*, I, pp. 142-46; P.W. Barnett, 'Apostle', *DPL*, pp. 45-51.

14. On Pauline chronology I may refer simply to my *Beginning from Jerusalem*, §28.1.

15. As indicated by Luke (Acts 9.26) and also hinted at by Paul himself (Gal. 1.18-20).

an 'apostleship' (ἀποστολήν).[16] And Paul's insistence that he was an apostle, the apostle to the Corinthian church, carries with it the clear indication that his apostolic status was not accepted by others: 'Am I not an apostle? Have I not seen our Lord?... If to others I am not an apostle, at least I am to you' (1 Cor. 9.1-2).

What is striking about Luke's restriction of the resurrection appearances to forty days in Jerusalem, then, is that *it excludes the appearance to Paul from the list of recognized resurrection appearances*. The assertion that the resurrection appearances came to an end after a relatively short period was not at issue. Paul also regarded the sequence of such appearances as having come to an end; the appearance to himself was 'last of all' (1 Cor. 15.8). The key factor, however, was that Luke shared with Paul the belief that the only ones who were qualified to bear the weighty title 'apostle' were those who had seen the risen Christ, and who thus could bear witness to the resurrection (Acts 1.22). Since, then, for Luke, the resurrection appearances had ended after forty days, *Paul did not meet that qualification and consequently could not be designated as 'apostle' of* the same category as Peter and the rest of 'the twelve'.[17]

Luke of course had no doubt as to the fact that Paul had been commissioned by Christ for his mission to the Gentiles. But should we see in Luke's conception of who counted as an apostle, a witness of Christ's resurrection, a holding back of the full designation of 'apostle' to Paul similar to what is suggested in Gal. 2.8? And if so, should this count as one of the points at which Luke's portrayal of Paul's status and mission has been influenced by a Jerusalem perspective?

16.   Whereas Peter's mission is designated as 'the apostleship (ἀποστολήν) of the circumcision', Paul's is described only as 'for the Gentiles' (ἀποστολήν is not repeated) (2.8). H.D. Betz, *Galatians* (Hermeneia; Philadelphia: Fortress Press, 1979), p. 82, states that 'The agreement must have recognized Peter's apostleship, but left Paul without a specific title' (and cf. p. 98). J.L. Martyn, *Galatians* (AB, 33A; New York: Doubleday, 1997), p. 203, describes the account as '...unmistakably failing to grant formal apostolicity to Paul's labors'.

17.   Luke's reference to Paul and Barnabas as 'the apostles' (14.4, 14) is somewhat puzzling, given the qualifications for apostleship laid down in 1.22, and that Luke uses the term elsewhere invariably to refer to the twelve in Jerusalem (within whose number Barnabas had not previously been included). The only obvious solution is that Luke's account reflects the story as told from an Antiochene perspective, Paul and Barnabas having been commissioned and sent forth as missionaries of that church (13.3). Similarly C.K. Barrett, *The Acts of the Apostles* (ICC; 2 vols.; Edinburgh: T. & T. Clark, 1994, 1998), I, pp. 666-67, 671-72. Paul also uses 'apostle' in the less weighty sense of emissary of a particular church (2 Cor. 8.23; Phil. 2.25), though he clearly regarded his own apostleship as wholly on a par with that of the Jerusalem apostles.

II. *The Sequel to Paul's Conversion*

Probably the strongest card in Linton's hand is the tension between Luke's and Paul's accounts of the sequel to Paul's conversion.

In Acts, Luke seems to suggest that the converted Saul left Damascus after a short time there and went directly to Jerusalem, where he was received by 'the apostles' (Acts 9.23-27). The juncture is even tighter in Acts 22, where Paul in his self-testimony, having recounted Ananias' call to him to be baptized, continues, 'After I had returned to Jerusalem…' (22.16-17). In contrast, Paul's testimony is sharply different—Gal. 1.16-20 (my translation):

> …in order that I might preach him among the Gentiles, I did not consult immediately with flesh and blood, nor did I go up to Jerusalem to those who were apostles before me, but I went away into Arabia and returned again to Damascus. Then, after three years, I did go up to Jerusalem to get to know Cephas, and I stayed with him fifteen days. Other of the other apostles I did not see, but only James the Lord's brother. What I write to you, please note, before God, I am not lying.

The overlap in the two accounts is almost as striking as the contrast. Paul was clearly protesting against a different version of the sequel to his conversion. Why did he deny that he consulted with flesh and blood? The obvious inference is that he was responding to a claim that he *had* done so. The parallel with Gal. 1.1 similarly implies that Paul found it necessary to contest (in his opening words!) a claim that his commission came from fellow humans and through human hands (rather than directly from God and through Jesus Christ). And why does he deny that he went up to Jerusalem to those who were apostles before him? The implication is the same: Paul was denying what others said about him, that he had derived his commission and his gospel from the Jerusalem apostles.[18] The point is that *this is precisely what Luke seems to say*: that soon after his conversion Paul went up to Jerusalem and consulted with the apostles. So Paul seems to be going out of his way to deny Luke's account!

Paul evidently found it necessary to continue laying out his version. It was only after three years[19] that he went up to Jerusalem, for the first time

---

18. The focus of Paul's defence suggests that 'the apostles' here in view were not the apostles (= missionaries) referred to in 1 Cor. 15.7, but those regarded by others as 'the apostles' (the Jerusalem leadership). This is the one time that Paul's usage comes close to that of Luke, which suggests both that Luke's usage was closer to that of Paul's critics, and that Paul wrote concessively here.

19. 'After three years (μετὰ ἔτη τρία)' is expressed in the normal Greek idiom (BDAG, pp. 637-38). It could denote an interval of fully three years; but since the

following his conversion. Even then he only stayed with Cephas (Peter) and otherwise saw only James. The assertion was so important to Paul, and so important to refute the alternative being circulated by others, that he takes a solemn oath on the point there and then: 'what (plural) I write to you, look, before God I am not lying' (1.20).[20] We should note that Paul does not deny contact with the Jerusalem leadership outright. The view which he was opposing was based on knowledge of at least some contact between Paul and the Jerusalem leadership. This is the view, presumably, on which Luke probably drew in drafting his own version of events (Acts 9.26-27).

What are we to make of this? There does not seem any way to avoid the conflict between the two accounts. Luke evidently saw the episode as a means of knitting the converted Saul into the Jerusalem leadership (Acts 9.27), and therefore of sustaining his theme of the centrality of Jerusalem for the beginnings of Christianity. And his account (9.19-25) does leave room for some period of time to have passed before Saul's inelegant exit from Damascus (by basket!).[21] But he hardly allows the impression that two to three years were to elapse (spent in Arabia) before Paul's departure for Jerusalem; and the Acts 22 account gives no hint of such a gap. Perhaps, then, what we have to recognize is that Acts is not simply or solely a defence of Paul, or, at least, not a defence of Paul in Paul's own terms. Luke evidently did not see himself simply as a spokesman for Paul but was familiar with other views of Paul, including the views of those who opposed Paul's mission and who had misgivings

---

year from which the counting began would be reckoned as the first year, the period could be anything from not much over two years.

20. 'I am not lying' has the force of a formula of affirmation (Job 6.28; 27.11; Ps. 89.35; *4 Macc.* 5.34; Plutarch, *Mor.* 1059A; BDAG, p. 1097; H. Conzelmann, *TDNT*, IX, p. 601). Paul uses the formula elsewhere (Rom. 9.1; 2 Cor. 11.31; also 1 Tim. 2.7). For the seriousness of lying within the Jewish tradition, see *TDNT*, IX, pp. 598-600. The addition of 'before God' gives the affirmation the force of a sacred oath, indicating that Paul was willing to stake his whole standing before God on the veracity of what he had just written; see further J.P. Sampley, '"Before God, I do not Lie" (Gal. 1.20): Paul's Self-Defence in the Light of Roman Legal Praxis', *NTS* 23 (1977), pp. 477-82.

21. Acts 9.19, 'after some (τινάς) days', is vague and imprecise; in 9.22 Saul engaged with 'the Jews who lived in Damascus' for some time; 9.23 makes reference to 'after many (ἱκαναί) days'. M. Hengel and A.M. Schwemer, *Paul between Damascus and Antioch* (London: SCM Press, 1997) read these differentiated time notes as positive indicators of Luke's responsible historiography: they 'mark Luke out as a historian and distinguish him from the producers of apostolic romances' (p. 402 n. 701).

about his gospel.[22] If Luke was fully aware of Paul's version he may even have thought there was too much special-pleading and *parti pris* in Paul's account of his relationship with Jerusalem. What we may well have, then, is Luke trying to construct an account which takes account of both views, but without excluding either.

III. *Paul's Visits to Jerusalem*

The most outrageous disagreement between Paul and Luke is on the number of visits Paul made to Jerusalem. Alternatively expressed, the issue is whether Luke's account of a 'famine relief visit' by Paul and Barnabas to Jerusalem (Acts 11.30) can be easily squared with Paul's insistence that his second visit to Jerusalem was to lay before the Jerusalem leadership the gospel which he preached (to Gentiles) (Gal. 2.1-2). The Acts 11.30 episode suffers from the same problems as afflicted Acts 9.26-30. It is not that historical records fail to record famines during the reign of Claudius (41–54): there are several such references.[23] Nor is it the implication that the Jerusalem church had many impoverished members; that is confirmed by Rom. 15.26. It is rather that Paul's own solemn affidavit (Gal. 1.18–2.1) does not allow room for any intermediate visit by Paul to Jerusalem. It is possible that Gal. 2.1-10 refers to that visit (Gal. 2.1-10 = Acts 11.27-30), but as we shall see, the match between Gal. 2.1-10 and Acts 15 is too close to allow them to be pulled apart.

More plausible, I suggest, is the likelihood that such a visit (as 11.30) was undertaken by Barnabas, alone,[24] or with some other(s), before he and Saul had become a team; and that, possibly confused by the fact that the two subsequently became such a close team, some of those ill-disposed towards Paul later assumed that Saul had accompanied Barnabas on the visit. Some attempt to represent Paul as visiting Jerusalem more frequently, and therefore as more dependent on/subservient to the Jerusalem leadership, is presumably what caused Paul to itemize his

---

22. Cf. Betz, *Galatians*, p. 79. Otherwise, Barrett indicates what can be said positively about the traditions drawn on by Luke (*Acts*, I, pp. 460-62).

23. Reviewed, for example, by C.J. Hemer, *The Book of Acts in the Setting of Hellenistic History* (WUNT, 49; Tübingen: Mohr Siebeck, 1989), pp. 164-65; Barrett, *Acts*, I, pp. 563-64; Hengel and Schwemer, *Paul*, pp. 240-41.

24. As suggested by M. Hengel, *Acts and the History of Earliest Christianity* (London: SCM Press, 1979), p. 111. Hengel and Schwemer consider the possibilities that Paul travelled with the delegation but kept out of Jerusalem, because there his life was still in danger or his presence would not have been welcome (*Paul*, pp. 242-43), or that he had been involved in the preparation of this collection in Antioch (p. 465 n. 1273).

Jerusalem visits so scrupulously. Paul's insistence that he remained unknown by sight to the churches of Judea, and that it was only after a further fourteen years that he went again to Jerusalem (Gal. 1.22; 2.1), is another way of saying emphatically, 'I did *not* go to Jerusalem during the intervening years.'

Acts 11.30 looks to be another passage, then, in which Luke has heard an account of Paul's relationship with Jerusalem which was at odds with Paul's own recollection, but which he has chosen to use (he may not have been familiar with Paul's account of the matter) in order to highlight the strength of continuity between the Jerusalem leadership and Paul's mission to the Gentiles.

IV. *The Jerusalem Meeting and the 'Apostolic Decree'*

Linton's thesis can also help make better sense of the differences between the accounts in Acts 15 and Gal. 2.1-10. The differences are such that the strong minority opinion appears very enticing: that the Jerusalem meeting referred to by Paul took place during the famine relief visit of Acts 11.30.[25] I remain unpersuaded principally for two reasons.

(1) Paul clearly regarded the Gal. 2.1-10 meeting as achieving a formal agreement with the key Jerusalem leadership (2.7-9), despite fierce opposition (2.4-5), an agreement which would have made further debate on the issue both unnecessary and retrograde.[26] The Galatians 2 = Acts 11 solution to the problem may be a case of sacrificing the integrity of the Jerusalem leadership in order to safeguard Luke's reliability.

(2) On the Galatians 2 = Acts 11 hypothesis, the attitude ascribed to Peter in Acts 15.10 is remarkably at odds with his conduct in Gal. 2.12, so that one has to envisage a Peter who learned that Jews may eat with Gentiles in Acts 10, was persuaded otherwise in Gal. 2.12, and then claimed that the law is a yoke which 'neither we nor our ancestors have been able to bear' (Acts 15.10).[27] It is also hard to imagine the Paul who wrote so dismissively of the Jerusalem apostles in Gal. 2.6, and was so

---

25. Notably W.M. Ramsay, *St. Paul the Traveller and the Roman Citizen* (London: Hodder & Stoughton, 1896), pp. 54-60, 154-55; F.F. Bruce, *Paul: Apostle of the Free Spirit* (Exeter: Paternoster Press, 1977), Chapters 15, 17; R.N. Longenecker, *Galatians* (WBC, 41; Dallas: Word, 1990)—full discussion on pp. lxxiii-lxxxviii.

26. In defending the Gal. 2 = Acts 11 option, E.J. Schnabel, *Early Christian Mission* (2 vols.; Downers Grove, IL: InterVarsity Press, 2004), argues that 'there was no in-depth discussion of circumcision during the consultation' (II, p. 991), ignoring the obvious implications of Gal. 2.3-6.

27. Peter 'is described here as something of a Paulinist, though the Paulinism is not accurately portrayed' (Barrett, *Acts*, II, p. 719).

outraged by the conduct of Peter and Barnabas in 2.11-16, acting so meekly as Acts 15.12, 22 and 25 implies.[28]

As an alternative, I suggest that once again Linton's thesis provides a more satisfactory solution to the problem: that Acts 15 is Luke's account of the Jerusalem consultation *from the perspective of the Jerusalem leadership*; and that Gal. 2.1-10 is Paul's recollection of the same consultation, from his own perspective. Here not least, in the understandable preference for Paul's eye-witness account over against Luke's somewhat more remote version, we should again avoid the assumption that Paul's account is that of an objective eye-witness. The fact that Barnabas, Paul's close colleague, fades almost wholly from sight, in an almost wholly first person singular account of the triumph achieved at that meeting, is itself sufficient warning that Paul's account is no dispassionate description.[29] In comparing Acts 15 with Galatians 2, *each* account may be as much special pleading as the other, both theological as well as historical.

Following Linton's hint, then, we can see that *Luke* relates the Jerusalem meeting from the perspective of the Jerusalemites. The lead actors are Peter and James (Acts 15.7-11, 13-21); Barnabas and Paul are passed over in a single sentence (15.12). He narrates it also from his own perspective, where Peter's decisive contribution (15.7-11) reflects the central importance Luke gave the Cornelius episode in his own narrative (10.1–11.18), and the importance he placed on Peter's acceptance of Cornelius as the determinative precedent for the whole Christian mission. *Paul*, on the other hand, recalled his own contribution to the decision not to require circumcision of Gentile believers as decisive. As already noted, the predominantly 'first person' account of Gal. 2.1-10 almost entirely eclipses the role of Barnabas; it was Paul through whom God had worked so effectively, the grace given to Paul that was recognized by the Jerusalem leadership, and Paul who had been entrusted with the gospel for the uncircumcision (2.7-9). Paul evinces here an ungraciousness which is only partly excusable in the light of Barnabas' subsequent lapse (2.13): perhaps Barnabas had not been so unyielding as Paul in the critical confrontation of 2.3-5; or possibly Paul wanted to suppress the fact that he and Barnabas went to Jerusalem as representatives of the Antioch church.[30]

---

28. Would Paul have accepted that the items listed in 15.20, 29 were 'essentials, compulsory (ἐπάναγκες)' (BDAG, p. 358)?

29. The predominantly 'first person' account of Gal. 2.1-10 ('I'/'me', 2.1, 2, 3, 6, 7, 8, 9, 10) almost entirely eclipses the role of Barnabas (2.1, [5], 9, [10]).

30. Martyn, *Galatians*, p. 209. M. Öhler, *Barnabas: die historische Person und ihre Rezeption in der Apostlegeschichte* (WUNT, 156; Tübingen: Mohr Siebeck, 2003), believes Barnabas was probably the chief respondent to the Jerusalemites (pp. 70-72).

When we look more closely at Acts 15 we can easily see that Luke has produced an account in line with his consistent intention to portray the beginnings of Christianity as essentially harmonious. He has *James* both affirm the precedent through *Peter*, and in rather *Pauline* terms.[31] Thus Luke was able to provide an account of the agreement reached by these three key figures in Christianity's beginnings and to promote the harmony which he was portraying. James agrees with Paul (15.19) that even for a non-Christian Jew, a genuine turning to God by a Gentile should be sufficient ground for the former to drop most of the ritual barriers to association with the latter and to stop bothering/harassing Gentile converts on the point.

More to the point here, however, are the indications that Luke has, once again, told his story more from the perspective of Jerusalem than that of Paul. That the precedent was provided by Peter and the determinative ruling given by James accords well with what we learn (also from Acts) of the shifting leadership in the Jerusalem church, as Peter became more committed to mission, leaving the leadership in Jerusalem primarily in James' hands. Also noticeable is that James is presented as finding confirmation of what Simeon/Peter had reported in scripture,[32] and in such terms as integrated the incoming of the Gentiles with the primary goal of the restoration of Israel.[33]

The terms of the 'apostolic decree' are also indicative of the 'solution' to the problems caused to most believing Jews by the growing number of Gentile believers. For they seem to be based not so much on the 'Noahide laws' (including the prohibition of idolatry, adultery and incest, bloodshed, and eating the flesh of a limb cut from a living animal) which may already have served to provide 'rules of association' between Jews and Gentiles.[34] However, it is now generally recognized that the principal

---

31. As already noted (n. 27), 15.10 also depicts Peter as speaking in Pauline terms.

32. R.J. Bauckham, 'James and the Jerusalem Church', in R. Bauckham (ed.), *The Book of Acts in its Palestinian Setting* (Grand Rapids: Eerdmans, 1995), pp. 415-80 (452), notes: 'The issue is a matter of *halakhah*, which can only be decided from Scripture (cf. *b. B. Mes.* 59b)'.

33. Bauckham ('James and the Jerusalem Church', pp. 453-55) justifiably argues that the 'rebuilt tent of David' would have been seen as a reference to the Jerusalem community as the eschatological Temple, the Amos prophecy being read in the 'context of prophecies which associate the eschatological conversion of the Gentile nations with the restoration of the Temple in the messianic age'.

34. On the Noahide laws, see particularly D. Novak, *The Image of the Non-Jew in Judaism: An Historical and Constructive Study of the Noahide Laws* (Lewiston, NJ: Edwin Mellen Press, 1983); M. Bockmuehl, *Jewish Law in Gentile Churches*

source of the 'apostolic decree' is the legislation regarding the 'resident alien', that is, the non-Jews who were permanently resident in the land of Israel, 'in the midst of' the people.[35] The apostolic decree, in other words, could be regarded as the Jerusalem church's solution to the problem of how to regard godfearers who became believers in Messiah Jesus and who (evidently) received the Spirit as Gentiles. That is, to treat them in effect as 'resident aliens', Gentiles in the midst of the people, while retaining their identity as Gentiles. Here we can see the more tradition-ist Jews, led by James, attempting to ensure that the albeit uncircumcised Gentile believers should maintain a pattern of living which fitted with the continuing priorities of the Jewish believers.[36]

Similarly the implication of Acts 15.21 (Jews of the diaspora heard Moses being read out sabbath by sabbath) is that knowledge and obser-vance of the law was well sustained in diaspora synagogues and was not at all threatened by the compromise proposed. The hope implicit in the 'apostolic decree', then, would be for a mutual respect within the extended communities between Jews who insisted on stricter practice and those who consorted with Gentiles on the basis of the rules just proposed. It should be noted, however, that the whole proposal is put from a Jewish perspective and is geared to maintaining relationships in mixed churches on Jewish terms. The thought is not of Christian com-munities as such, the basis of whose fellowship was their common faith in Christ (the absence of any overt reference to Jesus should not escape notice). The thought is rather of communities whose basis for fellowship would be continued respect for the law.

One further deduction can be made in regard to the historicity of Luke's account and the origin of the 'apostolic decree'. If Luke's account cannot be squared in detail with Paul's, and if it reflects so strongly a

(Edinburgh: T. & T. Clark, 2000), Chapter 7. Gen. 9.4-6 had already warned against both eating flesh in which the blood still adheres, and murder.

35.   Lev. 17.8-9, 10-14; 18.26; see Bauckham, 'James and the Jerusalem Church', pp. 458-62; and further J. Wehnert, *Die Reinheit des "christlichen Gottesvolkes" aus Juden und Heiden* (FRLANT, 173; Göttingen: Vandenhoeck & Ruprecht, 1997), pp. 209-38; Barrett, *Acts*, II, pp. 733-34. J. Taylor, 'The Jerusalem Decrees (Acts 15.20, 29 and 21.25) and the Incident at Antioch (Gal 2.11-14)', *NTS* 47 (2001), pp. 372-80, suggests that the Jerusalem decrees can be interpreted both as 'Noahide commandments', implicitly keeping the separation between Jews and Gentiles, and as analogous to the decrees for resident aliens, implicitly allowing Gentiles to asso-ciate with Jews under certain conditions; he argues that the two interpretations correspond to the attitudes towards Gentile believers at Antioch manifested by James and Cephas respectively.

36.   See again Bauckham, 'James and the Jerusalem Church', pp. 462-67.

Jerusalem perspective on the problems of mixed congregations, then the most likely inference to be drawn is that this was in fact Jerusalem's version of events, that indeed the theology (Acts 15.14-18) and the practice (15.19-20) were those insisted on by Jerusalem (and by James). But also that they were the theology and practice as they became clear and established in the years following the Jerusalem council. The origin of the 'apostolic decree' in fact is probably indicated by those to whom the letter conveying the decree was addressed (15.29)—the Gentile believers in Antioch, Syria and Cilicia (15.23). These were the churches which became established during the period when Paul still fully acknowledged the Jerusalem leadership's authority (Gal. 1.20; 2.1-2).

The decree, then, probably represents the practice which evolved in the mixed (Jew/Gentile) churches which continued under Jerusalem's and Antioch's direct supervision, probably at the direction (as a 'decree') of the Jerusalem leadership. How soon that practice became established is not at all clear, but it need not have been long after Paul's departure on his Aegean mission, and perhaps as a compromise to resolve the problems posed by the Antioch incident.[37] In any case, it would appear that Luke has done here what he did in describing the appointment of elders in the churches founded by the mission from Antioch (Acts 14.23). That is, viewing the events from the perspective of his own time, forty or fifty years later, Luke presents the agreed practice which had become established during the intervening years in the mission directed from Antioch (Syria and Cilicia) as the terms of association agreed at the Jerusalem council.[38]

This more negative judgment on Luke's account of the Jerusalem meeting carries with it a similar hesitation to take his account of the sequel as straightforward history—the delivery of the letter containing the 'decree', from 'the apostles and elders' (that is, the Jerusalem leadership) to the church in Antioch, and presumably subsequently to the churches of 'Syria and Cilicia' (15.30, 41) and Galatia (16.4). In other words, it is once again precisely in his description of Paul's dealings

---

37.   A.J.M. Wedderburn, 'The "Apostolic Decree": Tradition and Redaction', *NovT* 35 (1993), pp. 362-89 (388-89); Hengel and Schwemer, *Paul*, p. 442 n. 1084.

38.   This hypothesis accords with the majority view; see, for example, E. Haenchen, *The Acts of the Apostles* (trans. R.McL. Wilson; Oxford: Blackwell, 1971): 'a living tradition which was probably even then [at the time of Luke's writing] traced back to the Apostles... These prohibitions must have come into force in a strongly mixed community of the diaspora, where Jewish claims were more moderate and could be satisfied by the four commandments which Moses himself gave to the Gentiles' (pp. 470-72).

with 'the apostles' in Jerusalem, as in his account of Paul's first post-con-version visit to Jerusalem (Acts 9.26-30), that Luke's account becomes most difficult to square with Paul's attitude and clearly expressed senti-ments. Here too Luke was probably following a tradition which ema-nated from Jerusalem and which told a story more conducive to Luke's own point of view.

V. *Paul's Collection*

The only other sequence where Luke's account of Paul's mission and Paul's own letters seem to jar badly is the issue of Paul's collection for the poor among the believers in Jerusalem (Rom. 15.26). It was clearly a matter of considerable importance for Paul: the very fact that he devotes so much attention to it, and across three letters, puts it among his primary concerns.[39] So it obviously dominated much of his thought and planning during the Ephesus-based Aegean mission. Moreover, the correlation of the reference to 'church delegates' in speaking of the collection (1 Cor. 16.3; 2 Cor. 8.23), and the list of church representatives who were to accompany Paul on the journey to Jerusalem (Acts 20.4), presumably means that the three months in Corinth (20.3) were largely devoted to coordinating the organization of the gathering of these delegates, of their hospitality and sea passage to Israel, and of the security of the collection itself. In any case, it is clear beyond reasonable doubt that Paul's principal, indeed only real, goal in making his final trip to Jerusalem was to pass over to the leaders of the Jerusalem church the collection, presumably by which he hoped to re-establish the link between Jerusalem and the churches he had founded (Rom. 15.25-28).

The evident importance of the collection for Paul and of its safe delivery in person to Jerusalem, makes it all the more astonishing that Luke ignores the collection as completely as he does. Paul's enthusiasm to make the collection is never mentioned in Luke's account of the period when the collection was obviously one of Paul's primary concerns. Luke identifies Paul's companions on his last journey to Jerusalem as delegates from the churches of the Pauline mission (Acts 20.4), but he gives no hint that they accompanied Paul to reinforce the message of the collection or to provide the necessary security for its transport, as we may assume to have been the case. And in the Jerusalem encounter of Paul with the Jerusalem leadership, no hint whatsoever is given of the fact that Paul came bearing gifts to assist the Jerusalem church (21.17-26).

---

39. 1 Cor. 16.1-4; 2 Cor. 8–9; Rom. 15.25-32.

The only detectable allusion to the collection in Luke's account is the reference made by Paul in his defence before the Roman governor, Felix, in Acts 24. There Paul is represented as giving his reason for his return to Jerusalem: 'to bring alms to my nation and to offer sacrifices' (24.17). Whatever Luke's source for this speech, and if we may take it to be a reference to the collection, it would appear that once again Luke was interpreting the collection as seen through the eyes of the more tradition-alist Jerusalem believers. In this case the collection, which Paul himself had described as an act of 'righteousness' (2 Cor. 9.9-10), would have been understood according to the Jewish tradition of almsgiving as a central and crucial expression of covenant righteousness.[40] From this perspective 'almsgiving' and 'righteousness' could be regarded as synony-mous.[41] Since the primary act of righteousness for a godfearing Jew, the acceptance of circumcision, had been ruled out—both Luke and Paul are agreed on that (Acts 15.5, 7-11, 19-21; Gal. 2.1-9)—the next best alter-native would be for Gentile believers to accept the traditional Jewish obligation of almsgiving.[42] Arguably this was also the motivation behind the Jerusalem leadership's insistence on almsgiving as an integral part of the agreement made in Jerusalem (Gal. 2.10).[43]

Alternatively, or in addition, if accepted by the Jerusalem traditional-ists, the collection might well have been regarded as a fulfilment of the prophetic hope for Gentiles to come in bearing gifts to the Lord, a vision particularly prominent in Isaiah.[44] Paul himself certainly played on that idea in talking of his priestly commission to make 'the offering of the Gentiles acceptable' (Rom. 15.16). The passage echoes the Isaianic vision (Isa. 66.20), a verse which may well have contributed significantly to Paul's whole mission strategy.[45] The problem, from Paul's perspective, is

40. Dan. 4.27; Sir. 3.30; 29.12; 40.24; Tob. 4.10; 12.9; 14.11.

41. In the LXX, ἐλεημοσύνη, 'kind deed, alms, charitable giving', is frequently used to translate the Hebrew, צֶדֶק / צְדָקָה, 'righteousness' (G. Schrenk, 'δικαιοσύνη', *TDNT*, II, p. 196). Note, for example, the Midrash on Deut. 15.9: 'Be careful not to refuse charity, for everyone who refuses charity is put in the same category with idolaters, and he breaks off from him the yoke of heaven, as it is said, "wicked", that is, "without yoke"'.

42. K. Berger, 'Almosen für Israel: Zum historischen Kontext der paulinischen Kollekte', *NTS* 23 (1976–77), pp. 180-204, observes that almsgiving could be presented as a substitute for Temple sacrifice and circumcision.

43. See further my *Beginning from Jerusalem*, pp. 458-60.

44. Isa. 18.7; 45.14; 60.5-7, 9, 11, 13; 61.5-6.

45. See especially R. Riesner, *Paul's Early Period: Chronology, Mission Strategy, Theology* (trans. D. Stott; Grand Rapids: Eerdmans, 1998), pp. 249-50. See also D.J. Downs, '"The Offering of the Gentiles" in Romans 15.16', *JSNT* 29 (2006),

that Isaiah's vision could easily be interpreted in terms of glorifying the nation of Israel; the gifts brought by the Gentiles were to enrich the restored people of Israel. The vision was most naturally fulfilled by the Gentiles becoming proselytes.[46] But since full proselytization of Gentile believers had been ruled out as unnecessary, the next best option for more traditionalist Jerusalem believers would be to interpret the success of the Gentile mission along the lines of Isaiah's hope. This would be consistent with the resolution of James in the Jerusalem consultation: that the incoming of Gentiles was part of the restoration of Israel itself (Acts 15.16-17). The collection could even be presented as a Christian equivalent to the Temple tax, signifying the centrality of Jerusalem for the diaspora believers, and even the Jerusalem church's right to an equivalent to the Temple tax from the diaspora churches.[47]

Of course, we do not know whether the collection was accepted by the Jerusalem church. It is quite possible that it was rejected, however courteously or otherwise. Paul had feared that it might be so (Rom. 15.31). Alternatively, perhaps the acceptance of the collection was dependent, in James' view, on Paul proving his *bona fides* as a devout Jew (Acts 21.23-26), after which James would have been able to receive the collection understood in terms of the earlier agreement (Gal. 2.10). In which case, presumably, the failure of the compromise and the resultant riot would have made it virtually impossible for James to accept the collection; such acceptance would be too easily interpreted as James accepting the collection on *Paul's* terms, which would leave the Jerusalem leadership exposed to the outright hostility of the more extreme 'zealots'. Or was the collection actually accepted out of public gaze, and the delegates (Gentiles all) encouraged to go home quietly?[48]

In any of these cases, the outcome of Paul's collection mission would have been too embarrassing for Luke to narrate. He had, after all, passed

---

pp. 173-86, who argues that the phrase 'the offering of the Gentiles' should be read as a subjective genitive.

46. The texts are assembled in my *Jesus Remembered*, pp. 394-95 nn. 70, 71.

47. The point was pressed in a famous article by K. Holl, 'Der Kirchenbegriff des Paulus in seinem Verhältnis zu dem der Urgemeinde', in his *Gesammelte Aufsätze zur Kirchengeschichte* (3 vols.; Tübingen: J.C.B. Mohr, 1928), II, pp. 44-67. S. McKnight, 'Collection for the Saints', *DPL*, pp. 143-47, suggests that the collection might have been administered along with the Temple tax, Paul accompanying both funds to hand them over to the Temple and the Jerusalem community (p. 144).

48. D. Georgi, *Remembering the Poor: The History of Paul's Collection for Jerusalem* (Nashville: Abingdon Press, 1992 [ET of the original 1965 Heidelberg doctoral dissertation]) suggests that it 'was received as if "on the side", accompanied by whispers; quite a blow to the delegation'; hence Luke's silence on the subject (p. 126).

over in complete silence the Antioch incident (Gal. 2.11-14) and the threat to Paul's churches emanating from Jerusalem as indicated by several of Paul's letters (Galatians, Phil. 3, and probably 2 Cor. 10–13). And silence on the outcome of the collection, while hinting that the collection anyway could be seen both in terms of traditionalist emphasis on the importance of almsgiving and in terms of the hope for Gentiles bringing offerings to Jerusalem, provided an account of an uncomfortable episode consistent with a Jerusalem perspective on the Pauline mission.

VI. *Conclusion*

In short, this line of reflection helps us to see how eirenic and how subtle was Luke's portrayal of Paul and his relation to Jerusalem. He had no doubt of the significance and centrality of Paul's mission in the expansion of Christianity. But he evidently went out of his way to present Paul in terms which more traditionalist Jewish believers who nevertheless sympathized with outreach to Gentiles would probably have preferred. That is, he was ambiguous over the status of Paul's commission by the heavenly Christ and the status of his apostleship. He preferred Jerusalem's version of Paul's visits to Jerusalem and of the Jerusalem consultation. He emphasized Paul's continuing readiness to follow traditional Jewish practice (Acts 16.3; 18.18; 21.22-26), and, in the case of the collection, Paul's willingness to go along with a more traditionalist interpretation of such a substantial gift coming from Gentiles. The fact that this interpretation accords with what we may deduce both from Paul (Gal. 2.10) and from Luke (Acts 15.16-17) suggests that Luke was able to and chose to view this and other points in the earliest years of Christianity from a Jerusalem perspective.

Philological and Performative Perspectives on Pentecost[*]

Heidi J. Hornik and Mikeal C. Parsons

Loveday Alexander has bemoaned the fact that in much academic study of the Bible,

> the old, holistic activity of using the canonical texts creatively as a frame-work for making sense of religious and moral experience was left outside the academic matrix altogether, devolved down to a private, devotional or pietistic practice, a matter for the preacher or for the individual con-science.[1]

On the contrary, in the 'holistic' approach that Alexander advocates,

> the study of a canonic text always swings between the two poles…of 'philology' (which treats classic texts as 'dead' texts from the past to be explicated and dissected) and 'performance' (which treats them as scripts for live performance in the present).[2]

---

[*] We are pleased to contribute to this volume honoring our dear friend, Loveday Alexander. Loveday has been unfailing in her support of our work at the intersection of biblical studies and art history. With this essay, we recall especially and fondly the gracious hospitality that Loveday and Philip extended to our family during our brief stay in their home in October 2004 and Loveday's more recent trip to Baylor to deliver the endowed Drumwright Lecture in November 2008. This essay is part of a larger project intended to trace the history of the interpretation of Acts; see H. Hornik and M. Parsons, *Acts through the Centuries* (Blackwell Bible Commentary; Oxford: Blackwell, forthcoming).

1. L. Alexander, 'God's Frozen Word: Canonicity and the Dilemma of Biblical Studies Today', *ExpTim* 117 (2009), pp. 237-42 (240). This work was first delivered as lectures, first upon Loveday's appointment as Professor in Biblical Studies at the University of Sheffield in November 2003, and then two months later (January 2004) upon her appointment as Canon Theologian at Chester Cathedral. That she viewed the lecture as appropriate for both an academic and an ecclesial audience is itself illustrative of the holistic approach to which she is calling her fellow biblical exegetes.

2. Alexander, 'God's Frozen Word', p. 239. Alexander claims this holistic approach, which she herself experienced studying classics at Oxford in the 1960s, is rooted in the ancient Hellenistic schools.

For the biblical critic, 'philology' refers to understanding the Bible historically, as 'a product of its own culture', prioritizing the 'original sense' of the text as understood by its authors and first audience, and employing the full range of historical-critical methodologies to do so.[3] 'Performance', for Alexander, refers to 'after-effects of the text on a variety of readers, who might be quite different from those it was written for'.[4] While not excluding how the Bible is performed in film or popular culture, Alexander is concerned also about its use 'in the construction of religious or ethical discourse'.[5] She concludes that

> surely in a post 9/11 world we don't need to apologize for studying (among other things) precisely *how* our texts work as *religious texts*, how different religious groups and ideologies make sense of their canonic texts, use their canonic texts to make sense of their world.[6]

What follows is an attempt to explore both the philological aspects and the performance (with a special focus on the visualization) of one text, namely the miracle of Pentecost, as recorded in Acts 2.[7]

I. *Philological Perspectives on Pentecost*[8]

Luke associates the Pentecost event with the renewal of the Sinai covenant.[9] Pentecost or the Feast of Weeks in the Old Testament was a festival associated with the wheat harvest (Exod. 23.16; Deut. 16.9-12).

---

3. See Alexander, 'God's Frozen Word', pp. 238, 240. She borrows the term 'philology' and this understanding from G. Nagy, *Homeric Questions* (Austin, TX: University of Texas Press, 1996).

4. Alexander, 'God's Frozen Word', p. 240. Alexander acknowledges (influenced by F. Young, *Biblical Exegesis and the Formation of Christian Culture* [Cambridge: Cambridge University Press, 1997]) that what she is labeling 'performative biblical criticism' is known in other circles as 'reception history' or *Wirkungsgeschichte*.

5. Alexander, 'God's Frozen Word', p. 240.

6. Alexander, 'God's Frozen Word', p. 240.

7. Space limitations preclude our exploring in any detail the impact of Pentecost on the musical arts, but we should mention its prominence in music and liturgy from at least the time of *Veni, Sancte Spiritus*, known as the 'Golden Sequence', which, since the Middle Ages has been sung or chanted in Mass before the Gospel proclamation on Pentecost Sunday. The hymn begins: *Veni, Sancte Spiritus, et emitte caelitus lucis tuae radium* ('Come Holy Spirit, and send down from heaven the ray of your light'). Consider also, among others, *Veni, Creator Spiritus* attributed to Rabanus Maurus (776–856); or 'Come Holy Ghost, all quickening fire!' by Charles Wesley.

8. An earlier version of this material is found in M. Parsons, *Acts* (Paideia; Grand Rapids, MI: Baker Academic, 2008), pp. 36-41.

9. Though not all subsequent interpreters agree (see the following section)!

The writer of *Jubilees* (second century BCE), however, states that Moses is given the law at Sinai in the third month of the year (1.1) and later states that Pentecost (or *Shebuot*) is a festival observed in the third month of the calendar (6.1), thus suggesting an implicit link between the giving of the Law and Pentecost, an allusion that is made explicit by the time of rabbinic Judaism (*b. Pes.* 68b: 'It [Pentecost] is the day on which the Torah was given'). Clues in Acts 2 suggest Luke stands in this stream of thought that moves from *Jubilees* to rabbinic Judaism.[10] The sound, fire, and speech in the Pentecost narrative were phenomena associated with the Sinai theophany (Exod. 19.16-19; cf. Philo, *Dec.* 9.33). C.H. Talbert suggests:

> The Sinai theophany and the establishment of the Mosaic covenant were brought to mind as surely as would Elijah by the description of John the Baptist's dress in Mk. 1.6. The typology of Acts 2.1-11, then, is that of making a covenant. The Pentecostal events of Acts 2.1-11, however, are not just a Messianist renewal of the Sinai covenant. Luke–Acts thinks in terms of a new covenant.[11]

This 'new covenant' was foretold by Jesus at the Last Supper (Lk. 22.20) and echoes the 'new covenant' of Jeremiah (31.31-34). In his speech, Peter makes it clear that receiving the Holy Spirit at Pentecost is the fulfillment of the ancestral promise given to Abraham (Gen. 12.3; 22.18). The gift of the Spirit fulfills the promise not only for Peter's Jewish audience (and their children; cf. Acts 2.39), but now 'all the nations of the earth', whom Peter calls 'all that are far off', are also blessed (Acts 2.39; cf. 3.25; 22.21).

Just as the Holy Spirit descended on Jesus at the outset of his public ministry (Lk. 3.22; 4.1, 14), so now the Holy Spirit comes upon the disciples at the inauguration of their public ministry. To depict this, Luke uses a typical rhetorical strategy in employing language that appeals as much to the eye as to the ear. The rhetorical tradition refers to this strategy as an *ekphrasis*. Theon, for example, defines *ekphrasis* as 'bringing what is portrayed clearly before the sight'. What is portrayed could be 'of persons and events and places and periods of time' (*Prog.* 118; trans. Kennedy[12]). An *ekphrasis* of an event could include a description of

10. For additional evidence, see C.H. Talbert, *Reading Acts: A Literary and Theological Commentary on the Acts of the Apostles* (New York: Crossroad, 1997), pp. 40-41; J. Fitzmyer, *The Acts of the Apostles* (AB, 31; New York: Doubleday, 1998), pp. 233-35.

11. Talbert, *Reading Acts*, p. 43.

12. G.A. Kennedy, *Progymnasmata: Greek Textbooks of Prose Composition and Rhetoric* (Writings from the Greco-Roman World, 10, Leiden: Brill; Atlanta: SBL, 2003).

'war, peace, a storm, famine, plague, an earthquake' (*Prog.* 118; trans. Kennedy). Often an *ekphrasis* is a detailed, verbal description of a visual artifact (e.g. Achilles' shield in Homer [*Il.* 18] or Dido's murals in Carthage described in the *Aeneid* [1.642-699] or the canopy over the bed of Anthia and Habracomes described in the opening scene in the Greek novel, *The Ephesian Tale* [1.2.5-8]), but it is by no means limited to such description.

The function of an *ekphrasis* or ekphrastic language in a narrative is often to draw attention to the significance of the event thus described for the overarching argument of the narrative.[13] Such is certainly the case with the use of ekphrastic language in Luke and Acts, where vivid language is used at key moments in the life of Jesus. At Jesus' baptism, and in a phrase unique to Luke, the narrator reports that 'the Holy Spirit came down upon him *in bodily form* as a dove' (Lk. 3.22; our emphasis). At the transfiguration scene, Jesus' 'appearance of his face was changed, and his garment became dazzling white' (9.29). Later in the same scene 'a cloud came and overshadowed' Jesus and his disciples (9.34). In the ascension scene described in Acts, Jesus is taken from his disciples' sight by a cloud (1.9), and two men 'in white robes' stood by, rebuking the disciples for staring into heaven after Jesus (1.10-11). The use of ekphrastic language in the description of the Pentecost scene is to underscore the continuity between the founder of the 'Way' and his followers. As significant events in Jesus' life and ministry were depicted in language that appealed to the 'eye and not the ear', so also is the beginning of the disciples' 'public ministry' described in similarly vivid language, marking the disciples' reception of the Holy Spirit. The gift of the Holy Spirit empowers the disciples (Acts 1.4) and the early Christian movement is moved forward by the impetus of the Spirit.

II. *Performing Pentecost*

If we read her correctly, Loveday Alexander would insist that 'Reading Acts Today' also requires the interpreter, following the exegetical model of the Hellenistic schools, to take seriously the fact that 'texts from the past were always studied with a view to their performance in the present, as poetic texts to be read aloud, as rhetorical models to be imitated in writing or speaking, as repositories of ethical values...'[14] Few texts have

---

13. M. Krieger, *Ekphrasis: The Illusion of the Natural Sign* (Baltimore: The Johns Hopkins University Press, 1992), p. 7.

14. Alexander, 'God's Frozen Word', p. 239.

enjoyed as varied and colorful 'performances' as the story of Pentecost recorded in Acts 2! Indeed, few, if any, biblical events have lent their name to describe an entire religious movement; yet, this is exactly the case for Pentecost.

From the beginning, commentators were divided regarding whether to read the Pentecost narrative against the background of the giving of the law at Sinai.[15] St Gregory of Nazianzus observed: 'The Jews keep the festival as well as we, but only in the letter. For while following after the bodily Law, such a one has not attained unto the spiritual Law' (*Oration* 31, 'On Pentecost'; see also Jerome, *Ep.* 78.12; Augustine, *Contra Faustum* 32.12; St Leo the Great, *Sermo de Pentecoste* 1; St Cyprian, *Treatises* 101.555). Others, however, such as St Ambrose (*Sermo* 36.2) read the Pentecost event as a typological reversal of the story of Babel (Gen. 11): if pride caused the division of tongues at Babel, humility was the condition necessary for the coming of the Spirit at Pentecost (see also St Maximus of Tours, *De Solemnitate Sanctae Pentecostes*, PL 17.371-80, 629-42).

Not everyone in the story, however, understands the glossalalia. St Cyril of Jerusalem comments that those who heard but did not comprehend experienced

> a second confusion, replacing that first evil one at [*sic*] Babylon... For in that confusion of tongues there was division of purpose, because their hearts were at enmity with God. Here minds were restored and united, because the object on which they focused was of God. The means of falling were the means of recovery. (*Catechetical Lectures* 17.15, 17)

Cyril also observed that those who mocked the apostles by saying 'They are full of new wine' had actually 'spoke[n] truly though in mockery. For in truth the wine was new, even the grace of the New Testament; but this new wine was from a spiritual Vine which had oftentimes ere this borne

---

15. See 'Pentecost', in D. Jeffrey (ed.), *A Dictionary of Biblical Tradition in English Literature* (Grand Rapids: Eerdmans, 1992), p. 597. Many of the following references are taken from this article. For more on the history of interpretation of the Pentecost scene, especially in the Patristic period, see N. Adler, *Das erste christliche Pfingstfest. Sinn und Bedeutung des Pfingstberichtes Apg 2,1-13* (Neutestamentliche Abhandlungen, 18,1; Münster: Aschendorff, 1938); K. Welliver, 'Pentecost and the Early Church: Patristic Interpretation of Acts 2' (PhD dissertation, Yale, 1961); S. Müller-Abels, 'Der Umgang mit "schwierigen" Texten der Apostelgeschichte in der Alten Kirche', in T. Nicklas and M. Tilly (eds.), *The Book of Acts as Church History: Apostelgeschichte als Kirchengeschichte: Text, Textual Traditions and Ancient Interpretations. Text, Texttraditionen und antike Auslegungen* (BZNW, 120; Berlin: W. de Gruyter, 2003), pp. 347-71.

fruit in the Prophets, and had now blossomed in the New Testament'
(*Catechetical Lectures* 18-19).

John Calvin likewise sides with those who read Acts 2 as a reversal of
Babel:

> For whence came the diversity of tongues, save only that the wicked and
> ungodly counsels of men might be brought to nought? (Gen. 11.7). But
> God doth furnish the apostles with the diversity of tongues now, that he
> may bring and call home, into a blessed unity, men which wander here
> and there. These cloven tongues made all men to speak the language of
> Canaan, as Isaiah foretold (Isa. 19.18). (*Commentary on Acts* 2)

John Wesley, on the other hand, favored the interpretation connecting
Pentecost to Sinai:

> At the Pentecost of Sinai in the Old Testament, and the Pentecost of
> Jerusalem in the New, were the two grand manifestations of God, the legal
> and the evangelical; the one from the mountain, and the other from
> heaven, the terrible and the merciful one.[16]

Some versions of the Revised Common Lectionary resolved this intertextual issue in favor of Babel as the appropriate background for Pentecost by combining Gen. 11.1-9 with Acts 2.1-21.[17]

Later interpreters were less interested in connecting Pentecost with
creation than with consummation. The radical Anabaptist, Hans Hut,
predicted that the end of the world would occur on Pentecost in 1528 and
set about to 'ingather' the 144,000 faithful.[18]

In modern times, the fault lines have been different, but no less con-
tentious. On the one hand, the full-scale movement known as Pentecostalism dates from the series of meetings held in Azusa Street, Los

---

16. John Wesley, *Explanatory Notes on the New Testament* (1754), cited in
Jeffrey, 'Pentecost', p. 599.

17. *The Book of Common Prayer*, however, links Acts 2 with the Joel prophecy
(2.28-32). *The Book of Common Prayer* has its own interesting history with the Feast
of Pentecost. In 1549, the primary language of public worship in England was
changed from Latin to English. The (first) *Book of Common Prayer* was first used
on Pentecost Sunday, 9 June 1549, and the occasion is now commemorated 'on the
first convenient day following Pentecost'.

18. W. Klaassen, 'Eschatological Themes in Early Dutch Anabaptism', in Irvin B.
Horst (ed.), *The Dutch Dissenters: A Critical Companion to their History and Ideas*
(Kerkhistorische bidjragen, 13; Leiden: Brill, 1986), pp. 15-31 (16); see also Klaassen,
'Visions of the End in Reformation Europe', in H. Loewen and A. Reimer (eds.),
Visions and Realities Essays, Poems, and Fiction Dealing with Mennonite Issues
(Winnipeg: Hyperion, 1985), pp. 11-57.

Angeles, beginning in 1906. Pentecostalism was (and is) grounded on the belief, drawn from its interpretation of Acts 2, that speaking in tongues is the physical manifestation of a person's having received the baptism of the Holy Spirit, an experience distinct from and subsequent to conversion that empowers believers for witness.[19]

On the other hand, resistance to Pentecostalism has caused others to deny the ongoing effects of Pentecost, claiming that the 'tongues' described in Acts 2 were not a permanent endowment but were rather limited to the apostolic period as a necessary sign for the inauguration of the church's public ministry, but not an event that was required or even allowed in modern times. This view, called 'cessationism', also read the 'foundation of the apostles and prophets' in Eph. 2.20 as referring to the role of the apostles (including their miracle-working role and use of tongues) as foundational but not ongoing. With the passing of the last apostle (or in some variations, with the writing of the New Testament), so this view goes, miracles and glossalalia ceased.[20] A.T. Robertson went as far as to dismiss 'modern so-called tongues' as nothing but 'jargon and hysteria'.[21]

The 'performance' of Pentecost in Christian liturgy and visual arts has its own distinct interpretive shape. Loveday Alexander has astutely observed that Luke's vision

> was one that lent itself to liturgical performance: it became embedded in the daily and yearly cycles of Catholic and Orthodox devotion. And these cycles in turn form the underwater reef which gives their distinctive shape to the iconographic traditions of Eastern and Western religious art.[22]

This is certainly true in the case of the Pentecost episode.

---

19. J.D.G. Dunn, *Baptism in the Holy Spirit: A Re-Examination of the New Testament Teaching on the Gift of the Spirit in Relation to Pentecostalism Today* (London: SCM Press, 1970), p. 2.

20. The classic work of this view is by B.B. Warfield, *Counterfeit Miracles* (New York: Scribner, 1918).

21. A.T. Robertson, *Word Pictures in the New Testament* (3 vols.; New York: Harper & Brothers, 1930–33), III, p. 22. For a critique of cessationism, see J. Ruthven, *On the Cessation of the Charismata: The Protestant Polemic on Post-biblical Miracles* (JPTSup, 3; Sheffield: Sheffield Academic Press, 1993).

22. L.C.A. Alexander, 'What If Luke Had Never Met Theophilus?', *BibInt* 8 (2000), pp. 161-70 (170). She goes go on (p. 170) to conclude: 'It is not wholly inappropriate that Luke should have come to be claimed as the patron saint of artists, given the intrinsic connection between the artistic tradition and the liturgical tradition'.

Figure 1. *Pentecost,* illumination from the Syriac Evangeliary
of Rabbula, c. 586. Biblioteca Laurenziana, Florence, Italy.
Photo credit: Alinari/Art Resource, NY.

Perhaps the earliest visual depiction of Pentecost is that found in the
Rabbula Gospels (Fig. 1). A colophon near the end of this Syriac codex
dates the completion of the book by a monk named Rabbula to 586 CE,
and although there is disagreement on whether the 26 pages of illustrations preceding the Gospel text were part of the original manuscript or
inserted at the time of the colophon's composition, there is general
agreement that the illustrations date no later than the completion of the
manuscript in the late sixth century CE.[23] At the beginning of the
manuscript are 26 pages which include 19 pages of canon tables, with
illustrations of the life of Christ (fols. 3v-12v). Full-page illustrations
include the rarely depicted election of Matthias (fol. 1r, illustrating Acts
1.15-26) and the commonly depicted Virgin and Child (fol. 1v). The last

23. See especially D. Wright, 'The Date and Arrangement of the Illustrations in
the Rabbula Gospels', *Dumbarton Oaks Papers* 27 (1973), pp. 197-208.

two pages depict the crucifixion and empty tomb (fol. 13r), the ascension (fol. 13v), Christ enthroned (fol. 14r), and Pentecost (fol. 14v). D. Wright has argued that the original arrangement of illustrations (found in the canon tables) was a 'full Christological cycle in logical order'.[24] If this is the case, then it is striking that this life of Christ cycle concludes, not with the ascension of Jesus, but rather the scene of Pentecost, the birth of the Church. The image visually anticipates C.K. Barrett's aphorism, 'In Luke's thought, the end of the story of Jesus is the Church...'[25]

The other striking feature of the Rabbula depiction of Pentecost is the prominent place that Mary holds in the scene. While the text of Acts does not explicitly state that Mary (and other women and disciples) were present at Pentecost, neither does it preclude such an interpretation.[26] The reading that 'all those gathered' included the 120 mentioned in Acts 1.15 goes back at least to Chrysostom (*Homily IV on the Acts of the Apostles*) and has gained traction among recent commentators. Loveday Alexander, for example, comments: 'Luke uses several words to stress the togetherness of Jesus' followers on this occasion (v. 1), which makes it look as if he means to include all the 120 believers of 1.14-15 (including Jesus' family and the women) not just the Twelve'.[27]

The illustrator of the Rabbula Gospels, however, does not intend to stress Lukan inclusivity, but rather to highlight the prominence and significance of the Virgin Mary at Pentecost.[28] Mary is in the center of the illustration; her dark blue robe stands in contrast to the paler blue of the apostles, and her halo is golden in comparison with the understated violet of the apostles. Why does she hold such an important position? Herbert Kessler argues that it is the result of an ecclesiological focus that runs parallel to the christological emphasis of the Rabbula cycle (and is found in both the ascension and Pentecost scenes):

24. Wright, 'Date and Arrangement', p. 204. Wright there explains the anomaly of the selection of Matthias occurring at the beginning of the illustrations rather than between the ascension and Pentecost (where the dedication of Christ is now found) as the result of the artist confusing his models.

25. C.K. Barrett, *Luke the Historian in Recent Study* (London: Epworth, 1961), p. 57.

26. The fact that several mss (e.g. 326, 2495, etc.) insert 'the apostles' after 'all' (παντές) is indirect evidence that such an interpretation was acknowledged, and rejected, from early on.

27. L. Alexander, *Acts* (People's Bible Commentary; Oxford: Bible Reading Fellowship, 2006), p. 28.

28. Mary holds a similar position of importance in the Rabbula Gospels' depiction of the ascension (fol. 13v).

Mary's dominant presence is even more important; not mentioned in scriptural accounts of the Ascension, she stands for the Church, left behind as the custodian of Christ's law until the Second Coming. The last folio in the codex depicts Pentecost, the foundational moment of the Church; the Virgin is pictured again amid the apostles, there inspired by the Holy Spirit.[29]

Both aspects of the Rabbula Gospels' illustration of Pentecost (that Pentecost is the logical end to the life of Christ and the importance of Mary's representative role in symbolizing the Church) are brought together by the Holy Spirit in the form of a dove, hovering just above Mary in the Rabbula Pentecost. The dove echoes Jesus' baptism, illustrated earlier in the canon tables (fol. 4v).

Figure 2. Giotto di Bondone (c. 1267–1336), *Pentecost*,
1304–1306, Scrovegni Chapel, Padua, Italy.
Photo credit: Cameraphoto Arte, Venice/Art Resource, NY.

Both themes are also found in later art; we explore two of those examples, Giotto's *Pentecost* and Botticelli's *Descent of the Holy Ghost* in some detail.[30] The first point illustrated by the Rabbula Gospels' Pentecost (that

29. H. Kessler, 'The Word Made Flesh in Early Decorated Bibles', in Jeffrey Spier (ed.), *Picturing the Bible: The Earliest Christian Art* (New Haven: Yale University Press, 2007), pp. 140-68 (166).

30. We are not suggesting that the Rabbula *Pentecost* served as a source for either Giotto or Botticelli (although the Gospels were taken to Florence in the fifteenth century and conceivably could have been seen by Botticelli), but rather function as a

Pentecost is viewed as a logical conclusion to the life of Christ) is seen again in the 1304–1306 work of Giotto di Bondone in the Scrovegni Chapel at Padua (Fig. 2). This series of frescoes is considered to be the most complete series by Giotto done in his mature style. The chapel in Padua, a university town not far from Venice, is usually called the 'Arena Chapel' because it is constructed above an ancient Roman arena. A wealthy merchant and influential Paduan citizen, Enrico Scrovegni, acquired the original chapel, dedicated to the Virgin Annunciate, in 1300. He rebuilt it with the likely intention of atoning for his sins, and those of his father, Riginaldo, for usury.[31] The church was dedicated on 16 March 1305 to Saint Mary of Charity.

The chapel is very simple architecturally. It has a rectangular form with a starry sky in the barrel vault, a Gothic triple lancet window on the façade and narrow windows on the southern wall. The apse is in the east and the main entrance in the west. The iconographic program is intellectually complex. Theological advisers, who worked in consultation with the patron, directed Giotto. The frescoes follow three main themes: scenes in the lives of Mary's parents, Joachim and Anna; scenes from the life of the Virgin; and scenes from the life and death of Christ. A large number of the representations are from the *Legenda Aurea*, or *Golden Legend*, by Jacobus da Voragine in 1264.

The magnitude of the project required Giotto to obtain assistance from his workshop, although he executed the principal figures in each scene and devised each spatial composition. Giotto and his assistants painted from top to bottom. Moist plaster had to be applied only to as much surface as could be painted in a day. This area, known as a *giornata*, prevented a premature drying of the wall and assured a true *fresco* composition. Calculated by the *giornate* seams, scholars have determined the frescoes were painted in 852 days.[32]

Giotto was probably commissioned to decorate this chapel by Enrico Scrovegni because of the artist's contemporary reputation. The *Chronicle* of Giovanni Villani, written just a few years after Giotto's death,

---

precedent in the history of art. The placement of the Pentecost scene at the end of a life of Christ cycle is distinctive and, so far as we know, limited to the Rabbula Gospels and Giotto. Highlighting Mary's representative role at Pentecost is found in a number of other depictions, including Taddeo Gaddi (1300–1350) and Andrea Orcagna (1360–65).

31. In *The Divine Comedy*, Dante banishes Riginaldo Scrovegni to the seventh circle of hell, the part reserved for usurers.

32. John C. Richards, 'Giotto di Bondone', in Hugh Brigstocke (ed.), *The Oxford Companion to Western Art, Oxford Art Online* <http://www.oxfordartonline.com/subscriber/article/opr/t118/e1049> (accessed 9 September 2009).

described the artist as among the great personalities of the day. The Trecento humanist Boccaccio claimed that Giotto had 'brought back to light' the art of painting 'that for many centuries had been buried under the errors of some who painted more to delight the eyes of the ignorant than to please the intellect of the wise' (*Decameron* VI,5). Dante also predicted Giotto's fame and influence on contemporary culture in the *Divine Comedy* (*Purgatorio* 11.94). The Byzantine style of Giotto's teacher, Cimabue, would soon be discarded by Tuscan artists in favor of the style derived from nature as painted by Giotto.

Pentecost is the final scene of the life of Christ cycle and is located on the lowest level of the three bands of narratives on the northern wall. It is also the scene closest to the eastern altar. The arrangement around a table is organized similarly to the *Last Supper* that is directly opposite it on the south wall. This balance is typical of Giotto. The artist placed the figures inside an architectural space that is clearly defined by a succession of four pointed arches (that illusionistically create a vaulted ceiling under which the apostles are seated) and a right side that is half the length of the front with a two-arch colonnade. This created the illusion that the event occurred within a small church. Basil de Sélincourt suggested that the Gothic arch is used for the first time to symbolize the Christian church.[33]

Visual sources that came before Giotto are rare but it can be argued that this is the first time a visual depiction of Pentecost was painted in a prominent location. Giotto will repeat the subject in the Florentine church of Santa Croce in 1306–12. He extended the visual depiction of the story to include verses up to Acts 2.1-13, rather than stopping at Acts 2.1-4. This allowed him to include three figures outside the house. The Santa Croce cycle also included the tongues of fire over the apostles' heads and the Holy Spirit is represented as a dove. In the Scrovegni chapel speech is portrayed through 'the speaking hand'.[34] This allows the critical message of the biblical story, that the twelve all start speaking in different languages, to be conveyed in a silent picture. Giotto chooses the hand because it is able to communicate so many different meanings and emotions. Precedents of this speaking hand are the orators of Greek and Roman art. The Holy Spirit is represented through rays of light emanating from outside the room and above the painted ceiling. Giotto does not depict Mary among the twelve. Instead the church itself is inscribed in the architecture, in the 'church-like structure' encompassing, containing and protecting the event from the world outside.

33. B. de Sélincourt, *Giotto* (London: Duckworth, 1905), p. 149.
34. M. Barasch, *Giotto and the Language of Gesture* (New York: Cambridge University Press, 1987), pp. 15-17.

Figure 3. Sandro Botticelli (1445–1510), *The Descent of the Holy Ghost*, 1495–
1505, Birmingham Museums and Art Gallery, Birmingham, England.
Photo credit: Birmingham Museums and Art Gallery.

Two centuries later in 1495–1505, Sandro Botticelli executed *The
Descent of the Holy Ghost* (Fig. 3). Botticelli, a student of Fra Filippo
Lippi, is one of the best-known Florentine Renaissance masters due to
his famous works, the *Birth of Venus* and the *Primavera*, painted for the
Medici c. 1483. Botticelli received both secular and religious commis-
sions throughout his artistic career as an independent master, a career
that began in 1472 when he joined the Compagnia di San Luca in
Florence. Botticelli was the master of a successful workshop and was
included in major projects throughout the Italian peninsula including
three frescoes (*Temptations of Christ, Moses and the Daughters of Jethro*
and the *Punishment of the Korah*) on the walls of the Sistine Chapel in
1481 for Pope Sixtus IV della Rovere. Botticelli was in the personal and
professional company not only of the Popes and the Medici but also
with Michelangelo, Giorgio Vasari, Domenico Ghirlandaio and Pietro
Perugino. His works and opinions shaped the city of Florence. In 1491
Botticelli helped select the façade for the Santa Maria del Fiore with 25

artists and the church board. Botticelli's importance in Florentine society was again documented when he served on the board that decided the location of Michelangelo's David in 1505 along with Giuliano da San-gallo, Cosimo Rosselli, Leonardo da Vinci, Filippino Lippi and others.

Botticelli painted the *Descent of the Holy Ghost* or *Pentecost* scene between 1495 and 1505, when he was most influential in the Florentine Renaissance. It is considered a mature work as Botticelli died on 17 May 1510. Although Botticelli's early influences were Verrochio and Fra Filippo Lippi, he was also influenced by Girolamo Savonarola (1452–23 May 1498). In 1491, during Lent, Savonarola, a friar at San Marco, preached in Florence. In 1497 Botticelli may have provided drawings for Savonarola's *Triumphant Crucis*.[35] Savonarola was excommunicated in 1497 and executed by Pope Alexander VI in 1498 in Florence. *Pentecost* may have been influenced by Savonarola's writings. The painting is curr-ently located in the City Museum and Art Gallery in Birmingham, England. The work is oil on panel and is made of five poplar panels.[36] The painting has sustained damage and about twenty percent has been completely lost and another twenty percent has suffered over painting. A dove above the Virgin was added in the nineteenth century but has now been removed from the painting. The panel on the right hand side was also replaced at that time. There remain connoisseurship issues related to the painting. Some scholars believe it to be a workshop piece, while others, including Peter Cannon-Brookes, maintain an attribution to Botticelli.[37] Botticelli may have prepared the design and began the painting but allowed his workshop to complete it. This was typical at this time in major workshops.

The Virgin Mary and the twelve apostles are depicted in the paint-ing looking up toward the heavens. The Holy Spirit descends, and the moment in the narrative is v. 3. The disciples have not yet begun to speak—this comes in v. 4. The golden tongues of fire rest on the forehead of each person. Each individual has a halo with his or her name inscribed on it. Many of the inscriptions are no longer legible but the Birmingham

---

35. M. Levey and G. Mandel, *The Complete Paintings of Botticelli* (New York: Abrams, 1967), p. 97.

36. T. Heaven, Birmingham Museums and Art Gallery Picture Librarian, Personal correspondence with Diane Nelson, Baylor University student, during the Spring 2010 semester, who generously shared his letter (dated 13 April 2010) and attachments regarding the painting. The poplar panel is generally agreed upon; however, the painting appears as tempera on panel and oil on panel in various publications. Even the museum itself has published both.

37. P. Cannon-Brookes, 'Botticelli's Pentecost', *Apollo* 87 (1968), pp. 274-77.

Museum and Gallery have attempted an identification starting from the lower left and moving clockwise: Matthew, James, Andrew, Jude, Simon, John, Mary, James of Zebedee, Peter, Bartholomew, Barnabas, Matthias and Philip.

The visual depiction of Mary is considered to have a Savonarola influence. Botticelli's earlier depictions of Mary were more regal. Here she is painted with a modest air that is well suited to the chaste Virgin invoked by Savonarola.[38] An image of the Virgin as depicted in the earlier works by Botticelli prompted the address Savonarola gave to painters in 1496: 'Do you believe the Virgin Mary went dressed this way, as you paint her? I tell you she went dressed as a poor woman, simply, and so covered that her face could hardly be seen... You make the Virgin Mary seem dressed like a whore. Now it really can be said that the worship of God is corrupt!'[39] Savonarola's Mary is a woman of abnormal dimensions and dressed in poor garments, of an ashen and rather tarnished beauty: less and less a woman and more and more Ecclesia, she represents the renewed Church, authentically Christian and the bearer of hope, that Botticelli learned to cherish listening to the word of Savonarola and earlier still, reading those of Dante.[40] This formulates an important connection between the new visualization of Mary and her role as representing the Church, a symbol particularly rich within the Pentecost scene; this scene is appropriately referred to as the birth of the Church.

III. *Conclusion*

Acts 2 has exerted an enormous influence on subsequent Christian theology, liturgy, and practice, and we have not in these few pages been able to deal adequately with all the issues surrounding specifically the interpretation of the Pentecost scene.[41] Acts 2 has also held an important

---

38. A. Kroegel, 'The Figure of Mary in Botticelli's Art', in Doriana Comerlati and Daniel Arasse (eds.), *Botticelli From Lorenzo the Magnificent to Savonarola* (Milan: Skira, 2003), pp. 55-67.

39. Kroegel, 'Figure of Mary', p. 67.

40. Kroegel, 'Figure of Mary', p. 67.

41. For example, another powerful aspect of Pentecost is Luke's use of symbolic imagery, which was widely noted from very early on. John Chrysostom commented on the use of similes in the Lukan account and cautions against having 'gross sensible notions of the Spirit': 'Nor is this all; but what is more awful still, "And there appeared unto them", it says, "cloven tongues like as of fire". (*v.* 3.) Observe how it is always, "like as"; and rightly: that you may have no gross sensible notions of the Spirit. Also, "as it were of a blast": therefore it was not a wind. "Like as of fire". For

place in Loveday Alexander's understanding of the hermeneutical task. In fact, for her, Peter's 'this is that' statement in Acts 2.16 ('This [Pentecost event] is that which was spoken by the prophet Joel') provides the scriptural warrant and precedent for the kind of hermeneutic Alexander proposes for the Church today:

> Peter starts with what is happening now ('this'), and then goes back into Scripture to find a correspondence ('that'). The Scripture text, once identified, then provides a revelatory framework for reaching a better understanding of the present: so the Joel quotation in Acts 2 tells us (a) that the 'last days' are now; (b) that God is pouring out his Spirit on all humanity; and (c) that 'the promise is to you, and your children, and to all that are afar off' (2.39). These points in turn are crucial hermeneutical keys for understanding the rest of the narrative: the message of Acts is that we are living in the age of the Spirit. The experience of the Spirit continues both to drive the unfolding pattern of events and to provide the hermeneutical key for interpreting them through Spirit-inspired visions, tongues, and signs and wonders which function as revelatory events in their own right. So we have a dialectical pattern: God's self-revelation in the present ('this') is interpreted in light of God's self-revelation in the past ('that' = Scripture), which then provides the framework for interpreting where God is leading in the future ('What then shall we do?').[42]

If Phillip Jenkins is correct, the shift of Christianity to the Global South will be accompanied by a dramatic increase in the number of Pentecostal

---

when the Spirit was to be made known to John, then it came upon the head of Christ as in the form of a dove: but now, when a whole multitude was to be converted, it is "like as of fire. And it sat upon each of them". This means, that it remained and "rested upon them". For the sitting is significant of settledness and continuance' (*Homily II on the Acts of the Apostles*). Despite these caveats, artists faced a particularly difficult problem in visualizing the signs of Pentecost. The visual 'concretization' of the 'tongues of fire' in the visual tradition should not lead automatically to the assumption that the artists or their audience disagreed with Chrysostom's assessment. Still, the images of fire and wind are particularly poignant, as Loveday Alexander observes: 'The thing about a flame is that the more you divide it, the more there is to go round: split a flame in half and you get more, not less. So the coming of the Spirit is a gift of new life to the community, which brings out the individual gifts of each member, a gift that brings God's living word to articulate expression in a host of individual tongues' (*Acts*, p. 29). Not all 'performances' of the Pentecostal signs are quite so edifying, however! One need only consider the parody of the flatulent friar's 'mighty wind' in Chaucer's Summoner's Tale! (See A. Levitan, 'The Parody of Pentecost in Chaucer's Summoner's Tale', *University of Toronto Quarterly* 40 [1971], pp. 236-46.)

42. L. Alexander, '"This is That": The Authority of Scripture in the Acts of the Apostles', *Princeton Seminary Bulletin* 25 (2004), pp. 189-204 (192).

or charismatic Christians for whom Acts 2 is a touchstone text.[43] In addition to the biblical literalism that typifies charismatic exegesis, there is also, traditionally, a kind of dichotomy between this form of Christian spirituality and any kind of activism. In these regards, Alexander's proposed hermeneutic and her call to a performative biblical criticism might provide a needed antidote. We end by giving Loveday the last word. In her People's Bible Commentary on Acts, Alexander claims her first priority is to 'describe the journey itself from the point of view of the author and his first readers'; this is, of course, what she (and we) has elsewhere described as the 'philological' task. But she also claims that 'we need to move back into the twenty-first century (which of course we never really left) and ask how Luke's stories relate to our own stories'.[44] She does this in the commentary by ending each section with 'a question, a quotation or a prayer, suggesting ways to link up with some of the stories that belong to our lives today—things that are happening in the newspapers, or in our churches, or in our own spiritual lives'.[45] At the end of her reading of Acts 2.1-8 she has a brief prayer that draws on the Pentecostal imagery of wind and fire and tantalizingly suggests our need for the Spirit to empower us both in our inward spiritual devotion *and* in our outward call to mission, both fueled by the flame of God's love:

> Come, Holy Spirit. Blow away the cobwebs from our minds; blow us out on to the streets, and kindle our hearts with the fire of your love.[46]

43. See the various writings of Philip Jenkins on this subject, especially *The Next Christendom: The Coming of Global Christianity* (Oxford: Oxford University Press, 2002); *The New Faces of Christianity: Believing the Bible in the Global South* (Oxford: Oxford University Press, 2006).

44. Alexander, *Acts*, p. 13.

45. Alexander, *Acts*, p. 13.

46. Alexander, *Acts*, p. 29.

THE PLACE OF ACTS 20.28 IN LUKE'S THEOLOGY OF THE CROSS*

I. Howard Marshall

A number of scholars have argued recently that Luke has a theological programme that includes the playing down of the traditional understanding of the death of Christ as the key element in his saving activity (both as a sacrifice offered to God and as the overcoming of Satan) and the placing of an emphasis on his resurrection and exaltation as the occasion of God's declaration or appointment of him as the Lord and Messiah with authority to confer forgiveness and the gift of the Spirit on those who repent and believe.[1] Some go so far as to speak of eliminating atonement theology.[2] Four main points are offered by way of support:

1. In the Gospel Luke omits the story of the conversation in Mk 10.35-45, but has parallel material in the alternative versions of the baptism saying in Lk. 12.50 and the cup saying in Lk. 22.42 and in the briefer account of a dispute in Lk. 22.24-30 which omits the crucial soteriological statement in Mk 10.45b. Carpinelli states: 'It is striking that [Luke] has nothing equivalent to Mark 10.45'. He claims that

---

*   A while back I came across (and then lost) a list of attendees at a conference, at which I was one of the speakers, that was intended to encourage and help theological students who were interested in going on to do research; it included Loveday Earl (as she then was) and Michael Nazir-Ali. It has been a joy to see what Loveday has subsequently achieved over the many years. Since that occasion I have learned so much from Loveday's meticulous and original scholarship and join with the other contributors to this volume in thanking her for what she has taught us and expressing best wishes for her continuing life and work.

1. J. Tyson, *The Death of Jesus in Luke–Acts* (Colombia: University of South Carolina Press, 1986); B.D. Ehrman, *The Orthodox Corruption of Scripture: The Effect of Early Christological Controversies on the Text of the New Testament* (New York: Oxford University Press, 1993), pp. 197-227. Cf. K. Anderson, *'But God Raised Him from the Dead': The Theology of Jesus' Resurrection in Luke–Acts* (PBM; Milton Keynes: Paternoster Press, 2006), pp. 37-41.

2. Ehrman, *Orthodox Corruption*, p. 199.

'redemption' is a different salvific operation from atonement; for him, it follows atonement and is liberation from evil rather than from sin; he also suggests that the associations of ransom with barter and money may have led Luke to avoid use of the term.[3]

Whether the statement that 'Luke knew of the Markan saying but *chose* not to use it'[4] is justified may be questioned. The fact that the whole pericope is replaced by other material could mean that other factors were at work and the loss of this clause was an unintended result. The suggestion that Luke found Mark's manner of expression 'awkward' is not compelling.[5] Nevertheless, the absence of the statement requires explanation.

2. There is textual uncertainty regarding Lk. 22.19b-20, and, if the shorter reading is adopted, the sayings at the last supper make no reference to Christ's death being for his disciples.

3. In the evangelistic sermons in Acts there are no references to the death of Christ being for the disciples or for sin and no use of sacrificial imagery. The death can be plausibly understood simply as a necessary stage on the way to glorification, specifically as the culminating act of human rejection of Jesus by the Jewish authorities (who represent the people generally).

4. Only in the pastoral homily in Acts 20.28, where the church of God is that which he purchased with his own blood (or with the blood of his own [*sc.* son]), is there a surviving element of the instrumental significance of the death of Christ in what is commonly understood to be apparently atonement theology. Yet this isolated reference has been understood as a piece of tradition taken over by the author of Acts that does not represent his theology or figure centrally in it. Alternatively, the attempt has been made to interpret the saying in a non-atoning, non-sacrificial manner. For B. Ehrman, Acts 20.28 does not refer to something positively achieved by the death of Jesus. It is not an atoning act for sin; rather, 'the blood of Jesus produces the church because it brings the cognizance of guilt that leads to repentance'. For Ehrman, it would seem that the 'cost' of producing human repentance was letting Jesus be put to death.[6] Elsewhere in Luke–Acts 'blood' refers to violent death

---

3. F.G. Carpinelli, '"Do This as *My* Memorial" (Luke 22.19): Lucan Soteriology of Atonement', *CBQ* 61 (1999), pp. 74-91 (82).

4. H.D. Buckwalter, *The Character and Purpose of Luke's Christology* (SNTSMS, 89; Cambridge: Cambridge University Press, 1996), p. 146 (my italics).

5. Buckwalter, *The Character and Purpose of Luke's Christology*, pp. 147-48.

6. Ehrman, *Orthodox Corruption*, pp. 202-203. Ehrman builds on the wording of Acts 5.28 where 'bringing blood upon someone' refers to the guilt for committing a

as the fate of the persecuted. There is no Pauline doctrine of the atonement here.[7]

Our attention in the present study focusses on the last of these points, the significance of Acts 20.28.

I. *Some Preliminary Considerations*

Our doubts are aroused at the outset by the fact that Ehrman's understanding of Acts 20.28 is an extraordinary way of understanding the concept of divine 'purchase' of the church and sounds like a desperate attempt to get rid of anything in Luke–Acts that might be thought to stand against his arguments against the authenticity of the longer text of Lk. 22.19-20. Neither in its present context nor in any conceivable traditional setting does the saying appear to be concerned with the way in which sinners should respond to the death of Jesus (as is the case in Acts 2.36-37; 3.19; 5.28; 7.52). In its present co-text it is used rather to indicate the awesome responsibility of those called to shepherd the church in view of its high value in the sight of God, who did not spare his own Son but gave him up to death as the cost to be paid. And uses of similar language elsewhere in the New Testament are concerned with what God did to redeem his people rather than to make them aware of their guilt.

Ehrman's unconvincing reinterpretation of the text appears to have been forced upon him by the need to close the door against admitting that Luke's theology had room for the kind of understanding of the death of Jesus that is found in Lk. 22.19b-20. If his case against the authenticity

---

murder; similarly in Acts 20.26 Paul claims to be free from anyone's blood. But this is an idiomatic usage referring to guilt whereas the phrase in 20.28 refers to the cost of what God did through the death of Jesus. Ehrman further argues that we should read the speech without reading Pauline theology into it, but this overlooks the fact that Luke does deliberately try to use Pauline language and motifs when recording what Paul says; cf. the use of justification language in Acts 13.39 and the association of a 'Son' christology with Paul in Acts 9.20. S. Hagene, *Zeiten der Wiederherstellung. Studien zur lukanischen Geschichtstheologie als Soteriologie* (Münster: Aschendorff, 2003), pp. 10-11, skims lightly over the passage, saying that the theocentric nature of the expression makes it clear that with the death of Jesus Luke does not see a cornerstone of church history but rather a manifestation of the redeeming will of God that aims at Israel as a whole. But she says nothing more than this and does not develop what this manifestation might actually mean.

7. Ehrman, *Orthodox Corruption*, p. 202. Cf. E. Richard, 'Jesus' Passion and Death in Acts', in D.D. Sylva (ed.), *Reimaging the Death of the Lukan Jesus* (BBB, 73; Frankfurt: Hain, 1990), pp. 125-52. J. Roloff, *Die Apostelgeschichte* (Göttingen: Vandenhoeck & Ruprecht, 1981), p. 306, is more nuanced.

of the longer text of the Last Supper is not persuasive, clearly this forced interpretation of Acts 20.28 is no longer needed. It has admittedly won some scholarly following among textual critics, but it must not be assumed to be the last word on the matter. It has failed to convince two of the most recent major commentators on the Gospel,[8] and other solutions to the textual problem are possible.[9] Hence this major motivation for attempting to produce a monolithic rejection of atonement theology throughout Luke–Acts should not necessarily influence our understanding of Acts 20.28 and force us into a desperate reinterpretation of it.

Luke's omission of Mk 10.45b is sometimes taken to reflect a deliberate aversion to atonement theology that has led him to avoid reference to it.[10] If Acts is dated comparatively early and is by an erstwhile companion of Paul, then it can be argued that such an understanding of Luke's presentation puts it at odds with the early kerygma, as it is attested by Paul in 1 Cor. 15.3-5 and other statements which can be plausibly recognized as traces of early tradition. The point is, of course, not simply that statements about the significance of the death of Christ were current from an early period but that such statements were taken to express the heart of the gospel, and that attestation of them comes from a wide variety of New Testament documents.[11] If Acts is dated significantly later, then the author's ignorance of, or aversion to, atonement theology becomes all the more difficult to explain and all the more surprising.

---

8. H. Klein, *Das Lukasevangelium* (KEK; Göttingen: Vandenhoeck & Ruprecht, 2006), pp. 664-65; M. Wolter, *Das Lukasevangelium* (HKNT; Tübingen: Mohr Siebeck, 2008), p. 699.

9. See I.H. Marshall, 'History and the Last Supper', in D.L. Bock and R.L. Webb (eds.), *Key Events in the Life of the Historical Jesus* (Tübingen: Mohr Siebeck, 2009), pp. 481-588. Cf. S. Walton, *Leadership and Lifestyle: The Portrait of Paul in the Miletus Speech and 1 Thessalonians* (SNTSMS, 108; Cambridge: Cambridge University Press, 2000), pp. 137-39, for an admirably terse survey of the arguments on both sides.

10. See above. On the other side, see D.P. Moessner, *Lord of the Banquet: The Literary and Theological Significance of the Lukan Travel Narrative* (Minneapolis: Fortress Press, 1989), pp. 322-24; he cites W.G. Kümmel's verdict that Luke 'in no way deletes the atoning significance of the death of Jesus, but does not emphasize it' ('Lukas in der Anklage der heutigen Theologie', *ZNW* 63 [1972], pp. 149-65 [159]).

11. The point is sometimes made that Luke makes minimal reference to the saving function of the death of Jesus. To put this point in perspective, however (so far, at least, as the Gospel is concerned), it must be remembered that there are only two places in each of Mark (10.45; 14.22-25) and Matthew (20.28; 26.26-28) where this motif is explicitly present.

We are being asked, in short, to assume that there was a stream, attested by Luke, which was unaware of or opposed to atonement theology. To be sure, there may have been something of a falling away from the earlier, New Testament understanding of grace when we come to the Apostolic Fathers.[12] It is also arguable that Docetists, who denied the crucifixion of the heavenly being who inhabited Jesus until just before the cross, would have no place for a doctrine of atonement, and this would have been true of Gnostics. But Luke is precisely not a Docetist or Gnostic. Nor is any other scenario likely which would account for the aversion.[13]

II. *Acts 20.28 and Mark 10.45*

What, then, do we make of Acts 20.28? Its significance becomes apparent when we note that it is probably Luke's deliberate substitute for the saying in Mk 10.45b.

It is well established that Luke's method of using his sources for the Gospel includes the practice of replacement. There are several occasions when he omits material from Mark but has some more or less equivalent material elsewhere.[14] He omits the whole of Mk 6.45–8.26; 9.41–10.12; 10.35-45. In some cases the Markan material is repetitive; in others there are non-Markan equivalents.[15] These equivalents are usually in the Gospel itself, but occasionally they are found in Acts. In some places the text of the Gospel has been adjusted, as compared with that of Mark and

12.   T.F. Torrance, *The Doctrine of Grace in the Apostolic Fathers* (Edinburgh: Oliver & Boyd, 1948).

13.   P. Pokorný, *Theologie der lukanischen Schriften* (Göttingen: Vandenhoeck & Ruprecht, 1998), pp. 139-43. He sees Luke as stressing the soteriological significance of Jesus' life as a whole, believing that this was more intelligible to Gentiles: Jesus is God's representative who comes to seek and save the lost. But this accent need not replace the concept of representative dying, and it is not clear why non-Jews should have difficulty with the concept, especially when it does not appear to have caused Paul difficulties. To some extent Pokorný is influenced by Bultmann's rejection of atonement as meaningless to modern people and in need of reinterpretation, and finds in Luke an anticipation of this move.

14.   This material is most probably taken from other sources (whether Q or other sources peculiar to Luke; it is debated whether some of Luke's material represents heavily edited uses of Markan material). This practice contrasts with that of Matthew, who has the tendency to run together material from Mark and Q.

15.   This is a familiar Lukan procedure and seems to rest largely on a desire to incorporate the material he has gathered from other sources rather than from an aversion to the Markan material which is displaced.

Matthew, in the light of what was to follow in Acts. The text of the Gospel, as we have it, is thus edited in the light of its place in a two-book composition.[16]

Thus Luke omits the discussion of purity and the healing of a Gentile recorded in Mark 7, but he has related material not only in Lk. 11.37-41 (Q) but also in Acts 10–11, where Jewish purity laws are put in abeyance and a Gentile is brought to salvation. There is no parallel in the Gospel to the saying about the unknown date of the parousia in Mk 13.32, but there is an equivalent in Acts 1.7. Luke omits the prophecy of the destruction of the temple in the trial of Jesus and reserves it for the trial of Stephen. He curtails the citation of Isa. 6.9 in Lk. 8.10 and reserves fuller use for Acts 28.26-27.[17]

Acts 20.28 should be seen as such an equivalent to Mk 10.45b.[18] (The equivalent to Mk 10.45a is to be seen in Lk. 22.27.) It is true that another saying in the Gospel could also be regarded as a replacement. This is Lk. 19.10: 'The Son of Man came to seek and to save what was lost'. Both sayings have in common 'The Son of Man came' followed by an infinitive and an object, but Lk. 19.10 has no explicit reference to the death of the Son of Man. Certainly the shepherd imagery, which undoubtedly underlies the Lukan saying, could be developed in the direction of the shepherd who saves the lost by laying down his own life as in the Johannine shepherd imagery (Jn 10.11, 15, 17-18), but this thought does not appear to be present in Lk. 19.10.[19] It is only in Acts 20.28 that the

16. See especially C.K. Barrett, 'The Third Gospel as a Preface to Acts? Some Reflections', in F. Van Segbroek *et al.* (eds.), *The Four Gospels 1992: Festschrift Frans Neirynck* (BETL; 3 vols.; Leuven: Leuven University Press, 1991), II, pp. 1451-66.

17. So I.H. Marshall, 'Acts and the "Former Treatise"', in B.W. Winter and A.D. Clarke (eds.), *The Book of Acts in its First Century Setting. I. Ancient Literary Setting* (Carlisle: Paternoster Press; Grand Rapids: Eerdmans, 1993), pp. 174-75. See F.F. Bruce, *The Acts of the Apostles* (Grand Rapids: Eerdmans; Leicester: Apollos, 3rd edn, 1990), pp. 102, 249, 282; Wolter, *Lukasevangelium*, p. 30.

18. I.H. Marshall, *The Gospel of Luke* (NIGTC; Exeter: Paternoster Press; Grand Rapids: Eerdmans, 1978), p. 691. Against the suggestion that Luke picks up on a saying of Jesus in Acts, Wolter, *Lukasevangelium*, p. 31, states that Luke does not refer back to any sayings of Jesus found in his Gospel in Acts. But in this case what we would have is an equivalent to a saying of Jesus (one that is not quoted in the Gospel), not a citation from the Gospel. The lack of attribution to Jesus conforms to the attested practice of the early church in normally alluding to sayings of Jesus rather than quoting them in the epistolary literature. The comment, therefore, does not stand in the way of our hypothesis.

19. Shepherd imagery occurs in the parable in Lk. 15, and this can be applied to Jesus. However, it is no more than a comparison, standing as it does alongside the parable of the woman who searches her house.

death of the shepherd is explicit. Thus Mk 10.45b is the only significant part of the dialogue that does not have a close parallel in the Gospel of Luke, but this lack is supplied in Acts 20.28.

To establish their functional equivalence a comparison of the sayings may be helpful:

Connective	Subject	Action and characterization	Object
For	the Son of Man	came...to give his life a ransom	for many
	He	purchased with his own blood	the church of God
Καὶ γὰρ	ὁ υἱὸς τοῦ ἀνθρώπου	ἦλθεν...δοῦναι τὴν ψυχὴν αὐτοῦ λύτρον	ἀντὶ πολλῶν
(ἦν)		περιεποιήσατο διὰ τοῦ αἵματος τοῦ ἰδίου	τὴν ἐκκλησίαν τοῦ θεοῦ

It must be remembered that we are arguing for a similarity of function, not necessarily of wording and precise form, between the two sayings. Nor is there any suggestion that the Acts statement is derived from Mk 10.45b, in the way that we find a later form of the latter in 1 Tim. 2.8 or influence from it, as in Tit. 2.14.

In Acts 20.28 and Mk 10.45b we have the following similarities in form and content:

1. The subject: Son of Man/he. Luke's omission of 'Son of Man' is consistent with the general disuse of this designation outside the Gospels (except for the notable retention, for good reasons, in Acts 7.56). The implied subject is generally taken to be God (*sc.* the Father),[20] although the action is the death of Christ.

2. The action of dying. Whereas this is expressed by a verbal phrase in Mark, it is implied by the noun 'blood' in Acts.

3. The character of the death. Mark has the noun 'ransom', expressing the motifs of purchase and cost; Acts has a verb expressing purchase, but the phrase 'his own blood' brings out the cost.

4. The salvific effect of the death. Mark makes the point more negatively in terms of deliverance by the payment of a ransom, whereas Acts expresses more positively the creation of a new people (cf. Acts 15.14).

---

20.   The subject of the relative clause is generally assumed to be the last mentioned noun and not, as is sometimes said, the subject of the preceding clause (which is τὸ πνεῦμα τὸ ἅγιον). It is universally agreed that θεοῦ is the original text here (note the wording of LXX Ps. 73.1-2, which is being echoed here; cf. Walton, *Leadership*, pp. 94-95). See below for discussion of the difficulties raised by this.

5. The beneficiaries of the death: many/the church of God. The ways in which the beneficiaries are expressed are from different perspectives.[21] In Mark 'many' signifies the large number of captives for whom the Son of Man gave himself, and in Acts the church is the resulting new people of God (referring primarily to those already in it, but the doors are not closed). Here the objects of redemption are those in the church for whom the elders must care, in the same way as we might say that the hospital staff care for 'the patients' although the identity of these changes from day to day.

These points of comparison indicate that there is a broad correspondence in form and content between the two sayings, sufficient to justify the claim that Luke would have regarded the two sayings as equivalent.

A significant supporting factor may now be adduced. In Tit. 2.14 we have the description of Jesus Christ as the one ὃς ἔδωκεν ἑαυτὸν ὑπὲρ ἡμῶν ἵνα λυτρώσηται ἡμᾶς ἀπὸ πάσης ἀνομίας καὶ καθαρίσῃ ἑαυτῷ λαὸν περιούσιον, ζηλωτὴν καλῶν ἔργων. The first part of this

---

21. In the New Testament there are three ways of referring to the human beneficiaries (intended or actual) of the work of Christ: (1) Those in actual need of God's provision of redemption (the godless, unjust, the people, etc.; Rom. 5.6; 1 Pet. 3.18; Jn 11.50-52). The thought is of the large company who need salvation, whether or not they actually receive it; hence the term 'all' can be used (2 Cor. 5.14-15; 1 Tim. 2.6; Heb. 2.9). Their identity before redemption is expressed. This is the language of evangelism. However, the form 'for you' does not occur evangelistically with reference to those who are being persuaded to accept the good news, but is used of the saved (1 Pet. 2.21; cf. Rom. 14.15; 1 Cor. 1.13). (2) Those who have come into an experience of redemption. The terminology refers to the new status of those who have benefited from the provision (the saved, the found, the church). Often this is the language of confession by those who have received the benefit. 'Christ died for us' tends to be used of and by the people who have experienced the saving effect (Rom. 5.8; 8.34; cf. 2 Cor. 5.21; Gal. 2.20; 3.13). (3) The prospective and actual people who are the object of redemption. The terminology can thus refer collectively to the company that consists or will consist of the redeemed in general rather than to the individuals who compose it at any given time. When Christ purchases the church or gives himself up for her (Eph. 5.25) the thought is of the company of people who are being set up by his action rather than of the specific individuals who will compose it. We might compare the establishment of a parliament in a previously non-democratic state as distinct from the appointment of individuals to be members of it. The two actions are separable, and the parliament can be established constitutionally even though its actual membership is not yet determined or known. When God's people say, 'We have been redeemed', there is no implication that they are speaking only of those who have actually been redeemed at that point in time; rather, the 'we' is open to the inclusion of whoever else joins the company in the future.

statement is clearly based on a combination of Mk 10.45b and Ps. 130.8 (LXX 129.8) and the second part reflects Ezek. 37.23 and the Old Testament phrase λαὸς περιούσιος. What is significant for our purpose here is the merging of the motifs and vocabulary of the Markan and Lukan sayings in such a way that we have the self-giving of Christ leading to two results: the negative one of redemption from the power of lawlessness and the positive one of creating a people for the Lord.[22] This apparently independent merging of motifs shows that Luke could well have recognized in the wording of Acts 20.28 a functional equivalent to Mk 10.45b. He has used church language that was current in his own time and appears in the Pauline corpus.[23]

It is therefore likely that Luke omitted the Markan scene as a whole out of preference for the various pieces of tradition that he uses elsewhere, and that in doing so he regarded the material here and in Lk. 19.10 as equivalent to the ransom saying. The proposal that he deliberately omitted the saying out of an aversion to a *theologia crucis* is therefore to be rejected.[24]

III. *The Interpretation of Acts 20.28*

The unusual phrase διὰ τοῦ αἵματος τοῦ ἰδίου has been interpreted in various ways:

1. τοῦ ἰδίου may be understood as an independent subjective or possessive phrase, 'with the blood of [*or* shed by] his own [one]'. This is then a way of referring to Christ as 'his own Son' (Rom. 8.32; cf. 8.3;

---

22. It is true, of course, that λαὸς περιούσιος and the verb περιποιέομαι are from different roots, but both the adjective περιούσιος and the noun περιποίησις are each used once in the LXX to translate Heb. *segullah* (Exod. 19.5; Mal. 3.17); this indicates the kinship of meaning.

23. More specifically, L. Aejmelaeus, *Die Rezeption der Paulusbriefe in der Miletrede (Apg 20.18-35)* (Helsinki: Finnische Exegetische Gesellschaft, 1987), pp. 134-36, argues unconvincingly for echoes of 1 Thess. 5.9-12. He rejects use of a Florilegium or direct links with 1 Pet. 2.9, 25; 5.2-3 (pp. 139-41).

24. After the substance of this article was completed, I found U. Mittmann-Richert, *Der Sühnetod des Gottesknechts: Jesaja 53 im Lukasevangelium* (Tübingen: Mohr Siebeck, 2008), which explores the evidence for Luke being heavily influenced by Isaiah: 'Lukas [tritt] als derjenige unter den Evangelisten hervor, der den Kreuzestod Jesu als Tod des zur Entsühnung Israels und der Heiden in die Welt gesandten Gottesknechts in paulinischer Tiefe reflektiert und das Geschehen sühnender Stellvertretung in erzählerisch höchster Kunst zur Darstellung bringt' (p. viii). Her work is centred on the Gospel and she plans a second volume on Acts (p. 314). If her new perspective on Luke can be upheld, this provides a significantly new context for our understanding of Acts 20.28.

Jn 3.16); it uses the adjective as equivalent to a noun, which is grammatically possible but unparalleled.[25]

2. τοῦ ἰδίου is attributive, giving 'with his own blood'. One possible interpretation is then that the blood was that of God the Father, but this patripassian interpretation is generally regarded as anachronistic.

3. With the same construction an alternative interpretation is that the blood is that of Christ, understood as God's blood in that he is the Father of the one who shed it.[26]

4. All of these three interpretations assume that the subject of the relative clause should be the last mentioned noun in the main clause, that is, God (the Father), and this is probably the most natural interpretation.[27] However, the author could conceivably have brought together loosely two pieces of traditional phraseology, the phrase 'church of God'[28]

---

25. This interpretation has attracted wide support; so, for example, Walton, *Leadership*, pp. 96-98 (but with the suggestion that it is adopted because it raises the fewest difficulties rather than because it has most advantages); cf. also J. Jervell, *Die Apostelgeschichte* (KEK; Göttingen: Vandenhoeck & Ruprecht: 1998), p. 512. F.J.A. Hort raised the possibility of conjecturally emending the text by adding υἱοῦ; see the discussion and references in C.K. Barrett, *The Acts of the Apostles* (ICC; 2 vols.; Edinburgh: T. & T. Clark, 1994–98), II, pp. 976-77. H. Le Cornu (with J. Shulam), *A Commentary on the Jewish Roots of Acts* (Jerusalem: Academon, 2003), p. 1131, detects an allusion to Gen. 22.2 and finds that the concept of the aqedah is difficult to escape. She develops a sacrificial interpretation. But the aqedah refers primarily to the self-sacrifice of the donor (Abraham) in giving up his own son to possible death, and this element of cost may be all that is intended. Once the donor is God who gives up his Son, the idea of a sacrifice offered to God himself becomes problematic, unless the thought is of God providing a sacrifice which sinners may offer to him. Cf. Exod. 15.16; 4Q504 1-2.15; *Pseudo-Philo* 18.5.

26. Barrett, *Acts*, II, pp. 976-77, appears to accept a loose use of 'with his own blood' as a natural reading of Greek, and reminds us that Luke is not 'a trained theologian'. Nevertheless, he also mentions the next possibility as a good suggestion explaining how the statement arose.

27. The actual subject of the main clause is the Holy Spirit. To speak (as some do) of a change of subject in the relative clause from God (the Father) as the subject of the main clause is thus incorrect.

28. The phrase is found in 1 Cor. 1.2; 10.32; 11.16, 22; 15.9; 2 Cor. 1.1; Gal. 1.13; 1 Thess. 2.14; 2 Thess. 1.4; 1 Tim. 3.5, 15. This evidence is, however, entirely Pauline and one would need some evidence to show that these passages rested on tradition rather than reflecting Pauline phraseology. If we are prepared to allow that the present passage can contain Pauline elements, the case can still stand that Luke is using traditional material but not just early church tradition; rather, this is Pauline tradition. G. Schneider, *Die Apostelgeschichte* (2 vols.; Freiburg: Herder, 1980–82), II, p. 297 n. 50, follows Lohfink in claiming that 'church' may have replaced an earlier wording which had 'people' (cf. Isa. 43.21; 1 Pet. 2.9; Tit. 2.14).

and the statement 'he (*sc.* Christ) purchased the church with his own blood';[29] in constructing the relative clause he failed to make clear that Christ was the subject.[30]

The view that seems most likely is the third one, namely, that the reference is to God purchasing the church with his own blood (i.e. the blood of his Son; it is God's blood in that it is his Son's own blood).[31] This is the way that the phrase is used in Heb. 9.12 and 13.12, and the existence of this close parallel, which may well rest on tradition, seems to me to be a decisive argument in its favour. Luke regularly sees God the Father and Christ as so closely linked that the same functions can be ascribed to both.[32] The blood is that of Christ as a human being. There is no suggestion that God as God has blood or a spiritual equivalent.

What is the force of ἴδιος? The adjective can simply have the weak sense 'his' in Hellenistic Greek, but the slightly more emphatic place given to it here (attributive by repetition of the article) probably rules out that sense.[33] The stronger force is to be accepted. However, the sense need not be 'his own and not some other [human] person's'. When the same phrase is used elsewhere (Heb. 9.12), there is a contrast between the Jewish high priests who offered blood that was not their own but was the blood of animals and Jesus who offered his own blood rather than the blood of animals. Thus the contrast between animal and human sacrifices is made in order to emphasize both the superiority and the costliness of Christ's death. A similar point is made in 1 Pet. 1.18-19; here, redemption is obtained not by the payment of money but by precious blood that is like that of an animal, though it is in fact the blood of Christ. This same kind of sense is probably present here; Christ redeemed with his own blood, which represents the apex of sacrifice and cost by implicit contrast with the blood of animals. Thus the phrase in Hebrews echoes a more

---

29. For this type of procedure possible parallels include the doxology in 2 Tim. 4.18 according to the (unlikely) minority interpretation of J.N.D. Kelly, *The Pastoral Epistles* (BNTC; London: A. & C. Black, 1963), p. 220. Note also Heb. 13.21 and 1 Pet. 4.11 where in each case a doxology appears to be addressed to Christ as the last-mentioned person, but commentators generally assume that the relative pronoun in the doxology refers to the more distant God.

30. H. Conzelmann, *Die Apostelgeschichte* (Tübingen: Mohr Siebeck, 1963), pp. 118-19, discusses possibilities 1 and 2 without coming to a firm decision.

31. Alternatively view 4 is possible. I pass over other, highly unlikely interpretations summarized and criticized by Walton, *Leadership*, pp. 96-98.

32. Examples include the gifting of believers with the Spirit (Acts 2.33/11.17; 15.8).

33. The attributive form with repetition of the article is rare; see Acts 1.25; Jn 1.42; 5.43; 7.18. If there is any emphasis, it is at best faint.

widely known theologoumenon. Certainly in the present context the main thought is of the greatness of God's concern for the church: if God cares for the church so much as to purchase it at the cost of personal sacrifice, a weighty obligation rests upon the under-shepherds to care for it so that none are lost from it.

The divine saving action is characterized as purchase. In its present context the verb περιεποιήσατο must imply some kind of costly purchase by God to gain a possession which the elders must faithfully guard rather than bringing about a sense of guilt and repentance on the part of those who crucified Christ; the latter idea is totally alien to the passage. Thus the case that Luke has 'deliberately suppressed' atonement theology by adopting a phraseology which lacks this motif cannot be supported from this passage, any more than it can be deduced from the absence of Mk 10.45b from Luke's Gospel.[34]

The thought is of deliverance from some other owner to become God's own possession. Barrett picks up the important point that, although the verb can simply mean 'acquire', its meaning can also be 'to save alive, to rescue from destruction' (Isa. 31.5; 43.21; Ps. 74.2 [LXX 73.2]; Lk. 17.33).[35] An Isaianic background is likely; the text probably reflects the language of the new exodus which pervades Acts.[36] The background for under-standing is deliverance from an alien power, and this ties in with Acts 26.18-19 where Paul's own mission is to go to the Gentiles to open their eyes, so that they may turn from darkness to light and from the power of Satan to God, so that (second purpose clause probably dependent on the first) they may obtain forgiveness of sins and an inheritance among the sanctified by faith in me (*sc.* Christ). This might appear at first sight to suggest that salvation is a matter of revelation and knowledge, leading people to turn away from obeying Satan and commit themselves to God and Christ. But the reference to the power of Satan strongly suggests that there is a captivity from which people need to be delivered by superior might rather than simply a change of mind as to whom they will obey (cf. Lk. 1.71, 74; 4.18; 13.16).

The primary thought, then, is of deliverance from the power of Satan and darkness so that the people may become God's people. But this thought is quickly linked with the need for forgiveness. Those who have

34. B.S. Billings, *Do This in Remembrance of Me* (London: T&T Clark International, 2006), p. 40, argues that Luke is working to a different agenda rather than carrying out 'a wholesale rejection of the atonement theology'.

35. Barrett, *Acts*, II, p. 976.

36. Surprisingly it escaped the attention of D. Pao, *Acts and the Isaianic Exodus* (BSL; Grand Rapids: Baker Academic, 2002).

succumbed to Satan's power have disobeyed God and offended him, and need his forgiveness. For the first Christians, it is likely that this thought developed particularly in connection with the crucifixion. Once his followers believe that the crucified Jesus is the Messiah, God's chief agent, they realize that their own people, the Jews, as represented by their leaders, have committed the sin of crucifying God's agent (just as they killed the prophets earlier, Lk. 11.49-51), and this creates the need for repentance and forgiveness on their part.[37] This motif is not explicit in Acts 20, where the context is the care of the church, but it is essential in evangelism. The strategy of the sermons in Jerusalem is thus seen to be historically appropriate, whether or not the actual wording is based on tradition.

For the appeal in Acts 20.28a it is sufficient to think of the church as being set free and purchased at the cost of the cross. But once this is seen, the cross must be understood as the costly means of redemption and not simply as the path to resurrection and exaltation; there is no 'cost' attached to resurrection! There has to be a conflict with Satan leading to victory. In theory the conflict might have been won by Christ not dying, that is, by preventing Satan from being able to administer the coup de grâce rather than by undoing the death that was actually inflicted.

The same motif of overcoming Satan may be present in Mk 10.45. Here the ransom for many suggests a price paid to deliver captives. The deliverance again can be seen as deliverance from the power of Satan rather than a price paid.[38] The motif of *Christus Victor* is an integral part of the theology in Acts.

Can we speak of atonement in either context? A number of commentators seem to assume too easily that the concepts of redemption and atonement are more or less synonymous. The term *Sühnetod* ('atoning death') has been applied to Lk. 22.19 and to this passage.[39] Pesch follows Roloff in finding the concept of atonement presupposed here as more or less as self-evident, even if it plays no central role in Luke's own

---

37. This understanding is reached by Jewish Christians themselves, and is not an example of antisemitism. Gentiles also need to repent and seek forgiveness (Acts 17.30; cf. 10.42-43, where the summons to faith is extended from 'the people' to include Gentiles). See the discussion from opposite sides by J.T. Sanders, *The Jews in Luke–Acts* (London: SCM Press, 1987), and J.A. Weatherly, *Jewish Responsibility for the Death of Jesus in Luke–Acts* (JSNTSup, 106; Sheffield: Sheffield Academic Press, 1994).

38. The often-made point that no ransom is actually paid to Satan stands. The metaphor must not be pushed literalistically.

39. H.-J. Michel, *Die Abschiedsrede des Paulus an die Kirche Apg 20,17-38* (Studien zum Alten und Neuen Testaments, 35; Munich: Kosel-Verlag, 1973), pp. 88-89.

theology.[40] But this may be going too far. If these scholars mean that the cross has redemptive efficacy and is not simply something unfortunate that happened to Christ, then we cannot but agree. If they are thinking of sacrifice in the sense of an offering made to God, some substantiation is required.

Redemption is bound up with atonement in Rom. 3.24-25. It would appear to be the personal deliverance which makes justification possible, and this in turn appears to rest upon the death of Jesus as a sacrifice of atonement. The appointment of Christ Jesus as ἱλαστήριον through his blood is the presupposition or prerequisite for the redemption that is in him. Justification is for Paul tantamount to forgiveness (Rom. 4.6-8), but he prefers the former term at this point in his theological thinking.[41] In Eph. 1.7 and Col. 1.14, however, redemption is explicated as forgiveness of sins. Redemption is generally tied to deliverance from sin and its power but also from its fatal consequences.

That Jesus forgave sins by his own authority as Son of Man is clear from the Synoptic Gospels and from Luke in particular (Lk. 5.20-24; 7.47-49; cf. 23.34 *si vera lectio*), as is his instruction to disciples to forgive freely. What Acts does is to continue this theme of Jesus as the one with authority, now confirmed by his exaltation, to forgive. In this context the cost to the one who forgives is not part of the declaration, although repentance on the part of the offender is the condition for the offer to become effective.

The link between redemption and forgiveness is an intrinsic one, in that those who are under the sway of Satan are somehow voluntary offenders who need to repent of their sin. There is a paradox of constraint and voluntariness that some may see as comparable to that between divine constraint and free response to the gospel. Thus there is no sense of tension or contradiction between the concepts for Luke, and their conjunction is not a problem.

Further linked to this may be the motif of sanctification and cleansing (Acts 26.18), which is another way of expressing the problem of sinfulness and reconciliation with God. There is thus a complex intertwining of motifs for Luke and the New Testament writers generally.

Does the thought of atonement, specifically of sacrifice, find a place within this complex here in Acts, as it does in Paul? Barrett comments

40. Roloff, *Apostelgeschichte*, p. 306; R. Pesch, *Die Apostelgeschichte* (EKK 5; 2 vols.; Zurich: Benziger; Neukirchen–Vluyn: Neukirchener Verlag, 1986), II, pp. 204-205.

41. Cf. Luke's use of 'justification' in Acts 13.39 as a synonym for forgiveness in the preceding verse.

that mention of blood does not necessarily convey the motif of sacrifice (cf. Stephen in Acts 22.20).[42] This is true, but a reference specifically to the blood of *Christ* might have a different force. The phrase διὰ τοῦ αἵματος is used in Eph. 1.7; Col. 1.20; Heb. 9.12; 13.12; and Rev. 12.11[43] (cf. also 1 Jn 5.6).[44] This usage suggests a stereotyped piece of traditional language that was certainly current at the time Luke probably wrote.[45] It is notable that Heb. 9.12 and 13.12 include the adjective ἴδιος to give a contrast with animals in the context of the sacrifices made by the high priest. This may indicate that the phrase had developed an atoning sacrificial sense when used with reference to Christ rather than simply the thought of a self-sacrificial death. Certainly the term 'blood' was in use earlier to refer to the death of Jesus and in a context of sacrifice (Rom. 3.25; cf. 5.9). From an early date it is also associated with the Lord's Supper (1 Cor. 10.16; 11.25). Here it is appropriate to remind ourselves that readers of Luke–Acts should already have read Lk. 22.20 with its use of the same blood motif as in Paul. We must beware of arguing in a circle, but it becomes ever clearer that Lk. 22.20 does fit into the theology developing in Acts and there are no grounds in its Lukan co-text for rejecting it from the text of the Gospel.

It is thus most unlikely that Luke could use this language without the thought of atoning sacrifice resonating through it for his readers.

It has been noted that the statement is not made as a direct focussed affirmation but has the primary task of asserting the supreme value of the church to God. Glöckner mentions the view that as a piece of tradition the phrase referred to the atoning death of Jesus, which had no significance for Luke's theology.[46] But, as Michel rightly emphasizes, Luke would not do this by employing a theologoumenon with which he disagreed, and the way in which he takes for granted this understanding of

---

42. Barrett, *Acts*, II, p. 977.

43. Rev. 12.11 uniquely has διὰ τὸ αἵμα as the means of the victory of the martyrs alongside the word of testimony.

44. A. Weiser, *Die Apostelgeschichte Kapitel 13–28* (Gütersloh: Mohn; Würzburg: Echter Verlag, 1985), p. 572, includes the phrase in a list of traditional elements in the speech.

45. J.T. Squires, in *Eerdmans Commentary on the Bible* (Grand Rapids: Eerdmans, 2003), p. 1255, rightly says that 'blood of his own Son' is based on traditional material known to Paul (cf. Weiser, *Apostelgeschichte*, II, p. 572) and to Luke (Lk. 22.20); but when he adds that 'which he obtained' is non-Lukan and reflects a post-Pauline situation (Eph. 1.14; 1 Tim. 3.13), he seems to be chasing a *non sequitur*. He does not consider the evidence for Luke's use of the New Exodus theme.

46. R. Glöckner, *Die Verkündigung des Heils beim Evangelisten Lukas* (Mainz: Matthias-Grünewald-Verlag, 1975), p. 181.

the death of Jesus indicates his acceptance of it.[47] In my view its force is all the stronger for being brought in as a self-evident basis for the main point that Luke is making.

Glöckner himself prefers to think that its significance for Luke was as an indication of the cost to God rather than as an atoning sacrifice. He makes the valid point that the saying is about God setting an example of the cost that must be borne in caring for the church: Luke is not saying that the leaders must protect the church because it was delivered from sin and justified by the death of Christ. 'The comment that the church is purchased through the blood of Christ cannot be understood as an expression of a justifying atonement but it characterizes the crucifixion as a loving self-giving to the uttermost for the church.'[48] This statement is correct in its description of the function of the saying, but this is no reason for denying that the question as to why God had to do this to acquire the church is implicitly present: the saying presupposes the need for redemption and the satisfaction of that need. Glöckner recognizes that Acts 20.28 connects salvation with the death of Jesus, but asserts that this one text has no significant weight over against the general outlook of Acts.[49] This, it seems to me, is a classic case of determination resolutely to ignore the evidence that suggests that the theory is wrong.

It may be asked why Luke did not simply transplant the actual wording of Mk 10.45b to Acts 20 if he was in agreement with its theology. The suggestion that he may have had some objections to the precise wording on literary grounds has been made by Buckwalter.[50] Whether or not we find Buckwalter's proposal convincing, it can be said that Luke may not have wanted to attribute a saying of Jesus to another speaker, and he preferred this tradition. We may compare how, when Mk 10.45b is used in 1 Tim. 2.6 and Tit. 2.14, the wording is carefully edited.

How, then, is the absence of atonement language elsewhere in Acts to be explained? What seems to be emerging is that there was an early stage in Christian proclamation in which Jesus Christ is presented as the Messiah approved and appointed by God, and as such affirmed and vindicated by his resurrection from the dead. Such a divine agent is entitled to the respect which should be given to God but which has been replaced by crucifixion and rejection. Yet God has given Christ the authority to forgive sins, especially the sin of rejection.

47. Michel, *Abschiedsrede*, pp. 88-89.
48. Glöckner, *Verkündigung*, p. 183.
49. Glöckner, *Verkündigung*, p. 231 n. 90. But see now the very different exposition of Luke's theology by Mittmann-Reichert.
50. Buckwalter, *Character*, pp. 146-48.

This constituted the message of the first preachers. Within the church, however, the question of why God let his Son be crucified came to the fore, and various insights combined to produce the understanding of the death as the means of cancelling out sin. Romans 3 is one deposit of such motifs, binding together a host of various images. Clearly the working out of this theme was an intra-congregational enterprise rather than something worked out in an evangelistic context,[51] but it quickly spilled over into the latter and coloured the preaching. Very early the gospel was understood as 'Christ died for our sins according to the Scriptures' and 'Christ died for us'. He is the one who died and rose so that he might be Lord of the dead and the living, that is, of all. The Pauline collocation of died and rose and the use of 'for us' with both verbs must rest on early Christian usage.

IV. *Conclusion*

The present investigation has established that Acts 20.28 is to be understood as the Lukan equivalent to Mk 10.45b, the ransom-statement which was a victim of Luke's decision to drop the whole of Mk 10.35-45 when he included similar material from other sources in his Gospel. Accordingly, the charge that he deliberately downplays the theology of the cross is to be rejected. Luke uses the motif of the cost of redemption to underline the responsibility of congregational leaders to care for the church, but the statement in itself ties in with the traditional concept of redemption found elsewhere in the Pauline corpus and 1 Peter and reflects a sacrificial understanding of the death of Jesus. The material in Acts reflects the lack of exposition of the atoning significance of the cross in the early preaching, as also attested elsewhere in the New Testament, and the development of the motif in intra-church theologizing, in which redemption, forgiveness (and justification) and sacrificial atonement are linked together. Luke is to be acquitted of the charge of aversion to such theology; he assumes it rather than expounds it, but this is explicable in the light of the purpose of Acts.

---

51. Cf. Wolter, *Lukasevangelium*, p. 705: 'The lack of an interpretation of the death of Jesus as a saving death in the mission speeches in Acts thus corresponds very precisely with its absence in the summary of Paul's missionary preaching in 1 Thess. 1.9-10). Correspondingly, it occurs of all places in Acts in 20.28, in the Pauline farewell speech before the Ephesian elders in Miletus, i.e. in the one speech that has a Christian audience.' Similarly, C.F.D. Moule, 'The Christology of Acts', in L.E. Keck and J.L. Martyn (eds.), *Studies in Luke–Acts* (Philadelphia: Fortress Press, 1980), pp. 159-85 (171).

THE RESURRECTION AND ITS WITNESSES IN THE BOOK OF ACTS[*]

Daniel Marguerat

The author of Luke–Acts, close to the heart of Loveday Alexander, and widely present in her works,[1] has a definition of 'apostleship' of his own. Although a disciple of Paul, he does not ratify the definition adopted by the apostle to the Gentiles in accordance with early Christianity as a whole: an apostle is a person entrusted with a mission, once he or she has been called by the Resurrected One.[2] 'Am I not an apostle? Have I not seen Jesus, our Lord?' (1 Cor. 9.1). In this rhetorical question, the second

[*] I am grateful to Paul R. Voumard for preparing the English translation of this essay.

1.   Alluding to one of her articles ('"In Journeying Often": Voyaging in the Acts of the Apostles and in Greek', in C.M. Tuckett [ed.], *Luke's Literary Achievement: Collected Essays* [JSNTSup, 116; Sheffield: JSOT Press, 1995], pp. 17-49), few exegetes have walked with such talent and such varied interests through the book of Acts. After her monograph on Luke's preface (*The Preface to Luke's Gospel: Literary Convention and Social Context in Luke 1:1-4 and Acts 1:1* [SNTSMS, 78; Cambridge: Cambridge University Press, 1993]), Loveday Alexander wrote numerous contributions, some of which have been reproduced in her collection of articles: *Acts in its Ancient Literary Context: A Classicist Looks at the Acts of the Apostles* (LNTS, 298; London: T&T Clark International, 2005); the title of this collection fits in perfectly with the programme of her exegetical quest, nourished, as it is, by an extensive knowledge of ancient classical literature. On the other side, her attention to the theological and devotional dimensions of the reading is evident in her commentary, *Acts* (People's Bible Commentary; Oxford: Bible Reading Fellowship, 2006).

2.   Paul speaks in Gal. 1.17 of the 'apostles who were before me' to indicate those of Jerusalem; but he also qualifies Andronicus and Junias in Rom. 16.7 as 'eminent apostles'. In 2 Cor. 8.23, the ἀπόστολοι are the delegates of the churches. In Phil. 2.25, Epaphras is qualified by the title. In 2 Cor. 11.13, Paul accuses his rivals of being false apostles (ψευδαπόστολοι) for preaching a rival message to his in Corinth. On the use of the title in the New Testament, see J.-A. Bühner, 'ἀπόστολος', in *EWNT*, I, pp. 342-51. On its use in the Pauline and post-apostolic literature, see J. Frey, 'Paulus und die Apostel. Zur Entwicklung des paulinischen Apostelbegriffs und zum Verhältnis des Heidenapostels zu seinen "Kollegen"', in E.-M. Becker and P. Pilhofer (eds.), *Biographie und Persönlichkeit des Paulus* (WUNT, 187; Tübingen: Mohr, 2005), pp. 192-227.

clause is the basis of the first: the vision of the Resurrected One legiti-
mizes apostleship. The Pauline extension to the Jerusalem creed of 1 Cor.
15.3b-5 (or 7) confirms the definition: 'Last of all, he also appeared to me,
the runt. For I am the least among the apostles…' (1 Cor. 15.8-9a). In
short, Paul puts into words the consensus of the first Christians by laying
down the equation: apostleship = being sent by the Resurrected One.

Once again, Luke does not share this consensus. Within the frame of
a narrative episode of his own, the election of Matthias as thirteenth
apostle replacing Judas, Luke has Peter setting out the criteria, which a
candidate to apostleship must meet: 'Therefore, one among the men who
have accompanied us at all times when the Lord Jesus went in and out
among us, beginning with the baptism of John up to the day when he was
taken away from us, one of these should become with us a witness to his
resurrection' (Acts 1.21-22). Only a man who has followed all the public
activity of Jesus, from his baptism to the Ascension, can be considered
for completing the apostolic college; henceforth, he is authorized with the
Eleven to be a 'witness to his resurrection'.

Such a restrictive definition of apostleship is understandable in terms
of the periodization of salvation history as carried out by Luke, the
historian. Jesus' time (told in the Gospel) and the Church's time (told in
Acts) are structured around the Ascension (Lk. 24.52; Acts 1.9-11).[3]
Being careful to build up ties between these two periods, Luke sets up the
Twelve as an instrument of continuity: their presence at Jesus' side and at
the Easter event ensures the authority of their witness. This unique and
non-repeatable status—should we remind ourselves that any idea of
apostolic succession is foreign to Lukan theology?—leads the author of
Acts to refuse the title of ἀπόστολος to preachers subsequent to Christ,
be they Stephen the proto-martyr (Acts 6–7), Philip the evangelist (Acts
8), Barnabas the preacher of Antioch (Acts 11)…and even Paul! Paul,
even though Luke had the greatest admiration for him, is in fact granted
the title of witness (μάρτυς, Acts 22.15; 26.16) but not that of ἀπόστολος.
Still, it is interesting to note in passing that a *lapsus calami* does reveal
Luke's knowledge of the title of apostle given to Paul: in Acts 14.4 and
14.14, he mentions 'the apostles Barnabas and Paul'.[4] One may point out

3. I refer the reader to the commentary on these texts in my *Les Actes des apôtres
(1-12)* (CNT, 5a; Geneva, Labor et Fides, 2007), pp. 43-51.

4. The commentators hesitate on the reasons for this exception in Luke's writings, otherwise still so coherent. Four explanations have been suggested: (1) Luke
forgot himself in passing; (2) Luke knows he should not name Paul as apostle, but his
admiration for him is such that the title escaped him; (3) the title 'apostles' does not
apply here to Barnabas and Paul, but to a larger group; (4) the term ἀπόστολος is not
used in its Lukan sense here, but designates the messengers in the way of primitive

that this quotation, in the plural, is in conformity with the Pauline definition of apostleship; however, this is the only exception.

I return to the Lukan portrait of the apostle: he needs to be a 'witness of his resurrection'. What does 'witness of Jesus' resurrection' mean? How and in which format is the 'witness to the resurrection' to be understood? I address this question to the entire book of Acts by dedicating this study to my colleague Loveday Alexander. The present study is a concrete expression of the interest we both share in Luke–Acts; it is offered to her as a sign of affection and admiration for her work, which has often inspired me, and in gratitude for our collaboration.

I wish to show here that, in Acts, witnessing to the resurrection is in no way reduced to a repetition of the events that followed Jesus' death. Witnessing to the resurrection is diversified into four models. They consist in: (1) reading history theologically, (2) announcing the restoration of human beings, (3) guaranteeing the universality of salvation and (4) witnessing by one's own life.

I. *Witnessing to the Resurrection*
is to Read History Theologically

Reading Peter's Pentecost speech (2.14-36) holds a surprise: the speech does not unfold as one would have expected. The first argumentation period (2.15-21) interprets the event that has just occurred with the help of Joel 3.1-5: the Pentecost languages explosion corresponds to the eschatological appearance of the Spirit, announced by Joel as a prophetic arousal of the whole people. In Joel's text, this arousal of the Spirit is part of an ultimate cosmos convulsion: the people will prophesy and have dreams, the sun will darken and the moon become bloody and these are the early warning signs of the coming of the day of the Lord. By means of this inter-text, the line of argument puts forward the notion of fulfilment: the oracle of Joel testifies to the dimension, both prophetic and eschatological, of the Pentecost event.[5]

Christianity and of Paul (in this case, the use of the term is often attributed to an Antioch source). See C.K. Barrett, *The Acts of the Apostles* (ICC; 2 vols.; Edinburgh: T. & T. Clark, 1994, 1998), II, pp. 671-72. Solution (4) seems the more plausible to me, taking into account the use of the term in the plural (and not the singular which would designate Paul exclusively); the hypothesis of a documentary source is not obvious.

5.   On the programmatic function of the quotation of Joel 3.1-5 in the discourse of Acts 2, see K.D. Litwak, *Echoes of Scripture in Luke–Acts: Telling the History of God's People Intertextuality* (JSNTSup, 282; London: T&T Clark International, 2005), pp. 155-68.

The surprise crops up in the second argumentation period (2.22-36). Instead of focusing on pneumatology, it branches off towards a scriptural demonstration of Jesus' resurrection. A kerygmatic announcement recalls the signs accomplished by God in the activities of Jesus (2.22); it goes on by bringing up the death-resurrection: Jesus 'delivered up according to the definite plan and foreknowledge of God, you have hanged and eliminated him by the hand of lawless men; he is the one God has raised by loosening him from the pangs of death, due to the fact that it was not possible for him to be held by it' (2.23-24). This so-called contrast formula opposes the resurrecting action of God to the action of people slaying Christ; the formula reappears several times in Acts.[6] To credit it with an anti-Jewish effect is to badly misunderstand it: it testifies to the superiority of divine power over the deadly action of humans and its climax is not an accusation but an offer of forgiveness (2.38).

In this regard, one is aware of the overwhelming character of Luke's theocentrism, which recognizes at the same time that the cross is not foreign to the divine plan and that God inverts the work of death into life. The task of fitting the entire Passion–resurrection drama within God's plan here borders on paradox. Yet the essential is played out on the side of the resurrection: death could not triumph, for God had decided otherwise. This is what the quote from Ps. 16.8-11 supports, where the psalmist tells of his trust in the God who will not let 'his holy one see corruption' (2.27). Following the prophetic function, which Luke regards as having priority in Scriptures, David is here conscripted to be the proclaimer of Jesus' resurrection.

Having interpreted Pentecost as the eschatological emergence of the Spirit by means of Joel's oracle, then having found in Psalm 16 the announcement of the resurrection, Peter can now make the connection between pneumatology and Christology: 'Therefore, being exalted at[7] the right hand of God, he has received from the Father the promise of the Holy Spirit, he has spread out what you see and hear' (2.33).

This is where witnessing to the resurrection becomes reality as a theological reading of history: the surprising coming of the Spirit refers to an origin and this origin is the power conferred by God on the Resurrected One. In other words, the explosion of languages in the Pentecost

---

6. Acts 3.13-15; 4.10; 5.30-31; 10.39-40; 13.27-30; cf. 7.52-56.

7. The Greek is τῇ δεξιᾷ, which can have a local meaning ('on the right') or an instrumental meaning ('by the right'); the local meaning without preposition being rare in Greek, I opt for the instrumental meaning, contrary to v. 34 where the turn of phrase is not the same. For the opposite position; see M. Gourgues, '"Exalté à la droite de Dieu" (Actes 2.33; 5.31)', *ScEs* 27 (1975), pp. 303-27.

community bears the signature of the Resurrected One. This miracle of tongues, in fact, indicates that Jesus has not been swallowed up by death, but that, restored by God, he is henceforth in a position to invest human history with his acts of power.

Peter's speech thus witnesses to the resurrection by decoding the work of the Resurrected One in the Pentecost event.[8] The link is assured by an interesting recurrence of terms: whereas the recollection of the kerygma mentions 'mighty works, wonders and signs' achieved by Jesus (2.22), Joel's oracle speaks of 'wonders' and 'signs' occurring in heaven and on earth (2.19). The same wonders/signs pair (τέρατα/σημεῖα) describes the actions of the earthly Jesus as well as the Pentecost miracle, the initiative of which is credited to the Resurrected One;[9] the same formula actually refers to the same achiever. The recurrence of the vocabulary is to be understood as a narrator's signal intended for his reader; *the reading of history is christological; its key is found in the resurrection.*

In Acts 3, Peter's speech following the healing of the lame man at the Beautiful Gate presents us with the same phenomenon. The healing is the event to be interpreted and its origin, so Peter insists as he begins his speech, is not to be attributed to the power or the piety of the apostles (3.12). Now, after that negative statement, the speech passes immediately to the affirmation of the resurrection: 'The God of Abraham, of Isaac and of Jacob, the God of our fathers, has glorified his servant Jesus…' (3.13). What end is served by this reminiscence of Easter? Verse 16 points to it by describing the works of the 'author of life, whom God has awakened from among the dead'; 'by faith in his name, his name has strengthened the one you observe and know'. Therefore, it is to the 'name of the Lord' that the healing power, which manifested itself at the Beautiful Gate of the Temple, is to be traced back. What is this about? The 'name of the Lord' is a concept dear to Luke, one which he has inherited from the Hebrew theology of the divine Name; it designates the sphere of power within which Christ acts in the midst of history. One of the Lukan theological originalities is to trace the miracles back to Christology, via

---

8. On the relationship between Spirit and witnessing, see W.H. Shepherd, *The Narrative Function of the Holy Spirit as a Character in Luke–Acts* (SBLDS, 147; Atlanta: Scholars, 1994), pp. 160-67; J.-N. Aletti, 'Esprit et témoignage dans le livre des Actes. Réflexions sur une énigme', in E. Steffek and Y. Bourquin (eds.), *Raconter, interpréter, annoncer. Mélanges D. Marguerat* (Le Monde de la Bible, 47; Geneva: Labor et Fides, 2003), pp. 225-38.

9. The couple τέρατα/σημεῖα in Acts refers to Pentecost (2.19), to the miraculous activity of Jesus (2.22), to that of Moses (7.36) and to that of the apostles (2.43; 4.30; 5.12; 6.8; 14.3; 15.12). That recurrence reveals above all the christological origin of the miracles occurring by the hand of the apostles.

the concept of the Name,[10] and not to pneumatology as Paul and the majority of the early Christianity writings do. The speech of Acts 3 is a nice illustration of this Lukan theological structure: the healing of the lame man is not to be taken as the expression of charismatic power or exceptional piety, be it that of the apostles; *its origin lies in the historical action of the Resurrected One.* Once again, Peter witnesses to the resurrection by discerning the trace of the risen Christ in a historical event.

This theology, or rather this Lukan Christology of miracle, explains the presence in Acts of a formulation, which is unique in the New Testament. When he heals Aeneas, the paralytic of Lydda, the same Peter declares: 'Aeneas, Jesus Christ heals you. Get up and make yourself (your bed)' (9.34). The conviction that the healing force does not stem from the apostle, but from the risen Christ, is expressed with extreme linguistic conciseness. The apostle steps aside to the point of letting his 'I' disappear and thrusting forward the third party whose witness and spokesperson he is. The Resurrected One is referred to as a man of action in history, whose witness invites the reader to identify the active presence.

II. *Witnessing to the Resurrection is to Announce the Restoration of Human Beings*

It is well known that the resurrection language in the New Testament—and Luke does not escape this semantic particularity—proceeds from an ambiguity. There are two Greek verbs our Bibles translate as 'to resurrect' into English. The first is ἐγείρω, literally, 'to awaken, to rouse somebody from sleep', and figuratively, 'to rouse somebody from the sleep of death, to resurrect'. The second is ἀνίστημι, 'to raise up, to pick up'; in the passive ἀνίστημαι, 'to be raised up or picked up' and consequently, 'to be raised from death, to resurrect'.[11] The texts sometimes play on this ambivalence, as in the healing stories where raising the sick up is enhanced by a resurrection connotation (Lk. 4.39; 5.25; 8.55; Acts 9.34, 40; 14.10). From my point of view, an identical practice of semantic

---

10. On this question, see my *The First Christian Historian: Writing the Acts of the Apostles* (SNTSMS, 121; Cambridge: Cambridge University Press, 2002), pp. 109-28 (118-21).

11. On the resurrection language in the New Testament, see my *Résurrection. Une histoire de vie* (Poliez-le-Grand: Éditions du Moulin, 3rd edn, 2003), pp. 7-24; and J.-P. Michaud, 'La résurrection dans le langage des premiers chrétiens', in O. Mainville and D. Marguerat (eds.), *Résurrection. L'après-mort dans le monde ancien et le Nouveau Testament* (Le Monde de la Bible, 45; Geneva: Labor et Fides; Montréal Médiaspaul, 2001), pp. 111-28.

ambivalence can be perceived in the narrative of the Ethiopian eunuch conversion (8.26-40) to which we now pay attention.

This text is characterized by a long quotation from the servant song in Isaiah 53. However, this prophetic text, which we know has exercised considerable influence on the Christology of the first Christians, is only quoted explicitly once in the New Testament, namely here. Everywhere else, it is referred to only by a brief extract or in reminiscence. The question is: Why does the author of Acts, whom we know to be very conscientious in handling his writing, provide this story with a quotation from Isa. 53.7b-8c *in extenso*?

> Then the Spirit said to Philip: 'Approach and join the chariot'. Philip ran, heard the eunuch reading Isaiah the prophet and asked: 'Do you know what you are reading?' He said: 'Well, how could I be capable of that if no one guides me?' He invited Philip to climb up and sit with him. Now, the Scripture passage he was reading was this: '*As a sheep led to slaughter or a lamb dumb before its shearers, so he opened not his mouth. In his humiliation, justice was denied him; who will tell of his generation? For his life is taken away from the earth.*' Speaking up, the eunuch said to Philip: 'I pray you, about whom does the prophet say that? About himself or someone else?' Beginning with that Scripture, Philip opened his mouth and announced Jesus, the good news, to him. (8.31-35)

Before answering the question, let us note that this Lukan cutting in the fourth Servant Song (Isa. 52.13–53.12) is surgical. It avoids two allusions to the expiatory death of the servant, which precede (Isa. 53.7a) and immediately follow the extract (Isa. 53.8d). Luke is coherent with himself: the sacrificial reading of Jesus' death is not to his liking.[12]

Quoted in vv. 32-33, the Septuagint version of Isaiah's text begins by outlining the distress of the servant: he accepts without protest the violence inflicted on him (v. 32).[13] The prophet here sketches the figure of someone totally submitted to violence, affected in body and word: like a dumb lamb, not opening the mouth. For the reader of Luke–Acts, the application of this is without a doubt to the cross.

However, the understanding of the second part (v. 33) is uncertain—in the Septuagint already. At first sight, it confirms the suffering of the Servant: his right (κρίσις) has been removed from him (ἤρθη) and no one will be able to speak of his descendants (γενεά) 'for it is taken away (αἴρεται) from the land of the living'. Without anyone to defend him,

---

12. See F. Bovon, *Luc le théologien* (Le Monde de la Bible, 5; Geneva: Labor et Fides, 3rd edn, 2006), p. 275.

13. I summarize here the analysis presented in my commentary, to which I refer the reader for more details: *Actes*, pp. 284-313.

without anyone to survive him, the Servant's life is removed from among humans. Is this the only possible reading of the text? No, because the verb αἴρω means 'to take away, to remove' as much as 'to raise, to lift'. The first meaning can be read in Lk. 8.12 ('he removes the word from their heart'), the second in Lk. 4.11 ('they will lift you up on their hands'). If this second meaning is adopted, the last line of the quote sounds quite different: 'for it is lifted from the land of the living'. Now, with that meaning, the verb αἴρω contains the same paschal connotation as ἐγείρω and ἀνίσταμαι. One can in fact understand 'lifting' as a reference to Christ's resurrection, according to a christological humbling/exaltation pattern we come across in Phil. 2.6-11. In that light, the sense of the previous sentences can also be turned around: Because he was humbled, his judgment (another possible meaning of κρίσις) has been lifted, that is to say suspended by God (v. 33a); who will now be able to describe his spiritual progeny (γενεά), so countless it is (v. 33b)?

Which reading has Luke retained? Contrary to his custom,[14] the narrator does not develop his exegesis of Scripture here. He briefly writes that 'Beginning with that Scripture, Philip opened his mouth and announced Jesus, the good news, to him.' The verb for announcing used here is εὐαγγελίζομαι, 'to announce the good news'. To proclaim Jesus as good news is to announce the kerygma of death and resurrection.[15] Resorting to this verb thus puts Philip up as a witness to the resurrection. But once again, why does Luke hush up the contents of Philip's proclamation? Does he suppose that his reading of Isaiah 53 is known to his readers? This explanation is plausible but I propose another one: Luke counts on that ambiguity of Isaiah's ending. My proposal has the merit of being part of the author's custom: Luke quotes a text, deliberately preserving its ambivalence in order to legitimize the question of its understanding.[16] Of Christ alone can one effectively say that his life has been exalted (cf. 2.34; 13.34-37).

Thus, Philip is a witness to the resurrection in the measure to which he decodes the veiled reference to Christ's resurrection contained in Isaiah's prophecy. It is through this that he announces 'the good news'. However, one must immediately observe that this is not the only level of reading to

---

14. See 2.25-36; 4.25-28 or 13.34-37.

15. This verb is very Lukan within the Synoptic tradition (occurrences: Mark = no occurrences; Matthew = 1; Luke = 10; Acts = 15). In Acts, it represents the synthetic designation of the apostles and the witnesses: 5.42; 8.4, 12, 25, 35, 40; 10.36; 11.20; 13.32; 14.7, 15, 21; 15.35; 16.10; 17.18.

16. A similar narrative strategy rules the quotations of Acts 2.25-28; 4.25-26; 13.35.

which the quotation of Isaiah 53 lends itself. It is in fact remarkable that the prophetic text applies perfectly to the eunuch's situation. In spite of his high social rank, he too, in view of his sterility, has been a victim of belittling remarks against which he could not protest ('As a sheep led to slaughter or a lamb dumb before its shearers, so he opened not his mouth'). From him, too, the hope of an earthly progeny has been withdrawn ('In his humiliation, justice was denied him; who will tell of his generation?'). However, he can hope that God will lift him up from his humiliation and restore his life ('For his life is lifted up from the earth').

Therefore, three stories are superimposed on Isaiah's text in which the reader may, one by one, identify the destiny of the suffering servant, of Jesus or of the Ethiopian eunuch. The christological application does not exclude an actualization in the case of the Ethiopian eunuch whose paradoxical portrait the narrator has carefully dealt with in 8.27-28: he is powerful in Candace's court but despised, as were castrated men in general in antiquity; he administers the finances of the Ethiopian kingdom but, as eunuch, is barred from the Temple in Jerusalem where he had come to worship God. In short, this man, strong and fragile, feared and disdained at the same time, hears a prophetic word which echoes his own shortcomings. *By announcing the Christ to him, Philip the witness opens the perspective of his own restoration just like on the path of the Crucified—Resurrected Lord.* His request for baptism is unique in Acts and famous for its direct language: 'Here is water, what hinders me from being baptized?' (8.36b). The reader is able to rationalize that type of coarseness: by applying to oneself the words of Isaiah 53, having first referred it to Jesus, he or she has integrated the promise it contained. The demand for baptism is its existential translation. The word of the witness has actually opened a space where humans are no longer degraded because of their status, their misery or their body.

The same kind of witnessing centred on restoration can be read in the intervention of Ananias of Damascus during Saul's conversion (9.10-19a). Christ appears to him in fact to inform him that Saul of Tarsus is staying in the house of Judas, that he saw him, Ananias, in prayer, coming to lay his hands on him that he may recover his sight. Ananias protests, following the typical pattern of the prophetic vocation and expressing an objection to the divine mandate: 'Lord, I have heard many speaking of that man and all the harm he has caused your saints in Jerusalem' (9.13). But the Resurrected One overcomes that objection by revealing to him that Saul is the instrument he has chosen for evangelizing the nations and Israel. He gains the support of Ananias who goes to Saul and sets to work both in word (announcing the Resurrected One) and deed (laying hands, healing, baptizing): '"Saul, brother, the Lord has sent me, Jesus who appeared to you on the road where you walked, in order that you may see anew and be filled with the Holy Spirit"; and immediately, there were like scales falling from his eyes, he could see again, and being lifted up, he was baptized. After some nourishment, he regained his strength' (9.17b-19a). Announcing the resurrection cannot and must not be separated from that which validates it and sets it at the heart of human relationships: eyes healed, baptism sealed, body restored and Spirit received. In the literal sense of the term, the interpretation of the shock that occurred in Damascus by the revelation of the Resurrected One stands Saul up again and returns him to life.

III. *Witnessing to the Resurrection is to Unfold the Universality of Salvation*

The third type of witness to the resurrection is found in the episode which is one of the highest points (maybe the highest) of the book of Acts: the meeting between Peter and the centurion Cornelius in Caesarea (Acts 10). The episode is a theological peak: for the first time in Acts, a non-Jew is admitted to salvation without being a proselyte. To set up the meeting between the two men, the narrator has orchestrated a stream of supernatural interventions: an angelic apparition to Cornelius (10.3-6), a trance in Peter (10.11-16) and a message of the Spirit to go to the centurion (10.19-20). The narrative strategy is evident: the reader needs to grasp the extraordinary character of that event, but above all to realize that this unprecedented extension of salvation to the nations is not the result of an initiative by the apostles, but of an intervention by God who forces history to fit into his plan.

Surprised by the event, Peter, once inside Cornelius' house, delivers a speech where he theologically decodes what is going on. His line of argument has always surprised commentators because it justifies the universality of salvation without appealing to Scriptures. In particular, one would have expected Luke, very fond of entrenching the Christian novelty within a continuity of Israel's history, to resort to the Old Testament to make the point that this novelty meets the expectations of Israel. But there is nothing of the sort. Did not Luke have pertinent texts to argue the case? His way of using Scripture to support Jesus' resurrection makes one think he was not short of scriptural arguments.[17] I rather think that this scriptural silence conveys *the theological conviction that*

---

17. Reading Acts 2.22-36; 3.13-26; 13.32-41 will be convincing.

Christian universality is the result of Easter. The paschal event, which Luke repeats was authored by none other than the God of Abraham, of Isaac and of Jacob, has led Christians to open the covenant of salvation to those who were originally deprived of it.

Therefore, Peter does not argue from Scripture, but from the christological kerygma. The passage that follows clearly establishes the link between the apostolic witness of the resurrection and the universality of salvation: to witness that Jesus has been raised from the dead is to announce that he is the eschatological Judge of the whole humanity and that, from now on, forgiveness of sins is granted to whoever—Jew or not—believes in him.

> As for us, we are witnesses to all that he did both in the land of the Jews and in Jerusalem. They executed him by hanging him on a tree, but God raised him on the third day and allowed him to appear, not to all the people but to witnesses chosen by God in advance, to us, who ate and drank with him after he rose from the dead; he commanded us to preach to the people and to testify that he is the one ordained by God as judge of the living and the dead. All the prophets testify about him: that everyone who believes in him receives forgiveness of sins through his name. (10.39-43)

Let us examine more closely what constitutes here the status of witness to the resurrection. First of all, Peter cites a fact common to all canonical Gospels[18] and to Paul; that is to say that the Resurrected One did not appear in public, but to his friends, in order to confirm the legitimacy of their witness. Not only were they sole beneficiaries of the apparitions, but they were divinely chosen. It is true that Luke limits that privilege to the disciples chosen by Jesus, the 'apostles' by his specific definition, and does not report the tradition reported by the apostle Paul on the apparition of the Resurrected One 'to more that five hundred brothers at one time' (1 Cor. 15.6).

As for these chosen witnesses, the intimacy experienced with the Resurrected One is asserted in a strange way: they have been eating with him and drinking with him. If the reader moves upstream in the Lukan narrative, he will think of the Resurrected One eating in Lk. 24.41-43, or rather of the meal at the beginning of Acts (1.4); the eating of Luke 24 (in Emmaus), which precedes the disciples' 'disbelief for joy' (v. 41), is actually more demonstrative than convivial. But why recall the paschal fellowship around the table? This is where the reader needs to have a

---

18. The apocryphal *Gospel of Peter* (about 150 CE?) in particular presents the first literary attestation of the apparition of the Resurrected to an audience foreign to the disciples or sympathizers of Jesus; in the occurrence, Christ comes out of the tomb, in full view of the soldiers charged with guarding the tomb (*Gos. Pet.* 38-45).

sharp eye. What is at stake in the meeting of Peter and Cornelius? The ecstasy that takes Peter by surprise in Joppa (10.9-16) makes him see all kinds of mixed pure and impure animals with a heavenly voice commanding him to sacrifice and eat. Peter was to refuse energetically that tempting command three times: to consume meat in contact with impurity contravenes the age-old rules of the Jewish dietary ritual. Yet, the divinely orchestrated meeting with Cornelius leads him to a pagan home where he manages to decode theologically the meaning of the trance by applying it to human relationships: 'You yourselves know how unlawful it is for a Jew to be in contact with a foreigner or to get close to him; but God has shown me that I should not call anyone profane or unclean' (10.28). This he confirms soon after: 'I truly realize that God does not look at appearances, but that in every nation, anyone who fears him and does what is just is acceptable to him' (10.34-35). The jumble of animals offered to him in the ecstasy appears to him as the destruction of the age-old barrier that separated Jews from the nations. Henceforth, faith authorizes anyone to receive pardon for sins. The God of Israel, the God of Jesus Christ, is the God of all and of each one.

Let us return to the table fellowship: the link now becomes clear. The divine command to the Judeo-Christian Peter to eat and drink with Cornelius' household represents the sharing of salvation. The 'eating with' (συνεφάγομεν) and the 'drinking with' (συνεπίομεν) the Resurrected One thus serve as symbolic and concrete expression of the universality of salvation (10.41). The censure of the Jerusalem brothers against Peter brandishes the same verbs: 'you have eaten with them!' (συνέφαγες) (11.3). In order to justify himself for that daring fellowship at table, Peter does not have any scriptural exegesis at hand, but a reading of the resurrection. In other words: *to take on witnessing to the resurrection is to enter into a dynamic of salvation where other people are no longer a threat of impurity to the believer, but the beneficiaries of a boundless welcome.* Easter is for Christians the birth date of a consequent theology of the universal God.

IV. *When Life becomes a Witness to the Resurrection*

The first kind of witness to the resurrection which I have listed in the book of Acts is of a *cognitive* order: it permits a theological reading of history. The second kind registers the impact of the resurrection at the level of *existence*: rehabilitating humanity. The third kind has implications both *ethical and theological*: contravening the age old rites, which safeguarded the purity of Israel, extends sainthood to all humanity; the universal impact of salvation bears the signature of the God of Easter.

The fourth kind, which I tackle now, fits in, like the second, at the level of existence: *it is the witnesses' own life that becomes a witness to the resurrection*. This fourth type emerges throughout the narrative of Acts, but it becomes explicit with the apology of Paul before Agrippa in Acts 26.

Its presence in the course of the story is continuous, but implicit; it discloses itself in the tormented destiny of the apostles and of the messengers of Christ. What does in fact happen to the messengers? Their proclamation inevitably exposes them to insecurity and hostility. The apostles in Jerusalem are harassed by the Sanhedrin who imprison them, have them flogged and try to ban their word (4.1-22; 5.17-42). Stephen is lynched after a pseudo-trial (6.8–7.60). The evangelist Philip comes up against Simon the magician (8.5-13). As for Paul, the plots threatening his life in Damascus and Jerusalem right after his conversion (9.19b-30) are but the prelude to the long series of humiliations this privileged witness of Christ will suffer: recurring conflicts with the Jews (Acts 13–21), then imprisonment in Caesarea and shipwreck off Malta (Acts 23–27).[19]

Yet, the 'miracle' recurs each time: the witness escapes death thanks to the supernatural action of God or to the providential intervention of human agencies. The apostles in Jerusalem are miraculously delivered from prison (5.19-21; 12.6-11). Philip's preaching prevails over Simon's magic (8.12-13). Paul is constantly contradicted, assaulted, flogged, humiliated, imprisoned, but the hero always escapes thanks to the protection of Roman authorities or the shrewdness of his companions[20].

Stephen dies under a volley of stones, but the persecution triggered by his martyrdom causes an outpouring of evangelization from Jerusalem and the establishment of the Antioch community; the crisis turns into a stimulus for the growth of the Church (8.1b-4; 11.19-26). In short, the destiny of the witnesses follows a pattern based on a christological model: their life is a Passion, but the witness comes out victorious from that path of suffering—not by the witness' own strength or cleverness, but through external interventions where the providential hand of God is clear. The rhetorical process identifiable here is *syncrisis*, in which Luke models the destiny of the messengers after the destiny of the One they proclaim:[21] the

19. See S. Cunningham, *'Through Many Tribulations': The Theology of Persecution in Luke–Acts* (JSNTSup, 142; Sheffield: Sheffield Academic Press, 1997).

20. For this latter cause (the saving shrewdness of the companions), see Acts 9.23-25, 29-30; 17.13-14; 23.12-16; cf. 21.11-14. This reason is an echo of the network of collaboration Paul benefited from in his missionary endeavours; it ought to restrain the reader from having an image of Paul as a solitary hero.

21. I have presented the process of *syncrisis*, which Luke uses to model Peter and Paul on each other and both on Jesus, in *The First Christian Historian*, pp. 56-59; see

life of the witnesses is suffering, but that suffering has life overshadowing it. The failure encountered by witnesses is a providential failure since the triumphant march of the Word is woven throughout it. In summary, the life of the witness in its very difficulties refers us to a theology where life's victory can be seen amid a tissue of frailty and precariousness. Yet once again, this direction is implicit; it is up to the reader to make the connection between survival of witnesses and the Passion–resurrection of Jesus. It is true that the reader of Luke–Acts has a clue at hand given upstream within the Gospel: 'The disciple is not above his master, but every well-trained disciple will be like his master' (Lk. 6.40).

One needs to wait almost to the end of the story for the implicit to become explicit. The occasion arises in the interpretation of Paul's conversion during his apology before King Agrippa in Acts 26. The statement of the Resurrected One on the Damascus road takes on an original turn:

> But get up and stand on your feet. For I have appeared to you for this purpose, to appoint you in advance as servant and witness of the things you have seen and those in which I will appear to you, by rescuing you from the people and the nations to whom I am sending you, to open their eyes, to turn them away from darkness to light and from the power of Satan to God, so that they may receive forgiveness of sins and a heritage among those who are sanctified by faith in me. (26.16-18)

One would expect Paul to be established as witness of Christ, as one proclaiming the Messiah promised to Israel. Ananias' announcement of Paul's vocation in 9.15 points in that direction. In 22.15, he is established as witness 'before all people of what you will have seen and heard'; what is seen and heard is understood to be Christ's revelation he has just received. But here, in that final re-formulation of the Damascus event within the story of Acts, Paul is set to become 'witness of the things you have seen and those in which I will appear to you, by rescuing you from the people and the nations to whom I am sending you' (26.16b-17a). The object of Paul's witnessing is none other than his life, his tormented life, within which Jesus will manifest himself through visions and deliverance from his misfortunes. It is through the destiny of Paul the witness that the liberating intervention of Christ is to be seen. *The life of the witness becomes gospel.* As Jean-Noël Aletti writes, 'the life of Paul has become entirely that of witnessing because, by telling it, he reveals at the same

also M. Quesnel, 'Luc historien de Paul et de Jésus', in B. Pouderon and Y.-M. Duval (eds.), *L'historiographie de l'Église des premiers siècles* (Théologie historique, 114; Paris: Beauchesne, 2001), pp. 57-66.

time the forgiveness and the grace of his Lord: to announce it amounts to taking up the entire itinerary again.'[22]

In the shift we identify, witnessing moves from the life of Jesus to that of the witness. Does this constitute the first step leading from Gospel to hagiography? Would Luke be responsible for (or guilty of) distorting the kerygma by sliding from the figure of Christ into that of the saints? That step, by which the figure of Christ tends to be confused with that of the apostles, is taken in the *Apocryphal Acts of the Apostles*.[23] It would be premature and anachronistic to identify it here. Because, if Luke shows extraordinary care with human mediations through which the divine in human history manifests itself, he never loses sight of the fact that the destiny of the messengers is not significant as such, but that it becomes transparent to the work of Jesus. Christology remains dominant. Any confusion that may turn the distance between the Son and his witnesses porous is carefully avoided. This is the way one ought to understand the absence of any mention of the death of the two main heroes of the story, Peter and Paul. Peter fades out of the story on an enigmatic note (12.17) and Paul's death is only mentioned in the story by means of a veiled allusion (20.25). One death alone is salutary and must be kept in memory: that of Jesus. That is why we ought to be careful not to speak of a Passion–resurrection of Paul after the image of that of Jesus.[24] The witness does not relate back to himself, but to the One whose name he bears.[25]

The very essence of the witness is to be a pointer to news that does not emanate from him/her, but which precedes and generates his/her words. Witnessing in Acts matches the definition: all the way in one's life, all the way by one's life, the witness refers to a word not his/her own.

---

22. Aletti, 'Esprit', p. 237.

23. The confusion between Christ and the apostle is found in *Acts of Paul* (3.21). Similarly, Christ takes on the characteristics of Thomas in the *Acts of Thomas* (151–55), of a wonderful young man in the *Acts of Andrew* (32), of John and a young man in the *Acts of John* (87); in the *Acts of Peter*, he takes on the face of the apostle (22), of a stunningly handsome young man (5) or of a man of undefinable age (21).

24. M.D. Goulder (*Type and History in Acts* [London: SPCK, 1964], pp. 62-63), followed by several commentators, has defended this typological reading.

25. During the evangelization of Samaria, what differentiates Philip the evangelist from his rival Simon the magician lies precisely in that different dimension. Whereas Simon identifies himself as 'great' and exerts a fascination on the crowds that makes them want to become attached to him (8.9-10), Philip announces the Reign of Another and the word of Another: 'But when they believed Philip, who was proclaiming the good news about the kingdom of God and the name of Jesus Christ, they were baptized, both men and women' (8.12).

A SPIRITUALITY OF ACTS?[*]

Steve Walton

I. *Setting the Scene*

'Spirituality': now there's a vague, catch-all category! And yet, to engage with the New Testament writings, and more widely those of early Christianity, without considering how the early believers understood their engagement with God is to neglect a major dimension of the life of the earliest Christians. They understood themselves to be in communication with God and to be experiencing the life of God through the Spirit: thus to focus entirely on their beliefs (i.e. what we might call 'New Testament Theology') to the exclusion of their behaviour and experience is to miss something which they considered crucial.

When we consider the patristic period, questions about 'spirituality' have been considered, sometimes in some depth; whereas in the New Testament period little work has been done.[1] A search of the ATLA database in relation to Acts finds just one article tagged as concerning both Acts and spirituality[2]—and the results are not much greater when searching more widely for 'spirituality' and 'New Testament'.[3]

Two studies in the 1990s began to restore this balance by exploring the question of the earliest Christians' engagement with God: Luke Johnson's *Religious Experience in Early Christianity* and Stephen Barton's *The Spirituality of the Gospels*.[4]

---

[*] I am delighted to offer this study in honour of Loveday Alexander, whom I am privileged to count as a friend as well as my *Doktormutter* and colleague in the academy. This study seeks to work at the interface of academy and church, a place very like Loveday's role as Canon Theologian of Chester Cathedral.

1. For example, in R. Williams, *The Wound of Knowledge* (London: Darton Longman & Todd, 1979), only pp. 4-13 cover the New Testament.

2. J.B. Green, 'Doing Repentance: The Formation of Disciples in the Acts of the Apostles', *Ex Auditu* 18 (2002), pp. 1-23.

3. Recently, see N.A. Røsæg, 'The Spirituality of Paul: An Active Life', *StSp* 14 (2004), pp. 49-92.

4. L.T. Johnson, *Religious Experience in Early Christianity* (Minneapolis: Fortress Press, 1998); S.C. Barton, *The Spirituality of the Gospels* (London: SPCK, 1992); cf. this emphasis in the writings of Dunn, Turner and Hurtado, in the following: J.D.G.

Johnson sets out to restore a balance and argues that a bias in favour of 'the textually defined and the theologically correct' has skewed the academy's engagement with earliest Christianity to the extent that the content of the New Testament texts is actually ignored.[5] He thus proposes that much of the New Testament writings refer to, express and argue from human experience rather than propositions, specifically from experiences of external divine power which produces effects in human lives.[6] Hence New Testament study, Johnson argues, easily becomes reductionist, seeking 'nothing but' explanations of the religious experience of the earliest Christians in sociological or other terms. How far Johnson is successful in providing this perspective in his studies of baptism, meals and tongues speech later in the book may be debated, but that he raises a key issue seems clear.[7]

Barton's *The Spirituality of the Gospels* was ground-breaking when it appeared in 1992 in seeking to ask how the Gospels (and, to a lesser degree, Acts) express and encourage '*the sense of the divine presence and living in the light of that presence*', which is his working definition of 'spirituality'.[8] After a brief introduction clarifying his general approach, Barton goes on to study the spirituality of each of the four canonical Gospels in turn. We focus on his study of Luke–Acts, which majors on the Gospel, but takes some account of Acts where its content and emphases supplement those of the Gospel.

Barton begins by sketching what he sees as the key themes of Lukan theology, since he (rightly) sees Lukan spirituality as a 'response to divine grace revealed in Christ'.[9] He enumerates the major themes of Lukan theology as focusing on a new age which has dawned. This new age has dawned with the births of the Baptist and Jesus. It is the age of the

Dunn, *Baptism in the Holy Spirit* (London: SCM Press; Philadelphia: Westminster Press, 1970); *idem, Jesus and the Spirit: A Study of the Religious and Charismatic Experience of Jesus and the First Christians as Reflected in the New Testament* (London: SCM Press, 1975); M. Turner, '"Trinitarian" Pneumatology in the New Testament?—Towards an Explanation of the Worship of Jesus', *Asbury Theological Journal* 57 (2003), pp. 167-86; L.W. Hurtado, *Lord Jesus Christ: Devotion to Jesus in Earliest Christianity* (Grand Rapids: Eerdmans, 2003).

5. Johnson, *Experience*, p. 3.

6. Johnson, *Experience*, pp. 5-7.

7. See, for example, the following useful critical reviews: J.D.G. Dunn, Review of L.T. Johnson, *Religious Experience in Earliest Christianity*, *Anvil* 18 (2001), pp. 59-61; J. Meggitt, Review of L.T. Johnson, *Religious Experience in Earliest Christianity*, *JTS* NS 51 (2000), pp. 685-58.

8. Barton, *Spirituality*, p. 1 (his italics).

9. Barton, *Spirituality*, p. 72.

eschatological Spirit. It is a time of salvation prior to the coming of the End, and in particular it is a time of salvation for *all* people.[10]

Barton then considers seven elements of the human response to divine grace according to Luke.[11] In each case he outlines the textual evidence for the presence of the theme and then considers why Luke might be highlighting this point. His themes are: joy, repentance and conversion, faith, prayer, the presence of the exalted Lord by the Spirit, witness, and the 'motif of the journey' as the context for spirituality.

Barton's analysis has many strengths, not the least of which is his understanding of spirituality as response to divine grace. However, Barton's study also prompts a number of reactions and questions. We shall see below that the communal dimension is core to understanding the spirituality portrayed in Acts, and it appears that Barton rather neglects this emphasis. Barton also seems to focus on divine grace at the expense of divine initiative and divine intervention. As we shall see, Acts presents God as active and involved with the life of his people, rather than merely passively receiving from his people. It may be that this is unfair to Barton: however, his portrait seems at least partial and incomplete and requires rounding out; so to this task we turn.

II. *How People Engage with God in Acts*

A significant danger in studying this topic is that 'spirituality' becomes a catch-all category which includes everything about the Christian life, and therefore in practice lacks precision—as with definitions of Christian worship in similar vein. Accordingly, we shall consider the two sides of people engaging with God: the divine initiative and the human response. Our consideration of the divine initiative will focus on the means by which God is known and experienced, by contrast with Barton's rather more abstract 'theological' categories.

a. *The Divine Initiative*
That the book of Acts is a work driven by the divine initiative is becoming more widely understood. I myself have argued for such an understanding as a key to reading Acts,[12] as has Beverly Gaventa in her recent

---

10. Barton, *Spirituality*, pp. 71-74.

11. Barton, *Spirituality*, pp. 74-104.

12. S. Walton, 'The Acts—of God? What is the "Acts of the Apostles" All About?', *EvQ* 80 (2008), pp. 291-306; *idem*, 'Acts, Book of', in K.J. Vanhoozer, C.G. Bartholomew, D.J. Treier and N.T. Wright (eds.), *Dictionary for Theological Interpretation of the Bible* (London: SPCK; Grand Rapids: Baker Academic, 2005), pp. 27-31.

commentary.[13] The movement of the story is focused on what God does, but the means and agents used by God to accomplish the divine purpose are many and varied.

First, *angelic beings* are key elements at certain points in the story. Angels are divine agents who appear at key points in biblical narrative, mainly to deliver messages to people;[14] they also possess power to effect dramatic events.[15] The angels of Acts function in line with these precedents: Philip is sent to the desert road by an angel (8.26); Cornelius sees an angelic visitor as he prays who directs him to send for Peter (10.3-6); Paul receives angelic reassurance as he is in the midst of the storm at sea (27.23-24). In terms of dramatic events, Peter is twice freed from prison by angelic intervention (5.19; 12.7-11).

Secondly, as has been widely discussed, *the Spirit* is a key divine agent. As Turner has argued, the Spirit in Acts acts in ways characteristic of the 'Spirit of prophecy' in earlier biblical and Jewish writings. The Spirit, on this view, functions as the organ of communication between God and humans, summed up in five prototypical gifts: revelatory visions and dreams; revelatory instruction or guidance; charismatic wisdom or discernment; charismatic praise; and charismatic preaching or teaching.[16] Each of these is a means of divine communication and engagement with humans. Thus, 1.8, widely seen as programmatic for Acts,[17] characterizes the Spirit as bringing power for witness: through the Spirit's enabling, the divinely appointed witnesses (principally the Twelve, especially Peter, but

13. B.R. Gaventa, *Acts* (ANTC; Nashville: Abingdon Press, 2003), *passim*, but see especially pp. 27-39; see also *eadem*, 'Acts of the Apostles', in K.D. Sakenfeld (ed.), *New Interpreter's Dictionary of the Bible* (5 vols.; Nashville: Abingdon Press, 2006), I, pp. 33-47.

14. For example, to Abraham and Lot (Gen. 18–19); Gideon (Judg. 6); Balaam (Num. 22); Elijah (1 Kgs 19); Zechariah (*passim*).

15. For example, in the exodus (Exod. 14.19; 23.20), and the siege of Jerusalem (2 Kgs 19.35; Isa. 37.36).

16. M. Turner, 'The "Spirit of Prophecy" as the Power of Israel's Restoration and Witness', in I.H. Marshall and D. Peterson (eds.), *Witness to the Gospel: The Theology of Acts* (Grand Rapids: Eerdmans, 1998), pp. 327-48 (334); more fully, see M. Turner, *Power from on High: The Spirit in Israel's Restoration and Witness in Luke–Acts* (JPTSup, 9; Sheffield: Sheffield Academic Press, 1996), pp. 92-101. In addition, Turner argues (against R.P. Menzies, *Empowered for Witness: The Spirit in Luke–Acts* [JPTSup, 6; Sheffield: Sheffield Academic Press, 1994]) that the Spirit is the author of conversion to the new messianic faith, and of deeds of power.

17. E.g. L.T. Johnson, *The Acts of the Apostles* (SP, 5; Collegeville: Liturgical Press, 1992), pp. 10-11; R.I. Pervo, *Acts* (Hermeneia; Minneapolis: Fortress Press, 2009), pp. 43-44.

also Stephen, Philip and Paul)[18] declare the marvellous deeds of God. Further, the geographical development enumerated in 1.8 (ἔν τε 'Ιερουσαλὴμ καὶ ἐν πάσῃ τῇ 'Ιουδαίᾳ καὶ Σαμαρείᾳ καὶ ἕως ἐσχάτου τῆς γῆς, 'in Jerusalem, and in all Judaea and Samaria, and to the end of the earth') suggests that the Spirit will guide the expansion of the witness.

Such guidance can be amply illustrated in the rest of the book. Philip, having been sent to the desert road by an angel (8.26), is told by the Spirit to go up to the ἄρμα ('ox-cart')[19] of the Ethiopian eunuch (8.29). The Spirit then whisks him away at the end of the encounter (8.39), after the manner of Ezekiel's transportation by the Spirit (Ezek. 3.12, 14; 8.3; 11.1, 24; 37.1; 43.5), and he continues his evangelistic ministry in Azotus and in the towns *en route* to Caesarea (8.40).

Similarly, Peter hears the voice of the Spirit telling him to go down from the roof in Joppa and to go with Cornelius' envoys, who are arriving (10.19-20). To the suspicious circumcised believers in Jerusalem, Peter cites both this experience (11.12) and the Spirit having fallen on Cornelius' household leading to tongues-speech (11.15-16, echoing 10.44-47) as evidence that God had led him. Thus, prior activity by the Spirit in bringing Peter to Cornelius, and the Spirit's intervention in their meeting, provide guidance that God is acting to bring uncircumcised people into the believing community. Peter confronts the Jerusalem 'council' with the same evidence (15.8)—a testimony which cannot be gainsaid.

Agabus the prophet is a figure who twice appears in the book. At his first mention he gives warning διὰ τοῦ πνεύματος ('through the Spirit') of a famine to come (11.27-28). On his second appearance, he again warns about the future: Paul will be tied up and handed over to the Gentiles (21.11), and this saying is attributed directly to the Holy Spirit— τάδε λέγει τὸ πνεῦμα τὸ ἅγιον ('Thus says the Holy Spirit')—after the manner of Old Testament prophets.[20]

---

18.   P. Bolt, 'Mission and Witness', in Marshall and Peterson (eds.). *Witness to the Gospel*, pp. 191-214, argues cogently that the vocabulary of witness is limited to these people in Acts and not used for the church's role more widely.

19.   Usually translated 'chariot', but this misleadingly suggests a military form of transport, whereas the eunuch is a civilian official who would have ridden in a flat-bed cart most probably pulled by oxen; so also C.K. Barrett, *A Critical and Exegetical Commentary on the Acts of the Apostles* (ICC; 2 vols.; Edinburgh: T. & T. Clark, 1994, 1998), I, pp. 426-27; F.F. Bruce, *The Acts of the Apostles* (Leicester: Apollos, 3rd edn, 1990), p. 226.

20.   Cf. the frequent use of τάδε λέγει, 'thus says', in the LXX (over 300 uses) when Yahweh or his spokesperson is the speaker; e.g. Exod. 4.22; 5.1; 7.17; 8.1, 20 (and often on the lips of Moses); 1 Kgs 11.31; 12.24; 13.21; 17.14; Amos 1.9, 11, 13, etc.; Obad. 1; Nah. 1.12; Hag. 1.2, etc.; Zech. 1.3, 14, 16, etc.; Isa. 1.24; 3.16, etc.; Jer. 2.2, 5, etc.; Ezek. 2.4; 3.11, etc.

The clarity of the formula 'Thus says the Holy Spirit' in 21.11 suggests that the means of the Spirit speaking in 13.2 is also by an individual inspired to speak by the Spirit. εἶπεν τὸ πνεῦμα τὸ ἅγιον ('the Holy Spirit said') is probably shorthand for a process by which an individual spoke words which the community recognized as being the voice of the Spirit to them, akin to the process of 'weighing' described by Paul in 1 Cor. 14.29.[21] Gaventa observes that this occasion is unique in being the only time in Acts that the Spirit directly gives a command to a *church*, rather than an individual.[22] (Further guiding interventions of the Spirit relate specifically to Paul's mission.)

A third form of God's intervention in the story of Acts is through *visions and dreams*. Having programmatically set the coming of the Spirit in the age in which 'your young men shall see visions and your old men shall dream dreams' (2.17, quoting Joel 3.1 LXX [EVV 2.28]), Luke portrays examples of these as a means by which God speaks. Thus, Ananias is told by God in a vision to go to see Saul (9.10, 12), Cornelius sees an angel ἐν ὁράματι φανερῶς ('in a vision distinctly', 10.3), mirrored by Peter experiencing a vision on the rooftop in Joppa (10.17), and Paul's noctural vision at Troas (16.9).[23] All of these passages portray visions as bringing guidance from God.[24]

Pilch has recently considered such examples and argues that they are the tip of a large iceberg of what he calls 'altered states of consciousness' (ASCs), in which humans enter into 'alternate reality' where God is.[25] He cites Acts 1.9 (Jesus' departure), 7.55-56 (Stephen's vision of Jesus), 9.3-4 (Saul's Damascus road experience), 10.10 (Peter's vision in Joppa), and 10.30 (Cornelius' visitation by an angel) as initial examples of the phenomena he identifies. He suggests that there are four areas of human experience which are engaged by ASCs: healing, divination,

21. So also J.D.G. Dunn, *The Acts of the Apostles* (Epworth Commentaries; London: Epworth, 1996), p. 173.

22. Gaventa, *Acts*, p. 190.

23. Luke's choice of a passive construction, ὅραμα διὰ τῆς νυκτὸς τῷ Παύλῳ ὤφθη ('a dream during the night was seen by Paul'), suggests this may be a 'divine passive' denoting that the vision came from God. BDAG, p. 719, ὁράω §A.1.c, and Barrett, *Acts*, II, p. 771, see the passive with dative as meaning 'appeared to', but this view is still compatible with seeing the passive as 'divine'.

24. See now the judicious discussion of the role of dreams in divine guidance in Luke–Acts in J.B.F. Miller, *Convinced that God Had Called Us: Dreams, Visions, and the Perception of God's Will in Luke–Acts* (BibInt, 85; Leiden: Brill, 2007).

25. J.J. Pilch, *Visions and Healing in the Acts of the Apostles: How the Early Believers Experienced God* (Collegeville: Liturgical Press, 2004); see my review in *Review of Biblical Literature* [http://www.bookreviews.org] (2005) at: <http://www. bookreviews.org/BookDetail.asp?TitleId=4334> (accessed August 2010).

metamorphosis ('the blurring of boundaries between the human world and the realm of God'[26]), and sky/spirit journeys. His guiding light (if I may use that phrase in this context!) is Dr Felicitas Goodman, founder of the Cuymungue Institute. She has done extensive work since the 1970s on people's experience of entering 'alternate reality' today.

As Pilch's book progresses, the appeal to 'trance' and 'altered states of consciousness' is frequent. Pilch regularly asserts that these would be taken as normal features of the culture of the Mediterranean world in the first century C.E. Thus, he suggests that the use of the verb ἀτενίζω, usually rendered as 'look intently at' or something similar, should be seen as highlighting a person going into a state of trance, since intently focused attention on a particular thing or person is one means of entering into such a state.[27] This appears to be running beyond the evidence, however, and it seems that Pilch's recognition of some phenomena described in Acts which appear, *prima facie*, to have parallels in 'altered states of consciousness' has led him to use this erroneously—or at least, over-optimistically—as a global explanation of many other phenomena in Acts.

Pilch utilizes Goodman's work without apparently realizing that there may be problems in using research on twentieth-century people and treating the phenomena they experience as the same as those recorded in an ancient text. Further, 'trance' is invoked as something of a 'catch-all' category which is imprecise and unclear, as is 'altered state of consciousness' (especially since Pilch is generally not at all clear *which* altered state of consciousness is being entered into by the biblical characters in each case).

At the end of his discussions, it is not clear how Pilch's work moves our understanding on. He claims that experiences described in Acts exhibit the same kind of phenomena as, and occur in similar situations to, ASCs today. But what does this add to Luke's own explanation that the creator God has invaded his universe in person in Christ and by the Spirit, and makes himself known by touching people's lives in healing, deliverance from evil spirits and the like?

In sum, Pilch's book is something of a curate's egg:[28] there are some insights into individual passages and issues which allow us to consider

---

26. Pilch, *Visions*, p. 4.

27. E.g. Pilch, *Visions*, pp. 40-41, discussing Acts 3.4.

28. A phrase originating in the cartoon 'True Humility' in *Punch*, 9 Nov 1895, picturing a rather timid curate having breakfast with a bishop. The bishop says, 'I'm afraid you've got a bad egg, Mr Jones'. The curate responds, 'Oh, no, my Lord, I assure you that parts of it are excellent!' See <http://www.punchcartoons.com/p338/Cartoon:-True-Humility---Conversation-regarding-bad-eggs./product_info.html>, accessed August 2010.

the mechanisms by which (accepting Luke's perspective) God acted. However, Pilch falls into a number of traps along the way of his argument, and thus his book is frustratingly unsuitable both for a scholarly audience (for it is not argued rigorously enough) and for its intended 'popular' audience (for it misleads so much).

A fourth means of encountering God is *the interpretation of Scripture in the light of the life, death and resurrection of Jesus and the coming of the Spirit*—the phenomenon characterized as 'This is that' interpretation of Scripture (cf. 2.16 KJV). This interpretation frequently occurs in addresses by the key witnesses to the events, and leads to response. Thus Peter explains and interprets these recent events through the lens of Scripture in his Pentecost address, focusing on Joel 3.1-5 LXX (EVV 2.28-32) and Pss. 15.8-11 LXX (EVV 16.8-11); 132.11 and 109.1 LXX (EVV 110.1), and the crowd responds by asking in distress what they must do (2.37).

The voice of Scripture is treated as the voice of God regularly: for example, in 1.16 the Holy Spirit foretold the action of Judas in leading the arrest party to Jesus and now leads the community to replace him (1.20 citing Pss. 69.26 LXX [EVV v. 25]; 109.8); and in 4.25-27 the Holy Spirit inspired David to speak of the opposition to the anointed one (Ps. 2.1-2), and this understanding informs the community's prayers when Peter and John are told not to speak further in the name of Jesus. The theme of Scripture providing God's interpretation of the events taking place now is echoed at the end of Acts, too, for in the final scene of the book (28.25-27) Paul cites Scripture (here Isa. 6.9-10) as something which the Holy Spirit said concerning the limited response among the Jewish people of Rome to the gospel message, an interpretation which leads to the conclusion that the message is to be offered to the Gentiles (28.20).

The theme of Scripture as God's voice links to the wider theme of *the word of God/the Lord* in Acts, which denotes the gospel message, a message which transforms people. The expression 'the word [of the Lord/God]' is found widely in Acts and regularly achieves powerful effects, notably in the summaries of 6.7; 12.24; 13.49, where it almost appears to be hypostatized.[29] Thus the preaching of the witnesses is a major means by which people encounter God, for in that preaching the saving events of Jesus are recounted in order to invite people into the believing community.

Finally, *the name of Jesus* functions powerfully as a divine agent: it is the means of healing (3.6, 16; 4.10), signs and wonders (4.30; 8.12), forgiveness (10.43), deliverance from demonic power (16.18) and salvation

---

29. See the helpful discussion in D.W. Pao, *Acts and the Isaianic New Exodus* (BSL; Grand Rapids: Baker Academic, 2002), pp. 147-80.

(4.12). Thus people are baptised into the name of Jesus (2.38; 8.12, 16; 10.48; 19.5; 22.16),[30] a characteristic which may suggest the invocation of the name of Jesus over them leading to the people becoming the possessions of Jesus.[31]

b. *The Human Response*

What forms does the human response to God's initiative take and, especially, how do people engage with God? There is a sense in which this could be answered by an analysis of all the activities of the believers in Acts, but we are seeking here to look for ways they encounter God, rather than (for example) their evangelism or social care, which are focused on other people. This is not to deny that the earliest Christians had a passion to respond to God by taking the message to others and providing for those in need; it is simply to explain the focus of our investigation.

One feature which merits attention immediately is to note *how slow and partial the believers' response to God was*: in a number of significant cases they did not grasp what God wanted quickly at all. A major example is the admission of Gentiles to the believing communities. Luke presents events as masterminded by God, sometimes against the direction the believers themselves might have gone.

Thus Acts 8 presents Philip going to Samaria, a community long alienated from the Jews, and drawing many to faith in Jesus (v. 12)—but this happens because of the deeds of power performed by God (vv. 6-8). ἐν τῷ ἀκούειν αὐτοὺς καὶ βλέπειν τὰ σημεῖα ἃ ἐποίει ('when they heard and saw the signs which he did', v. 6) is causal, expressing the reason for the statement in v. 6a, προσεῖχον δὲ οἱ ὄχλοι τοῖς λεγομένοις ὑπὸ τοῦ Φιλίππου ('the crowds listened eagerly to the things said by Philip'); γάρ in v. 7 indicates the grounds for the statement in v. 6 that the crowds listened eagerly, and v. 8 expresses the result as 'joy', a characteristic Lukan response to God.[32]

---

30. Different prepositions are used (ἐπί, εἰς, ἐν), but with no discernible difference in meaning. See further discussion in L. Hartman, *'Into the Name of the Lord Jesus': Baptism in the Early Church* (SNTW; Edinburgh: T. & T. Clark, 1997), pp. 37-50, 142-45; E. Ferguson, *Baptism in the Early Church: History, Theology, and Liturgy in the First Five Centuries* (Grand Rapids: Eerdmans, 2009), pp. 182-83; J.A. Ziesler, 'The Name of Jesus in the Acts of the Apostles', *JSNT* 4 (1974), pp. 28-41 (29-32).

31. Originally argued by W. Heitmüller, *"Im Namen Jesu". Eine sprach.- u. religionsgeschichtliche Untersuchung zum Neuen Testament, speziell zur altchristlichen Taufe* (FRLANT, I/2; Göttingen: Vandenhoeck & Ruprecht, 1903); although see criticisms in Hartman, *Name*, pp. 39-44.

32. With Barton, *Spirituality*, p. 77; W.G. Morrice, *Joy in the New Testament* (Exeter: Paternoster, 1984), pp. 74, 96-99.

Philip is then sent at God's behest to the desert road to meet another man who is at most a 'fringe' member of the Jewish community (8.26), for as a eunuch he is not permitted to take a full part in temple worship (Deut. 23.1; cf. Josephus, *Ant.* 4.290-91; Philo *Spec. Leg.* 1.324-25). However, this man's baptism has no impact on the continuing story and, interestingly, is not referred to when Luke presents later debates about the admission of Gentiles.

The breakthrough which Luke presents as impacting the development of the Gentile mission most is the conversion of Cornelius and his household. The significance of the story for Luke can be seen from his threefold repetition of it.[33] This is a story of God's purposes being carried out against the initial resistance of the believing community: Peter both argues with God about the vision of the sheet (10.14) and is puzzled by the vision (10.17, 19), and the Judaean believers criticize Peter for sharing table fellowship with Gentiles (11.2-3). The argument rumbles on, in spite of the conclusion of 11.18, as some believers claim that circumcision is necessary for salvation (15.1-2, 5). Finally, from Luke's perspective, the conditions of Gentile participation in the believing community are resolved by the decision of the Jerusalem meeting (15.13-29).

Luke's realistic portrayal of the slowness of religious people to change— realistic at least to those of us involved in churches today!—highlights that Acts presents no portrayal of an unhindered progress of the gospel message from Jerusalem to Rome, but rather that it presents the believers, warts and all, in their engagement with and response to God.

In terms of the major features of response to God's initiative, 2.42-47 has often been proposed as 'programmatic' for the life of the believers, containing features of the life of the post-Pentecost community in their response to the new event of the Spirit's coming: the apostles' teaching, the fellowship, the breaking of bread, the prayers (all v. 42), fear (v. 43), sharing of goods (vv. 44-45), participation in the temple and shared meals (v. 46), and praise of God (v. 47)—all of which resulted in numerical growth (v. 47b). Many of these features can be 'mapped' as features of the believers in the remainder of Acts (and we shall go on to do so), but the one which can be underemphasized is that the response portrayed is *corporate* rather than individual. All of the activities described in 2.42-47 are activities of a *community*, and the verbs are consistently plurals. Thus, to consider another verse widely seen as programmatic for Acts, it is a mistake to see 2.38 alone as mapping the nature of the

33. 10.1-48; 11.4-17; 15.7-11. See the helpful discussion of R.D. Witherup, SS, 'Cornelius Over and Over and Over Again: "Functional Redundancy" in the Acts of the Apostles', *JSNT* 49 (1993), pp. 45-66.

response required to the gospel message, in listing repentance and water
baptism as leading to forgiveness and the gift of the Spirit. Acts 2.39
needs to be included as programmatic, too, for it speaks of a communal
response to the new event of the universal gift of the Spirit to believers:
the new move includes 'you and your children and those who are far off'.
As we consider some of the major features of 2.42-47, we shall highlight
this corporate perspective.

The apostles' teaching (2.42) is presented as response to what God has
done in the life, death and resurrection of Jesus and the gift of the Spirit.
More specifically still, when God intervenes in evangelistic contexts to
heal, for example, the evangelists' response is to speak of these central
events: for example, Peter does this following the healing of the man at
the Beautiful Gate (3.12-26). This feature is part of the wider themes in
Acts of witness and the word of God/the Lord; the believers' response to
God's activity among not-yet-believers is to testify about Jesus and to
invite them to become believers and to join (or to form) the community
of believers in that place.

The 'fellowship' (2.42) is by its nature corporate, of course. In its
setting, this phrase seems to point particularly to the sharing of goods
described in vv. 44-45; the sharing of goods is an expression of the
sharing of lives which have been brought together by God's action in
Jesus and through the Spirit.[34] This theme runs on through Acts and does
not die out in Jerusalem, as some have suggested. The response of the
Antiochene believers to God's word through Agabus concerning a forthcoming famine is to give as they are able (11.28-30); Lydia's response to
the gospel is to offer hospitality to Paul and Silas (16.15); and the
Philippian jailer's coming to faith issues in hospitality and practical care
(16.33-34).[35]

'The breaking of bread' (2.42)—again, a clearly corporate activity—
is an ambiguous phrase: should we understand it to be specifically
eucharistic? It is an activity which occurs a number of times in Luke–Acts
(Lk. 22.19; 24.30, 35; Acts 20.7, 11; 27.35), and sometimes in a meal
setting (Lk. 24.30 and probably Acts 27.35, where it is unlikely to be
eucharistic because of the pagan setting). However, the first use of the
phrase in Lk. 22.19, in the setting of the inauguration of the eucharist,
combined with the precise wording τῇ κλάσει τοῦ ἄρτου from Lk. 24.35
being echoed in Acts 2.42, suggests that the mere mention of 'the breaking of bread' with the definite article τῇ in Acts 2.42 is likely to be
a specific thing. The use of the infinitive κλάσαι in 20.7 expressing

---

34. See the useful brief discussion in Green, 'Repentance', pp. 14-16.
35. See also 18.3; 20.33-35; 28.1-2, 7-10.

purpose—the believers met *in order to* break bread—suggests again that a specific act is meant here, rather than simply a shared meal. This is not to deny that shared meals were important to the earliest Christians, but it is to suggest that a shared eucharist in more and less formal settings was a feature of their life together in responding to God's action in giving the Spirit as a result of the work of Jesus.

'*The prayers*' (2.42) connects with a number of issues in Acts' spirituality. Prayer—that is, addressing God in various ways (praise, petition, confession, intercession, etc.)—is clearly central to our theme of the spirituality of Acts, and it is widely recognized that it represents a Lukan emphasis.[36] It is notable how frequent and pervasive Acts' emphasis on the believers' praying is, by contrast with Luke's Gospel, where the disciples are taught how to pray (Lk. 11.1-13) and told to pray (Lk. 22.40), but are never portrayed as actually praying (in the garden they even fall asleep while Jesus prays, Luke 22.45-46). The death and resurrection of Jesus and the coming of the Spirit transform the disciples into pray-ers in a way not previously highlighted by Luke.

The language of prayer is widely used in Acts,[37] but the plural articular use of the noun form ταῖς προσευχαῖς in 2.42, uniquely in the book,[38] suggests that *specific* prayers are being denoted.[39] The cotext, which highlights the community's participation in the temple (2.46) and Peter and John entering the temple precisely ἐπὶ τὴν ὥραν τῆς προσευχῆς τὴν ἐνάτην ('at the hour of prayer, the ninth [hour]', 3.1), strongly suggests that at least the temple prayers are being referred to in 2.42, perhaps with the community's own additional prayers (which would reflect their faith in Jesus as Messiah and be addressed to him, presumably).[40]

---

36. E.g. P.T. O'Brien, 'Prayer in Luke–Acts', *TynBul* 24 (1973), pp. 111-27; A.A. Trites, 'The Prayer Motif in Luke–Acts', in C.H. Talbert (ed.), *Perspectives on Luke–Acts* (Edinburgh: T. & T. Clark, 1978), pp. 168-86; D. Crump, *Jesus the Intercessor: Prayer and Christology in Luke–Acts* (WUNT, II/49; Tübingen: Mohr Siebeck, 1992); S.F. Plymale, *The Prayer Texts of Luke–Acts* (American University Studies: Series VII: Theology & Religion, 118; New York: Peter Lang, 1991); J.B. Green, 'Persevering Together in Prayer: The Significance of Prayer in the Acts of the Apostles', in R.N. Longenecker (ed.), *Into God's Presence: Prayer in the New Testament* (McMaster New Testament Studies; Grand Rapids: Eerdmans, 2001), pp. 183-202.

37. The προσευχή word group occurs 25 times in Acts and 47 times in Luke–Acts, from a total of 113 New Testament uses.

38. 10.4 is the only other use of the noun in the plural, but this is in reference to Cornelius' prayers: αἱ προσευχαί σου. The denotation may be the same as we argue below for 2.42, that is, a reference to specific corporate regular prayers.

39. With Dunn, *Acts*, p. 35.

40. Cf. Green, 'Persevering', pp. 186-88.

We may also notice how frequently the response to divine intervention is to pray[41]—and normally in a corporate context. Thus, 1.14 shows the community at prayer prior to Pentecost as they wait for the Father's promise as instructed during an appearance of the risen Jesus (1.4), and they pray particularly for God's guidance in choosing a replacement for Judas (1.24). The language is strong here, for Luke writes οὗτοι πάντες ἦσαν προσκαρτεροῦντες ὁμοθυμαδὸν τῇ προσευχῇ ('these all were devoting themselves with one heart[42] to prayer'). Further, when people are commissioned for particular tasks by the community in response to the call of God, prayer is a normal part of this process, notably in 13.3 (where the call itself comes as the body prays, 13.2). More broadly, when people are appointed, prayer is a key feature of their commissioning (6.6; 14.23).

Individual prayer is less common in Acts, but it is found. Saul is praying alone following his encounter with the exalted Jesus on the Damascus road (9.11). Peter sends others out of the room when he prays for Tabitha (9.40), although Luke does not explain why.[43] Peter is praying alone on the roof in Joppa when he sees the vision of the sheet coming down from heaven (10.4). Lest we think of prayer in terms from our day, we should remind ourselves that prayer, like reading, was spoken aloud in the ancient world—our concept of 'silent prayer' appears not to exist in ancient Judaism.[44]

Developing our consideration of prayer, we may also note that as well as prayer being a response to divine intervention, it is also found as the context for divine intervention. For example, Cornelius and Peter are both praying when they receive messages from divine agents (an angel, a vision) which bring them together (10.2, 4, 9; 11.5), and we have already observed that God's call to Barnabas and Saul comes as the group is praying (13.2). Thus, as Green graphically expresses it, it is as believers pray that they 'get in sync with and participate in what God is doing'.[45]

41.   Also noted in the rather brief treatment in O. Cullmann, *Prayer in the New Testament* (London: SCM Press, 1995), pp. 112-13.

42.   For this translation, see S. Walton, "Ὁμοθυμαδόν in Acts: Co-location, Common Action or "Of One Heart and Mind"?', in P.J. Williams, A.D. Clarke, P.M. Head, and D. Instone-Brewer (eds.), *The New Testament in its First Century Setting: Essays on Context and Background in Honour of B.W. Winter on His 65th Birthday* (Grand Rapids: Eerdmans, 2004), pp. 89-105 (101).

43.   J. Jervell, *Die Apostelgeschichte* (KEK; Göttingen: Vandenhoeck & Ruprecht, 17th edn, 1998), p. 297, notes parallels in 2 Kgs 4.33 and Mk 5.40, although in Mark (and Lk. 8.51-53) Jesus is not *alone* with the dead body, for the child's parents and some of his disciples are there too.

44.   G.D. Fee, *God's Empowering Presence: The Holy Spirit in the Letters of Paul* (Peabody, MA: Hendrickson, 1994), pp. 579-81.

45.   Green, 'Persevering', p. 194.

Prayer is also a significant response when the believers experience suffering or persecution. As an example we may highlight Acts 4. After Peter and John are forbidden by the Sanhedrin from speaking or teaching in the name of Jesus (v. 18) and are released, the response of the believing community is to pray (vv. 24-30). This prayer is strongly theocentric, focussing on God's power and authority as δέσποτα ('Master', v. 24), an address which leads to acknowledgment of God's creative power (v. 24) and his inspired word in the Scriptures (vv. 25-26, quoting Ps. 2.1-2 LXX). The reading of Scripture is then used to interpret the recent history of Jesus and (by implication) the believers' present experience as being under the sovereign control of God (vv. 27-28), and this forms the launch pad for their request that the Lord (now κύριε, v. 29) would 'pay attention' to their threats (rather than remove the threats, interestingly), empower the believers to speak, and continue to perform[46] signs and wonders by Jesus' name (vv. 29-30). Thus persecution is not treated as evidence that the believers are somehow 'getting it wrong'; rather, it is to be faced and endured with God's help.

The pair of persecution events in Acts 12 shows that some may die (James, v. 2) and some may be spared by divine intervention (Peter, vv. 3-17), but there is no suggestion that James died because the believers did not pray. The humorous touch of the believers' amazement when Peter appears at the gate of Mary's house (vv. 12-16)[47] suggests, rather than unbelief by the believers, that they are praying for Peter (thus v. 12b) and perhaps asking God for his release (for Peter has already been freed from prison previously, 5.17-20—interestingly, prayer is not mentioned in this setting), but with an openness concerning what God might do.

We noted earlier that 2.47 picks out praise as a particular kind of prayer which marked the life of the earliest community. Here the verb is αἰνέω, from a relatively rare word-group in the New Testament (eleven New Testament uses, of which seven are in Luke–Acts and three in Acts). The other Acts uses are 3.8, 9, both describing the response of the man at the Beautiful Gate to God healing him in Jesus' name. While this specific form of prayer is not mentioned frequently afterwards,[48] the programmatic role of other items from 2.42-47 suggests that Luke is leading us

46. ἐκτείνειν and γίνεσθαι are both present infinitives and thus suggest ongoing action—and God has already been acting in this way, not least in 3.1-10 in the healing of the man at the Beautiful Gate.

47. Note the helpful survey of humour in Acts in J. Goldingay, 'Are they Comic Acts?', *EvQ* 69 (1997), pp. 99-107, beginning with consideration of this incident.

48. Although note the extolling of God in tongues (μεγαλυνόντων τὸν θεόν, 10.46), and Paul's thanksgiving to God (εὐχαριστήσας τῷ θεῷ) in 28.15.

to expect this to be a typical response to God's activity in Jesus and by the Spirit.

Finally, *fear* is a feature of the early community in 2.43, and this can be traced as a reaction to God's intervention in other places. Three incidents stand out.[49] First, in response to the Ananias and Sapphire incident, people respond in fear (5.5, 11). Secondly, Luke summarizes the state of the churches of Judaea, Galilee and Samaria as πορευομένη τῷ φόβῳ τοῦ κυρίου ('walking in the fear of the Lord', 9.31), a usage which strongly echoes Old Testament use of the 'fear of the Lord'.[50] Thirdly, the response of the people of Ephesus to the incident with the sons of Sceva is to fear. The following phrase καὶ ἐμεγαλύνετο τὸ ὄνομα τοῦ κυρίου Ἰησοῦ ('and the name of the Lord Jesus was honoured', 19.17) suggests that the 'fear' has at least an element of respect for the power of the name of Jesus when it is invoked rightly.

As we have studied each of the elements of human response in 2.42-47, we have found patterns of echo and repetition in the rest of Acts which suggest that it is right to see this short section as programmatic for the book. Luke is portraying the life of the earliest community here in colours which will reappear throughout his story. Green rightly proposes that such repetition suggests that Luke's readers should be seeing models of the Christian response to God's actions, both in Jesus and more locally and recently, in these stories.[51] From a narrative-critical perspective, Luke is painting portraits of the earliest believers which invite his readers to identify with those believers and to live and respond to God in similar ways.

III. *Conclusion*

Miller writes, 'If it is important to notice that Luke–Acts is about God and the plan of God, it is equally important to notice that the story is also about God's people and their attempt, their struggle, to understand God's will'.[52] Miller's study of the role of dream-visions in Luke–Acts emphasizes the important role of human, believing interpretation in discerning God's will, and highlights a key overarching theme in the spirituality of

---

49. Excluding places where 'fear' is human fear of a situation or people, or used in reference to the so-called godfearers.

50. E.g. Pss. 34.11; 111.10; Prov. 1.7, 29; 2.5, which characterize the godly life as 'the fear of the Lord'. The one anointed by the Spirit in Isa. 11.2, 3 displays the fear of the Lord.

51. Green, 'Repentance', especially pp. 1-3.

52. Miller, *Convinced*, p. 242.

Acts: that is, that God does not reveal himself in a way that leaves no space for human engagement, interpretation and appropriate response. The Christian life, according to Acts, is a life of walking with God in company with others in response to God's initiative, but without always having a crystal-clear vision of God's purpose in a specific place or time beyond God's broad purpose to draw people to know him in Christ and by the Spirit.

Those of us who seek to live as Christian people today, following in the footsteps of our ancestors in the faith as described in Acts, find ourselves facing many of the same issues and questions. We have many of the same resources and forms of communication provided by God and need to continue to seek God's initiative in our own and our churches' lives. Alongside these 'means of grace', the need for human, believing engagement and discernment has not decreased—and Acts calls and invites believers today to continue that process.

BIBLIOGRAPHY

Abbott, H.P., *The Cambridge Introduction to Narrative* (Cambridge: Cambridge University Press, 2002).

Adler, N., *Das erste christliche Pfingstfest. Sinn und Bedeutung des Pfingstberichtes Apg 2,1-13* (Neutestamentliche Abhandlungen, 18,1; Münster: Aschendorff, 1938).

Aejmelaeus, L., *Die Rezeption der Paulusbriefe in der Miletrede (Apg 20.18-35)* (Helsinki: Finnische Exegetische Gesellschaft, 1987).

Aletti, J.-N., 'Esprit et témoignage dans le livre des Actes. Réflexions sur une énigme', in E. Steffek and Y. Bourquin (eds.), *Raconter, interpréter, annoncer. Mélanges D. Marguerat* (Le Monde de la Bible, 47; Geneva: Labor et Fides, 2003), pp. 225-38.

Alexander, L.C.A., *Acts* (People's Bible Commentary; Oxford: Bible Reading Fellowship, 2006).

—'Acts and Ancient Intellectual Biography', in Winter and Clarke (eds.), *The Book of Acts in Its Ancient Literary Setting*, pp. 31-63.

—*Acts in Its Ancient Literary Context: A Classicist Looks at the Acts of the Apostles* (LNTS, 298; London/New York: T&T Clark International, 2005).

—'Ancient Biography and the Social Function of Luke–Acts', *EvQ* 66 (1994), pp. 73-76 (repr.: *European Journal of Theology* 3.1 [1994], pp. 84-86).

—'Benefaction Gone Wrong: The "Sin" of Ananias and Sapphira in Context', in S.G. Wilson and M. Desjardins (eds.), *Text and Artifact in the Religions of Mediterranean Antiquity: Essays in Honour of Peter Richardson* (Studies in Christianity and Judaism, 9; Waterloo: Wilfrid Laurier University Press, 2000), pp. 91-110.

—'Fact, Fiction and the Genre of Acts', *NTS* 44.3 (1998), pp. 380-99.

—'Formal Elements and Genre: Which Greco-Roman Prologues Most Closely Parallel the Lukan Prologues?', in Moessner (ed.), *Jesus and the Heritage of Israel*, pp. 9-26.

—'God's Frozen Word: Canonicity and the Dilemma of Biblical Studies Today', *ExpTim* 117 (2009), pp. 237-42.

—'"In Journeyings Often": Voyaging in the Acts of the Apostles and in Greek', in *Acts in Its Ancient Literary Context*, pp. 69-96.

—'The Living Voice: Scepticism towards the Written Word in Early Christian and in Greco-Roman Texts', in D.J.A. Clines, S.E. Fowl and S.E. Porter (eds.), *The Bible in Three Dimensions* (JSOTSup, 87; Sheffield: JSOT Press, 1990), pp. 221-47.

—'Marathon or Jericho? Reading Acts in Dialogue with Biblical and Greek Historiography', in D.J.A. Clines and S.D. Moore (eds.), *Auguries: The Jubilee Volume of the Sheffield Department of Biblical Studies* (JSOTSup, 269; Sheffield: Sheffield Academic Press, 1998), pp. 92-125.

—'The Passions in Galen, Chariton and Xenophon', in J.T. Fitzgerald (ed.), *Passions and Moral Progress in Greco-Roman Thought* (New York: Routledge, 2008), pp. 175-98.

—'The Preface to Acts and the Historians', in Witherington III (ed.), *History, Literature, and Society in the Book of Acts*, pp. 73-103.

—*The Preface to Luke's Gospel: Literary Convention and Social Context in Luke 1:1-4 and Acts 1:1* (SNTSMS, 78; Cambridge: Cambridge University Press, 1993).

—'"This is That": The Authority of Scripture in the Acts of the Apostles', *Princeton Seminary Bulletin* 25 (2004), pp. 189-204.

—'What If Luke Had Never Met Theophilus?', *BibInt* 8 (2000), pp. 161-70.

Anderson, K., *'But God Raised Him from the Dead': The Theology of Jesus' Resurrection in Luke–Acts* (PBM; Milton Keynes: Paternoster Press, 2006).

Annand, R., 'Papias and the Four Gospels', *SJT* 9 (1956), pp. 46-62.

Aristotle, *Poetics* (ed. Stephen Halliwell; LCL, 199; Cambridge, MA: Harvard University Press, 1995).

Athanassakis, A.N., *The Homeric Hymns: Translation, Introduction, and Notes* (Baltimore: The Johns Hopkins University Press, 1976).

Aune, D.J., *The New Testament in Its Literary Environment* (Philadelphia: Westminster Press, 1987).

Baily, M., 'The Shepherds and the Sign of a Child', *ITQ* 31 (1964), pp. 1-23.

Balch, D.L., 'ΜΕΤΑΒΟΛΗ ΠΟΛΙΤΕΙΩΝ—Jesus as Founder of the Church in Luke–Acts: Form and Function', in Penner and Vander Stichele (eds.), *Contextualizing Acts*, pp. 137-86.

Barasch, M., *Giotto and the Language of Gesture* (New York: Cambridge University Press, 1987).

Barnett, P.W., 'Apostle', in Hawthorne and Martin (eds.), *Dictionary of Paul and His Letters*, pp. 45-51.

Barr, D.L., and Judith L. Wentling, 'The Conventions of Classical Biography and the Genre of Luke Acts: A Preliminary Study', in C.H. Talbert (ed.), *Luke–Acts: New Perspectives from the Society of Biblical Literature Seminar* (New York: Crossroad, 1984), pp. 63-88.

Barrett, C.K., *A Critical and Exegetical Commentary on the Acts of the Apostles* (ICC; 2 vols.; Edinburgh: T. & T. Clark, 1994, 1998).

—*Luke the Historian in Recent Study* (London: Epworth, 1961).

—'The Third Gospel as a Preface to Acts? Some Reflections', in F. Van Segbroek *et al.* (eds.), *The Four Gospels 1992: Festschrift Frans Neirynck* (BETL; 3 vols.; Leuven: Leuven University Press, 1991), II, pp. 1451-66.

Bartchy, S.S., 'Community of Goods in Acts: Idealization or Social Reality?', in B.A. Pearson (ed.), *The Future of Early Christianity: Essays in Honor of Helmut Koester* (Minneapolis: Fortress Press, 1991), pp. 315-18.

Bartlet, J.V., 'Papias' "Exposition": Its Date and Contents', in H.G. Wood (ed.), *Amicitiae Corolla* (London: University of London Press, 1933), pp. 15-44.

Barton, Stephen C., 'Can We Identify the Gospel Audiences?', in Bauckham (ed.), *The Gospels for All Christians*, pp. 173-94.

—*The Spirituality of the Gospels* (London: SPCK, 1992).

Bauckham, R.J. (ed.), *The Gospels for All Christians: Rethinking the Gospel Audiences* (Grand Rapids: Eerdmans, 1998).

—'James and the Jerusalem Church', in R. Bauckham (ed.), *The Book of Acts in Its Palestinian Setting* (Grand Rapids: Eerdmans, 1995), pp. 415-80.

—*Jesus and the Eyewitnesses: The Gospels as Eyewitness Testimony* (Grand Rapids: Eerdmans, 2006).

Becker, U., 'Gospel', *NIDNTT*, II, pp. 107-15.

Bede, The Venerable, *Homilies on the Gospels* (2 vols.; Cistercian Studies Series, 110-111; Kalamazoo, MI: Cistercian, 1991).

Belfiore, E.S., *Tragic Pleasures: Aristotle on Plot and Emotion* (Princeton, NJ: Princeton University Press, 1992).

Berger, K., 'Almosen für Israel: Zum historischen Kontext der paulinischen Kollekte', *NTS* 23 (1976-77), pp. 180-204.

Betz, D., 'Apostle', in *ABD*, I, pp. 309-11.

Betz, H.D., *Galatians* (Hermeneia; Philadelphia: Fortress Press, 1979).

Billings, B.S., '"At the Age of 12": The Boy Jesus in the Temple (Luke 2:41-52), the Emperor Augustus, and the Social Setting of the Third Gospel,' *JTS* NS 60 (2009), pp. 70-89.

—*Do This in Remembrance of Me* (London: T&T Clark International, 2006).

Bird, M.F., 'The Unity of Luke–Acts in Recent Discussion', *JSNT* 29 (2007), pp. 425-48.

Bockmuehl, M., *Jewish Law in Gentile Churches* (Edinburgh: T. & T. Clark, 2000).

Bolt, P., 'Mission and Witness', in Marshall and Peterson (eds.), *Witness to the Gospel*, pp. 191-214.

Bovon, F., *Luc le théologien* (Le Monde de la Bible, 5; Geneva: Labor et Fides, 3rd edn, 2006).

Brown, G., and G. Yule, *Discourse Analysis* (Cambridge Textbooks in Linguistics; Cambridge: Cambridge University Press, 1983).

Brown, N.O., *Hermes the Thief* (New York: Norton, 1947).

Brown, R.E., *The Birth of the Messiah* (Anchor Bible Reference Library; New York: Doubleday, updated edn, 1993).

Bruce, F.F., *The Acts of the Apostles* (London: Tyndale, 1951).

—*The Acts of the Apostles* (Leicester: Apollos, 3rd edn, 1990).

—*Paul: Apostle of the Free Spirit* (Exeter: Paternoster Press, 1977).

Bryan, C., *Render to Caesar: Jesus, the Early Church, and the Roman Superpower* (Oxford/New York: Oxford University Press, 2005).

Buckwalter, H.D., *The Character and Purpose of Luke's Christology* (SNTSMS, 89; Cambridge: Cambridge University Press, 1996).

Bühner, J.A., 'ἀπόστολος', in *EDNT*, I, pp. 142-46.

Burke, E., *A Philosophical Inquiry into the Origin of the Ideas of the Sublime and Beautiful* (Oxford World's Classics; Oxford: Oxford University Press, 1990).

Burridge, R.A., 'About People, by People, for People: Gospel Genre and Audiences', in Bauckham (ed.), *The Gospels for All Christians*, pp. 113-45.

—*What Are The Gospels? A Comparison with Graeco-Roman Biography* (SNTSMS, 70; Grand Rapids: Eerdmans, 2nd edn, 2004).

—'Who Writes, Why and for Whom?', in D.A. Hagner and M. Bockmuehl (eds.), *The Written Gospel* (Cambridge: Cambridge University Press, 2005), pp. 99-115.

Cadbury, H.J., *The Making of Luke–Acts* (with a new introduction by Paul N. Anderson; Peabody, MA: Hendrickson, 2nd edn, 1958 [1st edn, 1927]).

Campbell, W.S., 'The Narrator as "He", "Me", and "We": Grammatical Person in Ancient Histories and in the Acts of the Apostles', *JBL* 129 (2010), pp. 385-407.

—*The 'We' Passages in the Acts of the Apostles: The Narrator as Narrative Character* (StBL, 14; Atlanta: Scholars Press, 2007).

Cannon-Brookes, P., 'Botticelli's Pentecost', *Apollo* 87 (1968), pp. 274-77.

Capper, B.J., '"In der Hand des Ananias…": Erwägungen zu 1 QS VI,20 und der urchristlichen Gütergemeinschaft', *RevQ* 12 (1986), pp. 223-36.

—'The Interpretation of Acts 5.4', *JSNT* 19 (1983), pp. 117-31.

Carpinelli, F.G., '"Do This as *My* Memorial" (Luke 22.19): Lucan Soteriology of Atonement', *CBQ* 61 (1999), pp. 74-91.

Carter, W., *Matthew and Empire: Initial Explorations* (Harrisburg, PA: Trinity Press International, 2001).

—*Matthew and the Margins: A Sociopolitical and Religious Reading* (Maryknoll, NY: Orbis Books, 2000).

—*The Roman Empire and the New Testament: An Essential Guide* (Nashville: Abingdon, 2006).

Chatman, S., *Story and Discourse: Narrative Structure in Fiction and Film* (Ithaca, NY: Cornell University Press, 1978).

Chen, D.G., *God as Father in Luke–Acts* (StBL, 92; New York: Peter Lang, 2006).

Chester, S.J., *Conversion at Corinth: Perspectives on Conversion in Paul's Theology and the Corinthian Church* (SNTW; London: T&T Clark International, 2003).

Chong-Gossard, J.H. Kim On, *Gender and Communication in Euripides' Plays: Between Song and Silence* (Boston: Brill, 2008).

Cohick, L.H., *Women in the World of the Earliest Christians* (Grand Rapids: Baker Academic, 2009).

Collins, A.Y., 'Genre and the Gospels', *JR* 75 (1995), pp. 239-46.

Conzelmann, H., *Acts of the Apostles* (Hermeneia; Philadelphia: Fortress Press, 1987).

—*Die Apostelgeschichte* (Tübingen: Mohr Siebeck, 1963).

—*Theology of St. Luke* (trans. Geoffrey Buswell; San Francisco: Harper & Row, 1960).

Le Cornu, H., with J. Shulam, *A Commentary on the Jewish Roots of Acts* (Jerusalem: Academon, 2003).

Crawford, T.G., 'The Promised Land: Luke's Use of Joshua as a Christian Foundation Story', *RevExp* 95 (1998), pp. 255-57.

Crook, Z.A., *Reconceptualizing Conversion: Patronage, Loyalty, and Conversion in the Religions of the Ancient Mediterranean* (BZNW, 130; Berlin: W. de Gruyter, 2004).

Crossan, J.D., and J.L. Reed, *In Search of Paul: How Jesus's Apostle Opposed* (San Francisco: HarperSanFrancisco, 2004).

Crump, D., *Jesus the Intercessor: Prayer and Christology in Luke–Acts* (WUNT II/49; Tübingen: Mohr Siebeck, 1992).

Cullmann, O., *Prayer in the New Testament* (London: SCM Press, 1995).

Cunningham, S., *'Through Many Tribulations': The Theology of Persecution in Luke–Acts* (JSNTSup, 142; Sheffield: Sheffield Academic Press, 1997).

Damasio, A., *Looking for Spinoza: Joy, Sorrow, and the Feeling Brain* (Orlando: Harcourt, 2003).

—*The Feeling of What Happens: Body and Emotion in the Making of Consciousness* (Orlando: Harcourt, 1999).

Daube, D., *The Sudden in the Scriptures* (Leiden: Brill, 1964).

De Selincout, B., *Giotto* (London: Duckworth, 1905).

Derrett, J.D.M., 'The Manger at Bethlehem: Light on St. Luke's Technique from Contemporary Jewish Religious Law', in his *Studies in the New Testament* (2 vols.; Leiden: Brill, 1978), II, pp. 39-47.

—'The Manger: Ritual Law and Soteriology', in his *Studies in the New Testament* (2 vols.; Leiden: Brill, 1978), II, pp. 48-53.

Dibelius, M., *Studies in the Acts of the Apostles* (London: SCM Press, 1956).

—*Studies in the Acts of the Apostles* (ed. K.C. Hanson; London: SCM Press, updated edn, 2004).

Donaldson, T.L., 'Israelite, Convert, Apostle to the Gentiles: The Origin of Paul's Gentile Mission', in Longenecker (ed.), *The Road from Damascus*, pp. 62-84.

—*Paul and the Gentiles: Remapping the Apostle's Convictional World* (Minneapolis: Fortress Press, 1997).

—'Zealot and Convert: The Origin of Paul's Christ-Torah Antithesis', *CBQ* 51 (1989), pp. 655-82.

Downing, G., Review of G. Sterling, *Self-Definition: Josephos, Luke–Acts and Apologetic Historiography*, and of R. Burridge, *What Are the Gospels? JTS* NS 44 (1993), pp. 238-40.

Downs, D.J., '"The Offering of the Gentiles" in Romans 15.16', *JSNT* 29 (2006), pp. 173-86.

Dunn, J.D.G., *The Acts of the Apostles* (Epworth Commentaries; London: Epworth, 1996).

—*Baptism in the Holy Spirit: A Re-Examination of the New Testament Teaching on the Gift of the Spirit in Relation to Pentecostalism Today* (London: SCM Press, 1970).

—*Beginning from Jerusalem* (Grand Rapids: Eerdmans, 2009).

—*The Epistle to the Galatians* (BNTC; London: A. & C. Black; Peabody, MA: Hendrickson, 1993).

—*Jesus and the Spirit: A Study of the Religious and Charismatic Experience of Jesus and the First Christians as Reflected in the New Testament* (London: SCM Press, 1975).

—*Jesus, Paul and the Law: Studies in Mark and Galatians* (Louisville, KY: Westminster/John Knox Press, 1990).

—*Jesus Remembered* (Grand Rapids: Eerdmans, 2003).

—*The New Perspective on Paul: Collected Essays* (WUNT, 185; Tübingen: Mohr Siebeck, 2005).

—*The Partings of the Ways Between Christianity and Judaism and Their Significance for the Character of Christianity* (London: SCM Press; Philadelphia: Trinity Press International, 1991).

—'Paul and Justification by Faith', in Longenecker (ed.), *The Road from Damascus*, pp. 85-101.

—Review of L.T. Johnson, *Religious Experience in Earliest Christianity*, *Anvil* 18 (2001), pp. 59-61.

—*The Theology of Paul the Apostle* (Grand Rapids: Eerdmans, 1998).

Edwards, M.J., 'Quoting Aratus: Acts 17,28', *ZNW* 83 (1992), pp. 266-69.

Ehrman, B.D., *The Orthodox Corruption of Scripture: The Effect of Early Christological Controversies on the Text of the New Testament* (New York: Oxford University Press, 1993), pp. 197-227.

Eisenbaum, P., *Paul Was Not a Christian: The Original Message of a Misunderstood Apostle* (New York: HarperCollins, 2009).

Elliott, M.A., *Faithful Feelings: Rethinking Emotion in the New Testament* (Grand Rapids: Kregel, 2006).

Farrar, F.W., *The Gospel According to St Luke* (Cambridge: Cambridge University Press, 1910).

Fee, G.D., *God's Empowering Presence: The Holy Spirit in the Letters of Paul* (Peabody, MA: Hendrickson, 1994).

Ferguson, E., *Baptism in the Early Church: History, Theology, and Liturgy in the First Five Centuries* (Grand Rapids/Cambridge: Eerdmans, 2009).

Fisher, P., *The Vehement Passions* (Princeton, NJ: Princeton University Press, 2002).

Fitzmyer, J.A., *The Acts of the Apostles* (AB, 31; New York: Doubleday, 1998).

—*The Gospel According to Luke* (AB, 28; 2 vols.; New York: Doubleday, 1981, 1985).

Fletcher, J., 'A Trickster's Oaths in The *Homeric Hymn to Hermes*', *American Journal of Philology* 129 (2008), pp. 19-46.

Fortenbaugh, W.W., *Aristotle on Emotion* (London: Duckworth, 2nd edn, 2002).

Fredriksen, P., 'Judaism, the Circumcision of Gentiles, and Apocalyptic Hope: Another Look at Galatians 1 and 2', *JTS* NS 42 (1991), pp. 532-64.

—'Judaizing the Nations: The Ritual Demands of Paul's Gospel', *NTS* 56 (2010), pp. 232-52.

—'Mandatory Retirement: Ideas in the Study of Christian Origins Whose Time Has Come to Go', *SR* 35.2 (2006), pp. 231-46.

—'Paul and Augustine: Conversion Narratives, Orthodox Traditions, and the Retrospective Self', *JTS* NS 37 (1986), pp. 3-34.

Frey, J., 'Paulus und die Apostel. Zur Entwicklung des paulinischen Apostelbegriffs und zum Verhältnis des Heidenapostels zu seinen "Kollegen"', in E.-M. Becker and P. Pilhofer (eds.), *Biographie und Persönlichkeit des Paulus* (WUNT, 187; Tübingen: Mohr, 2005), pp. 192-227.

Friesen, S.J., 'Satan's Throne, Imperial Cults and the Social Settings of Revelation', *JSNT* 27 (2005), pp. 351-73.

Gasque, W.W., *A History of the Criticism of the Acts of the Apostle* (Tübingen: Mohr, 1975).

Gaventa, B.R., *Acts* (ANTC; Nashville: Abingdon Press, 2003).

—'Acts of the Apostles', in *NIDB*, I, pp. 33-47.

—*From Darkness to Light: Aspects of Conversion in the New Testament* (OBT; Philadelphia: Fortress Press, 1986).

—'Galatians 1 and 2: Autobiography as Paradigm', *NovT* 28 (1986), pp. 309-26.

Georgi, D.,'God Turned Upside Down', in *Paul and Empire: Religion and Power in Roman Imperial Society* (Harrisburg, PA: Trinity Press International, 1997), pp. 148-57.

—*Remembering the Poor: The History of Paul's Collection for Jerusalem* (1965; ET; Nashville: Abingdon Press, 1992).

Gill, C., 'The Character–Personality Distinction', in Pelling (ed.), *Characterization and Individuality in Greek Literature*, pp. 1-31.

—'The Question of Character-Development: Plutarch and Tacitus', *CQ* 33 (1983), pp. 469-87.

Glöckner, R., *Die Verkündigung des Heils beim Evangelisten Lukas* (Mainz: Matthias-Grünewald-Verlag, 1975).

Goldingay, J., 'Are They Comic Acts?', *EvQ* 69 (1997), pp. 99-107.

Goold, G.P. (ed.), *Pindar I* (LCL; Cambridge, MA: Harvard University Press, 1997).

Gourgues, M., '"Exalté à la droite de Dieu" (Actes 2.33; 5.31)', *Science et Esprit* 27 (1975), pp. 303-27.

—'La Literatura Profana en el Discourse de Atenas (He 17,16-31): ¿Expedient Cerrado?', *Anámnesis* 13, no. 2 (2003), pp. 15-45.

Graver, M., *Cicero on the Emotions: Tusculan Disputations 3 and 4* (Chicago: University of Chicago Press, 2002).

Green, Joel B., 'Doing Repentance: The Formation of Disciples in the Acts of the Apostles', *Ex Auditu* 18 (2002), pp. 1-23.

—'Internal Repetition in Luke–Acts: Contemporary Narratology and Lucan Historiography', in Witherington III (ed.), *History, Literature, and Society in the Book of Acts*, pp. 283-99.

—'Neglecting Widows and Serving the Word? Acts 6:1-7 as a Test Case for a Missional Hermeneutic', in J. Laansma, G. Osborne and R. Van Neste (eds.), *Jesus Christ, Lord and Savior* (Carlisle: Paternoster Press; Eugene, OR: Wipf & Stock, in press).

—'Persevering Together in Prayer: The Significance of Prayer in the Acts of the Apostles', in R.N. Longenecker (ed.), *Into God's Presence: Prayer in the New Testament* (McMaster NT Studies; Grand Rapids: Eerdmans, 2001), pp. 183-202.

—'The Problem of a Beginning: Israel's Scriptures in Luke 1–2', *BBR* 4 (1994), pp. 61-85.

—Review of P. Walters, *The Assumed Authorial Unity of Luke and Acts: A Reassessment of the Evidence*, Review of Biblical Literature [http://www.bookreviews.org] (2009), http://www.bookreviews.org/pdf/7084_7695.pdf, accessed September 2010.

—*The Theology of Gospel of Luke* (New Testament Theology; Cambridge: Cambridge University Press, 1995).

Gregory, A., 'Looking for Luke in the Second Century: A Dialogue with François Bovon', in C.G. Bartholomew, J.B. Green and A.C. Thiselton (eds.), *Reading Luke: Interpretation, Reflection, Formation* (Scripture and Hermeneutics, 6; Grand Rapids: Zondervan, 2005), pp. 401-13.

—*The Reception of Luke and Acts in the Period before Irenaeus: Looking for Luke in the Second Century* (WUNT, II/169; Tübingen: Mohr Siebeck, 2003).

Gross, D.M., *The Secret History of Emotion: From Aristotle's Rhetoric to Modern Brain Science* (Chicago: University of Chicago Press, 2006).

Grube, G.M.A., 'Euripides and the Gods', in Erich Segal (ed.), *Euripides* (Englewood Cliffs, NJ: Prentice–Hall, 1968), pp. 34-50.

Guthrie, W.K.C., *The Greeks and Their Gods* (Boston: Beacon, 1950).

Güttgemanns, E., 'In welchen Sinne ist Lukas Historiker? Die Beziehung von Luk 1:1-4 und Papias zur antiken Rhetorik', *Linguistica Biblica* 54 (1983), pp. 9-26.

Gutwenger, E., 'Papias: Eine chronologische Studie', *ZKT* 69 (1947), pp. 385-416.

Haenchen, E., *The Acts of the Apostles* (trans. R. McL. Wilson; Oxford: Blackwell, 1971).

Haft, A., 'The Mercurial Significance of Raiding', *Arion* 4 (1996), pp. 27-48.

Hagene, S., *Zeiten der Wiederherstellung. Studien zur lukanischen Geschichtstheologie als Soteriologie* (Münster: Aschendorff, 2003).

Halliwell, S., 'Traditional Greek Conceptions of Character', in Pelling (ed.), *Characterization and Individuality in Greek Literature*, pp. 32-59.

Hartman, L., *'Into the Name of the Lord Jesus': Baptism in the Early Church* (SNTW; Edinburgh: T. & T. Clark, 1997).

Havelaar, H., 'Hellenistic Parallels to Acts 5.1-11 and the Problem of Conflicting Interpretations', *JSNT* 67 (1997), pp. 63-82.

Hawthorne, G.F., and R.P. Martin (eds.), *Dictionary of Paul and His Letters* (Downers Grove: InterVarsity Press, 1993).

Heitmüller, W., *"Im Namen Jesu". Eine sprach.- u. religionsgeschichtliche Untersuchung zum Neuen Testament, speziell zur altchristlichen Taufe* (FRLANT, I/2; Göttingen: Vandenhoeck & Ruprecht, 1903).

Hemer, C.J., *The Book of Acts in the Setting of Hellenistic History* (WUNT, 49; Tübingen: Mohr Siebeck, 1989).

Hengel, M., *Acts and the History of Earliest Christianity* (London: SCM Press, 1979).

—*The Pre-Christian Paul* (in collaboration with R. Deines; trans. J. Bowden; London: SCM Press; Philadelphia: Trinity Press International, 1991).

Hengel M., and A.M. Schwemer, *Paul Between Damascus and Antioch* (London: SCM Press, 1997).

Hill, C.E., 'What Papias Said about John [and Luke]: A "New" Papian Fragment', *JTS* NS 49 (1998), pp. 582-629.

Hine, D., *Works of Hesiod and the Homeric Hymns* (Chicago: University of Chicago Press, 2005).

Holl, K., 'Der Kirchenbegriff des Paulus in seinem Verhältnis zu dem der Urgemeinde', in *Gesammelte Aufsätze zur Kirchengeschichte* (3 vols.; Tübingen: J.C.B. Mohr, 1928), II, pp. 44-67.

Hornik, H., and M. Parsons, *Acts through the Centuries* (Blackwell Bible Commentary; Oxford: Blackwell, forthcoming).

Horsley, R.A., *Galilee: History, Politics, People* (Valley Forge, PA: Trinity Press International, 1995).

—*Jesus and Empire: The Kingdom of God and the New World Disorder* (Minneapolis: Fortress Press, 2003).

—(ed.), *Paul and Empire* (Harrisburg, PA: Trinity Press International, 1997).

—(ed.), *Paul and Politics* (Harrisburg, PA: Trinity Press International, 2000).

—(ed.), *Paul and the Roman Imperial Order* (Harrisburg, PA: Trinity Press International, 2004).

Howell, J., 'The Imperial Authority and Benefaction of Centurions and Acts 10.34-43', *JSNT* 31.1 (2008), pp. 25-51.

Hultgren, A.J., 'Paul's Pre-Christian Persecutions of the Church: Their Purpose, Locale, and Nature', *JBL* 95 (1976), pp. 97-111.

Hurtado, L.W., 'Convert, Apostate or Apostle to the Nations: The "Conversion" of Paul in Recent Scholarship', *SR* 22 (1993), pp. 273-84.

—*Lord Jesus Christ: Devotion to Jesus in Earliest Christianity* (Grand Rapids/Cambridge: Eerdmans, 2003).

Jeffrey, D.L. (ed.), 'Pentecost', in *A Dictionary of Biblical Tradition in English Literature* (Grand Rapids: Eerdmans, 1992), p. 597.

Jenkins, P., *The New Faces of Christianity: Believing the Bible in the Global South* (Oxford: Oxford University Press, 2006).

—*The Next Christendom: The Coming of Global Christianity* (Oxford: Oxford University Press, 2002).

Jervell, J., *Die Apostelgeschichte* (KEK; Göttingen: Vandenhoeck & Ruprecht, 17th edn, 1998).

Johnson, L.T., *The Acts of the Apostles* (SP, 5; Collegeville: Liturgical Press, 1992).

—'Literary Criticism of Luke–Acts: Is Reception-History Pertinent?', *JSNT* 28 (2005), pp. 159-62.

—'On Finding the Lukan Community: A Cautious Cautionary Essay', in *SBLSP* (1979), I, pp. 87-100.

—*Religious Experience in Early Christianity* (Minneapolis: Fortress Press, 1998).

Just, A.A., Jr. (ed.), *Luke* (Ancient Christian Commentary on Scripture, 3; Downers Grove, IL: InterVarsity Press, 2003).

—'Visions of the End in Reformation Europe', in Harry Loewen and Al Reimer (eds.), *Visions and Realities* (Winnipeg: Hyperion, 1985), pp. 11-57.

Kelly, J.N.D., *The Pastoral Epistles* (BNTC; London: A. & C. Black, 1963).

Kennedy, G.A., *Progymnasmata: Greek Textbooks of Prose Composition and Rhetoric* (Writings from the Greco-Roman World, 10; Leiden: Brill; Atlanta: SBL, 2003).

Kessler, H., 'The Word Made Flesh in Early Decorated Bibles', in J. Spier, H.L. Kessler, S. Fine and M. Charles-Murray (eds.), *Picturing the Bible: The Earliest Christian Art* (New Haven: Yale University Press, 2009), pp. 140-66.

Kim, H.-S., *Die Geisttaufe des Messias: Eine kompositionsgeschichtliche Untersuchung zu einem Leitmotiv des lukanische Doppelwerks: Ein Beitrag zur Theologie und Intention des Lukas* (Studien zur klassischen Philologie, 81; Frankfurt-am-Main: Peter Lang, 1993).

Kim, S., *Christ and Caesar: The Gospel and the Roman Empire in the Writings of Paul and Luke* (Grand Rapids: Eerdmans, 2008).

—*The Origin of Paul's Gospel* (Grand Rapids: Eerdmans, 1982).

—*Paul and the New Perspective: Second Thoughts on the Origin of Paul's Gospel* (Grand Rapids: Eerdmans, 2002).

Klaassen, W., 'Eschatological Themes in Early Dutch Anabaptism', in Irvin B. Horst (ed.), *The Dutch Dissenters* (Leiden: Brill, 1986), pp. 15-31.

Klauck, H.-J., *Judas: Un disciple de Jésus: Exégèse et répercussions historiques* (trans. Joseph Hoffmann; LD; Paris: Éditions du Cerf, 2006).

Klein, H., *Das Lukasevangelium* (KEK; Göttingen: Vandenhoeck & Ruprecht, 2006).

Konstan, D., *The Emotions of the Ancient Greeks: Studies in Aristotle and Classical Literature* (Toronto: University of Toronto Press, 2006).

Korn, M., *Die Geschichte Jesu in Veränderter Zeit: Studien zur bleibenden Bedeutung Jesu im lukanischen Doppelwerk* (WUNT, II/51; Tübingen: Mohr Siebeck, 1993).

Körtner, U.H.J., *Papias von Hierapolis: Ein Beitrag zur Geschichte des früher Christentums* (FRLANT, 133; Göttingen: Vandenhoeck & Ruprecht, 1983).

Kovacs, D., 'Ion', in D. Kovacs (ed.), *Euripides* (LCL; Cambridge, MA: Harvard University Press, 1999), pp. 313-511.

Krieger, M., *Ekphrasis: The Illusion of the Natural Sign* (Baltimore: The Johns Hopkins University Press, 1992).

Kroegel, A., 'The Figure of Mary in Botticelli's Art', in Doriana Comerlati and Daniel Arasse (eds.), *Botticelli from Lorenzo the Magnificent to Savonarola* (Milan: Skira, 2003), pp. 55-67.

Kuhn, K.A., *The Heart of Biblical Narrative: Rediscovering Biblical Appeal to the Emotions* (Minneapolis: Fortress Press, 2009).

LaVerdiere, E., 'Wrapped in Swaddling Clothes', *Emmanuel* 90 (1984), pp. 542-46.

Leat, S.J., 'Artificial Intelligence Researcher Seeks Silicon Soul', *Research News and Opportunities in Science and Theology* 3.4 (2002), pp. 7, 26.

LeDoux, J., *The Emotional Brain: The Mysterious Underpinnings of Emotional Life* (New York: Simon & Schuster, 1996).

—*The Synaptic Self: How Our Brains Become Who We Are* (London: Penguin, 2002).

Levey, M., and G. Mandel, *The Complete Paintings of Botticelli* (New York: Abrams, 1967).

Levitan, A., 'The Parody of Pentecost in Chaucer's Summoner's Tale', *University of Toronto Quarterly* 40 (1971), pp. 236-46.

Lietaert Peerbolte, L.J., *Paul the Missionary* (CBET, 34; Leuven: Peeters, 2003).

Lightfoot, J.B., *Essays on the Work Entitled Supernatural Religion* (London: Macmillan, 1889).

Linton, O., 'The Third Aspect: A Neglected Point of View', *ST* 3 (1949), pp. 79-95.

Litwak, K.D., *Echoes of Scripture in Luke–Acts: Telling the History of God's People Intertextuality* (JSNTSup, 282; London: T&T Clark International, 2005).

Longenecker, R.N., *Galatians* (WBC, 41; Dallas: Word, 1990).

—(ed.), *The Road from Damascus: The Impact of Paul's Conversion on His Life, Thought, and Ministry* (McMaster NT Studies; Grand Rapids: Eerdmans, 1997).

MacDonald, D.R., *Does the New Testament Imitate Homer? Four Cases from the Acts of the Apostles* (New Haven: Yale University Press, 2003).

—'Paul's Farewell to the Ephesian Elders and Hector's Farewell to Andromache: A Strategic Imitation of Homer's *Iliad*', in Penner and Vander Stichele (eds.), *Contextualizing Acts*, pp. 189-203.

—'The Shipwrecks of Odysseus and Paul', *NTS* 45 (1999), pp. 88-107.

Maddox, R., *The Purpose of Luke–Acts* (Göttingen: Vandenhoeck & Ruprecht, 1982).

Malina, B.J., and J.J. Pilch, *Social-Science Commentary on the Book of Acts* (Minneapolis: Fortress Press, 2008).

Marguerat, D., 'La Mort d'Ananias et Saphira (Ac 5.1-11) dans la Stratégie Narrative de Luc', *NTS* 39 (1993), pp. 222-26.

—*Les Actes des apôtres (1–12)* (CNT, 5a; Geneva: Labor et Fides, 2007).

—*Résurrection. Une histoire de vie* (Poliez-le-Grand: Éditions du Moulin, 3rdd edn, 2003).

—*The First Christian Historian: Writing the Acts of the Apostles* (SNTSMS, 121; Cambridge: Cambridge University Press, 2002).

Marshall, I.H., 'Acts and the "Former Treatise"', in Winter and Clarke (eds.), *The Book of Acts in Its Ancient Literary Setting*, pp. 162-83.

—'History and the Last Supper', in D.L. Bock and R.L. Webb (eds.), *Key Events in the Life of the Historical Jesus* (WUNT II/106; Tübingen: Mohr Siebeck, 2009), pp. 481-588.

—*The Gospel of Luke* (NIGTC; Exeter: Paternoster Press, 1978).

Marshall, I.H., and D. Peterson (eds.), *Witness to the Gospel: The Theology of Acts* (Grand Rapids/Cambridge: Eerdmans, 1998).

Martin, W., *Recent Theories of Narrative* (Ithaca, NY: Cornell University Press, 1986).

Martyn, J.L., *Galatians: A New Translation with Introduction and Commentary* (AB, 33A; New York: Doubleday, 1997).

Matill, A.J., Jr., 'The Jesus–Paul Parallels and the Purpose of Luke–Acts', *NovT* 17 (1975), pp. 15-46.

—'The Purpose of Acts: Schneckenburger Reconsidered', in W. Ward Gasque and R.P. Martin (eds.), *Apostolic History and the Gospel* (Exeter: Paternoster Press, 1970), pp. 108-22.

Matlock, R.B., Review of S. Chester, *Conversion at Corinth* and S. Gathercole, *Where is Boasting?*, *JSNT* 26 (2003), pp. 251-55.

McKeon, R. (ed.), *The Basic Works of Aristotle* (Modern Library; New York: Random House, 2001).

McKnight, S., 'Collection for the Saints', in Hawthorne and Martin (eds.), *Dictionary of Paul and His Letters*, pp. 143-47.

Mealand, D.L., 'Style, Genre, and Authorship in Acts, the Septuagint, and Hellenistic Historians', *Literary and Linguistic Computing* 14.4 (1999), pp. 479-506.

Meggitt, J., Review of L.T. Johnson, *Religious Experience in Earliest Christianity*, *JTS* NS 51 (2000), pp. 685-58.

Menken, Maarten J.J., *Matthew's Bible: The Old Testament Text of the Evangelist* (BETL, 173; Leuven: Leuven University Press, 2004).

Menzies, R.P., *Empowered for Witness: The Spirit in Luke–Acts* (JPTSup, 6; Sheffield: Sheffield Academic Press, 1994).

Michaud, J.-P., 'La résurrection dans le langage des premiers chrétiens', in O. Mainville and D. Marguerat (eds.), *Résurrection. L'après-mort dans le monde ancien et le Nouveau Testament* (Geneva: Labor et Fides, 2001), pp. 111-26.

Michel, H.-J., *Die Abschiedsrede des Paulus an die Kirche Apg 20,17-38* (Studien zum Alten und Neuen Testaments, 35; Munich: Kosel-Verlag,1973).

Mikalson, J.D., 'The Tragedians and Popular Religion', in *Greek Drama* (Bloom's Period Studies; Philadelphia: Chelsea House, 2004), pp. 277-87.

Miller, J.B.F., *Convinced That God Had Called Us: Dreams, Visions, and the Perception of God's Will in Luke–Acts* (BibInt, 85; Leiden: Brill, 2007).

Mittmann-Richert, U., *Der Sühnetod des Gottesknechts: Jesaja 53 im Lukasevangelium* (Tübingen: Mohr Siebeck, 2008).

Moessner, D.P. (ed.), *Jesus and the Heritage of Israel* (Harrisburg, PA: Trinity Press International, 2000).

—*Lord of the Banquet: The Literary and Theological Significance of the Lukan Travel Narrative* (Minneapolis: Fortress Press, 1989).

Momigliano, A., *The Development of Greek Biography* (Cambridge, MA: Harvard University Press, 1971).

Morgenthaler, R., *Statistik des neutestamentlichen Wortschatzes* (Zurich: Gotthelf, 1958).

Morrice, W.G., *Joy in the New Testament* (Exeter: Paternoster Press, 1984).

Most, G.W. (ed.), *Hesiod: Theogony, Works and Days, Testamonia* (LCL; Cambridge, MA: Harvard University Press, 2006).

Moule, C.F.D., 'The Christology of Acts', in L.E. Keck and J.L. Martyn (eds.), *Studies in Luke–Acts* (Philadelphia: Fortress Press, 1980), pp. 159-85.

Müller-Abels, S., 'Der Umgang mit "schwierigen" Texten der Apostelgeschichte in der Alten Kirche', in T. Nicklas and M. Tilly (eds.), *The Book of Acts as Church History. Apostelgeschichte als Kirchengeschichte: Text, Textual Traditions and Ancient Interpretations. Text, Texttraditionen und antike Auslegungen* (BZNW, 120; Berlin: W. de Gruyter, 2003), pp. 347-71.

Munck, J., 'Die Tradition über das Matthäusevangelium bei Papias', in W.C. van Unnik (ed.), *Neotestamentica et Patristica. Eine Freundesgabe H. Prof. Dr.O. Cullmann zu seinem 60. Geburtstag überreicht* (NovTSup, 6. Leiden: Brill, 1962), pp. 249-60.

Nagy, G., *Homeric Questions* (Austin, TX: University of Texas Press, 1996).

Neagoe, A., *The Trial of the Gospel: An Apologetic Reading of Luke's Trial Narratives* (SNTSMS, 116; Cambridge: Cambridge University Press, 2002).

Nehamas, A., 'Pity and Fear in the *Rhetoric* and the *Poetics*', in Rorty (ed.), *Essays on Aristotle's Poetics*, pp. 291-314.

Newman, C.C., *Paul's Glory-Christology: Tradition and Rhetoric* (NovTSup, 69; Leiden: Brill, 1992).

Nickelsburg, G.W., ʿΑπ´Εκτρωμα, Though Appointed from the Womb: Paul's Apostolic Self-Description in 1 Corinthians 15 and Galatians 1', *HTR* 79 (1986), pp. 198-205.

Nolland, J., *Luke 1–9:20* (WBC, 35a; Dallas: Word, 1989).

Norelli, E., *Papia di Hierapoli, Esposizione degli oracoli del Signore. I frammenti* (Letture cristiane del primo millennio, 36. Milan: Paoline, 2005).

Novak, D., *The Image of the Non-Jew in Judaism: An Historical and Constructive Study of the Noahide Laws* (Lewiston, NJ: Edwin Mellen Press, 1983).

Nussbaum, M.C., *The Fragility of Goodness: Luck and Ethics in Greek Tragedy and Philosophy* (Cambridge: Cambridge University Press, 1986).

—'Tragedy and Self-Sufficiency: Plato and Aristotle on Fear and Pity', in Rorty (ed.), *Essays on Aristotle's Poetics*, pp. 261-90.

—*Upheavals of Thought: The Intelligence of Emotions* (Cambridge: Cambridge University Press, 2001).

O'Brien, P.T., 'Prayer in Luke–Acts', *TynBul* 24 (1973), pp. 111-27.

—'Was Paul Converted?', in D.A. Carson, P.T. O'Brien and M.A. Seifrid (eds.), *Justification and Variegated Nomism. II. The Paradoxes of Paul* (WUNT, II/181; Tübingen: Mohr Siebeck; Grand Rapids: Baker Academic, 2004), pp. 361-91.

Öhler, M., *Barnabas: die historische Person und ihre Rezeption in der Apostlegeschichte* (WUNT, 156; Tübingen: Mohr Siebeck, 2003), pp. 70-72.

Olbricht T.H., and J.L. Sumney (eds.), *Paul and Pathos* (SBLSymS, 16; Atlanta: SBL, 2001).

O'Toole, R.F., 'Luke's Position on Politics and Society in Luke–Acts', in Richard J. Cassidy (ed.), *Political Issues in Luke–Acts* (Maryknoll, NY: Orbis Books, 1983), pp. 1-17.

—'"You Did Not Lie to Us (Human Beings) but to God" (Acts 5,4c)', *Biblica* 76 (1995), pp. 202-209.

Palmer, D.W., 'Acts and the Ancient Historical Monograph', in Winter and Clarke (eds.), *The Book of Acts in Its Ancient Literary Setting*, pp. 1-29.

Pao, D.W., *Acts and the Isaianic New Exodus* (BSL; Grand Rapids: Baker Academic, 2002).

Parsons, M.C., *Acts* (Paideia; Grand Rapids: Baker Academic, 2008).

—'Reading a Beginning/Beginning a Reading: Tracing Literary Theory on Narrative Openings', *Semeia* 22 (1991), pp. 11-31.

Parsons, M.C., and R.I. Pervo, *Rethinking the Unity of Luke and Acts* (Minneapolis: Fortress Press, 1993).

Pelling, C.B.R. (ed.), *Characterization and Individuality in Greek Literature* (Oxford: Oxford University Press, 1990).

—'Plutarch's Adaptation of his Source Material', *JHS* 100 (1980), pp. 127-40.

—'Plutarch's Method of Work in the Roman Lives', *JHS* 99 (1979), pp. 74-96.

—'Truth and Fiction in Plutarch's Lives', in D.A. Russell (ed.), *Antonine Literature* (Oxford: Oxford University Press, 1990), pp. 19-52.

Penner, T., and C. Vander Stichele (eds.), *Contextualizing Acts: Lukan Narrative and Greco-Roman Discourse* (SBLSymS; Atlanta: Scholars Press, 2003).

Pervo, R.I., *Acts* (Hermeneia; Minneapolis: Fortress Press, 2009).

—*Dating Acts: Between the Evangelists and the Apologists* (Santa Rosa: Polebridge Press, 2006).

—'Direct Speech in Acts and the Question of Genre', *JSNT* 28 (2006), pp. 285-307.

—'Israel's Heritage and Claims upon the Genre(s) of Luke and Acts: The Problems of a History', in Moessner (ed.), *Jesus and the Heritage of Israel*, pp. 127-43.

—*Luke's Story of Paul* (Minneapolis: Fortress Press, 1990).

—'Must Luke and Acts Belong to the Same Genre?', in *SBLSP* (1989), pp. 309-16.

—*Profit with Delight: The Literary Genre of the Acts of the Apostles* (Philadelphia: Fortress Press, 1987).

Pesch, R., *Die Apostelgeschichte (Apg 1-12)* (EKK; Neukirchen–Vluyn: Neukirchener Verlag, 1995).

Phillips, T.E., *Acts Within Diverse Frames of Reference* (Macon: Mercer University Press, 2009).

—The Genre of Acts: Moving Toward a Consensus?', *CBR* 4 (2006), pp. 365-96.

—*Paul, His Letters and Acts* (LPS; Peabody, MA: Hendrickson, 2009).

—'Subtlety as a Literary Technique in Luke Characterization of Jews and Judaism', in R.P. Thompson and T.E. Phillips (eds.), *Literary Studies in Luke–Acts* (Macon, GA: Mercer University Press, 1998), pp. 314-26.

Pietersen, L.K., 'Despicable Deviants: Labelling Theory and the Polemic of the Pastorals', *Sociology of Religion* 58.4 (1997), pp. 343-52.

Pilch, J.J., *Visions and Healing in the Acts of the Apostles: How the Early Believers Experienced God* (Collegeville: Liturgical Press, 2004).

Pippen Burnett, A., *Ion* (Greek Drama Series; Englewood Cliffs, NJ: Prentice–Hall, 1970).

—*Pindar* (Ancients in Action; London: Bristol Classical Press, 2008).

Plymale, S.F., *The Prayer Texts of Luke–Acts* (American University Studies: Series VII: Theology and Religion, 118; New York: Peter Lang, 1991).

Pokorný, P., *Theologie der lukanischen Schriften* (Göttingen: Vandenhoeck & Ruprecht, 1998).

Porter, S.E., 'The Genre of Acts and the Ethics of Discourse', in Thomas E. Phillips (ed.), *Acts and Ethics* (Sheffield: Sheffield Phoenix Press, 2005), pp. 1-15.

Prieur, A., *Die Verkündigung der Gottesherrschaft: Exegetische Studien zum lukanischen Verständnis von βασιλεία τοῦ θεοῦ* (WUNT, II/89; Tübingen: Mohr Siebeck, 1996).

Prince, G., *Dictionary of Narratology* (Lincoln: University of Nebraska Press, 1987).

—*Narrative as Theme* (Lincoln: University of Nebraska Press, 1992).

Quesnel, M., 'Luc historien de Paul et de Jésus', in B. Pouderon and Y.-M. Duval (eds.), *L'historiographie de l'Église des premiers siècles* (Théologie historique, 114; Paris: Beauchesne, 2001), pp. 57-66.

Rabinowitz, P.J., *Before Reading: Narrative Conventions and the Politics of Interpretation* (Ithaca, NY: Cornell University Press, 1987).

Race, W.H., *Pindar* (Twayne World Author Series, 773; Boston: Twayne Publishers, 1986).

Ramsay, W.M., *St. Paul the Traveller and the Roman Citizen* (London: Hodder & Stoughton, 1896).

Richard, E., 'Jesus' Passion and Death in Acts', in D. de Sylva (ed.), *Reimaging the Death of the Lukan Jesus* (BBB, 73; Frankfurt: Hain, 1990), pp. 125-52.

Richards, J.C., 'Giotto di Bondone', in Hugh Brigstocke (ed.), *The Oxford Companion to Western Art* (*Oxford Art Online*). Http://www.oxfordartonline.com/subscriber/article/opr/t118/e1049 (accessed 9 September 2009).

Richardson, N.J., 'The *Homeric Hymn to Hermes*', in P.J. Finglass, C. Collard and N.J. Richardson (eds.), *Hesperos* (New York: Oxford University Press, 2007), pp. 83-91.

Riesner, R., *Paul's Early Period: Chronology, Mission Strategy, Theology* (trans. D. Stott; Grand Rapids: Eerdmans, 1998).

Robertson, A.T., *Word Pictures in the New Testament* (3 vols.; New York: Harper & Brothers, 1930–33).

Robin, C., *Fear: The History of a Political Idea* (Oxford: Oxford University Press, 2006).

Robinson, J.M., P. Hoffmann and J.S. Kloppenborg (eds.), *The Critical Edition of Q: A Synopsis Including the Gospels of Matthew and Luke and Thomas with English, German and French Translations of Q and Thomas* (Hermeneia; Minneapolis: Fortress Press, 2000).

Roloff, J., *Die Apostelgeschichte* (Göttingen: Vandenhoeck & Ruprecht, 1981).

Rorty, A.O. (ed.), *Essays on Aristotle's* Poetics (Princeton, NJ: Princeton University Press, 1992).

—*Essays on Aristotle's* Rhetoric (Berkeley: University of California Press, 1996).

Røsæg, N.A., 'The Spirituality of Paul: An Active Life', *StSp* 14 (2004), pp. 49-92.

Rowe, C.K., 'History, Hermeneutics and the Unity of Luke–Acts', *JSNT* 28 (2005), pp. 131-57.

—'Literary Unity and Reception History: Reading Luke–Acts as Luke and Acts', *JSNT* 29 (2007), pp. 449-57.

—'Luke–Acts and the Imperial Cult: A Way Through the Conundrum?', *JSNT* 27 (2005), pp. 279-300.

Ruthven, J., *On the Cessation of the Charismata: The Protestant Polemic on Post-biblical Miracles* (JPTSup, 3; Sheffield: Sheffield Academic Press, 1993).

Sadler, M.F., *The Gospel According to St. Luke* (New York: James Pott & Co., 1890).

Said, E.W., *Beginnings: Intention and Method* (New York: Basic Books, 1975).

Sampley, J.P., '"Before God, I do not Lie" (Gal. 1.20): Paul's Self-Defence in the Light of Roman Legal Praxis', *NTS* 23 (1977), pp. 477-82.

Sanders, E.P., *Paul and Palestinian Judaism: A Comparison of Patterns of Religion* (Philadelphia: Fortress Press, 1977).

Sanders, J.T., *The Jews in Luke–Acts* (London: SCM Press, 1987).

Schmidt, D.D., 'Rhetorical Influences and Genre: Luke's Preface and the Rhetoric of Helle-
    nistic Historiography', in Moessner (ed.), *Jesus and the Heritage of Israel*, pp. 27-60.
Schwartz, D.R., 'The End of the Line: Paul in the Canonical Book of Acts', in William S.
    Babcock (ed.), *Paul and the Legacies of Paul* (Dallas: SMU Press, 1991), pp. 3-24.
Segal, A.F., *Paul the Convert: The Apostolate and Apostasy of Saul the Pharisee* (New
    Haven: Yale University Press, 1990).
Segal, C., 'Euripides' *Ion*: Generational Passage and Civic Myth', in Mark W. Padilla (ed.),
    Rites of Passage in Ancient Greece: Literature, Religion, Society (Lewisburg: Bucknell
    University Press, 1999), pp. 42-77.
Sélincourt, A. de, *Herodotus: The Histories* (Baltimore: Penguin Books, 1954).
Sellner, H.G., *Das Heil Gottes: Studien zur Soteriologie des lukanischen Doppelwerkes*
    (Berlin: W. de Gruyter, 2007).
Shepherd, W.H., *The Narrative Function of the Holy Spirit as a Character in Luke–Acts*
    (SBLDS, 147; Atlanta: Scholars Press, 1994).
Smith, D.E., 'Narrative Beginnings in Ancient Literature and Theory', *Semeia* 22 (1991),
    pp. 1-9.
Sokolon, M.K., *Political Emotions: Aristotle and the Symphony of Reason and Emotion*
    (DeKalb: Northern Illinois University Press, 2006).
Spencer, F.S., *Journeying through Acts: A Literary-Cultural Reading* (Peabody, MA:
    Hendrickson, 2004).
—*The Portrait of Philip in Acts: A Study of Roles and Relations* (JSNTSup, 67; Sheffield:
    Sheffield Academic Press, 1992).
Spencer, P.E., 'The Unity of Luke–Acts: A Four-Bolted Hermeneutical Hinge', *CBR* 5
    (2007), pp. 341-66.
Spier, J. (ed.), *Christian Art* (New Haven: Yale University Press, 2007).
Squires, J.T., 'Acts', in J.D.G. Dunn and J.W. Rogerson (eds.), *Eerdmans Commentary on
    the Bible* (Grand Rapids: Eerdmans, 2003), pp. 1213-67.
Stendahl, K., *Paul among Jews and Gentiles and Other Essays* (Philadelphia: Fortress Press,
    1976).
Sterling, G.E., *Self-Definition: Josephos, Luke–Acts and Apologetic Historiography*
    (NovTSup, 64; Leiden: Brill, 1992).
Stoddard, K., *The Narrative Voice in the Theogony of Hesiod* (Boston: Brill, 2004).
Story, I.C., and A. Allan, *A Guide to Ancient Greek Drama* (Malden, MA: Blackwell, 2005).
Strauss Clay, J., *The Politics of Olympus: Form and Meaning in the Major Homeric Hymns*
    (Princeton, NJ: Princeton University Press, 1989).
Swanson, R.A., *Pindar's Odes* (Library of Liberal Arts; New York: Bobbs-Merrill, 1974).
Talbert, C.H., 'The Acts of the Apostles: Monograph or *Bios*?', in Witherington III (ed.),
    History, Literature, and Society in the Book of Acts, pp. 58-72.
—*Literary Patterns, Theological Themes, and the Genre of Luke–Acts* (SBLMS, 20;
    Missoula, MT: Scholars Press, 1974).
—*Reading Acts: A Literary and Theological Commentary on the Acts of the Apostles* (New
    York: Crossroad, 1997).
—*What Is a Gospel? The Genre of the Canonical Gospels* (Minneapolis: Fortress Press,
    1977).
Talbert, C.H., and P.L. Stepp, 'Succession in Mediterranean Antiquity, Part 1: The Lukan
    Milieu' and 'Part 2: Luke–Acts', in *SBLSP* (1998), pp. 148-68, 169-79.
Taylor, J., 'The Jerusalem Decrees (Acts 15.20, 29 and 21.25) and the Incident at Antioch
    (Gal 2.11-14)', *NTS* 47 (2001), pp. 372-80.

Thompson, L.L., *The Book of Revelation: Apocalypse and Empire* (Oxford: Oxford University Press, 1990).

Thompson, R.P., *Keeping the Church in Its Place: The Church as Narrative Character in Acts* (New York/London: T&T Clark International, 2006).

Toolan, M.J., *Narrative: A Critical Linguistic Introduction* (London: Routledge, 1988).

Torrance, T.F., *The Doctrine of Grace in the Apostolic Fathers* (Edinburgh: Oliver & Boyd, 1948).

Trites, A.A., 'The Prayer Motif in Luke–Acts', in C.H. Talbert (ed.), *Perspectives on Luke–Acts* (Edinburgh: T. & T. Clark, 1978), pp. 168-86.

Turner, M., *Power from on High: The Spirit in Israel's Restoration and Witness in Luke–Acts* (JPTSup, 9; Sheffield: Sheffield Academic Press, 1996).

—'The "Spirit of Prophecy" as the Power of Israel's Restoration and Witness', in Marshall and Peterson (eds.), *Witness to the Gospel*, pp. 327-48.

—'"Trinitarian" Pneumatology in the New Testament? Towards an Explanation of the Worship of Jesus', *Asbury Theological Journal* 57 (2003), pp. 167-86.

Tyson, J.B., *The Death of Jesus in Luke–Acts* (Colombia: University of South Carolina Press, 1986).

—'From History to Rhetoric and Back: Assessing New Trends in Acts Studies', in Penner and Vander Stichele (eds.), *Contextualizing Acts*, pp. 23-42.

Walaskay, P.W., *And So We Came to Rome* (SNTSMS, 49; Cambridge: Cambridge University Press, 1983).

Walcot, P., 'Cattle Raiding, Heroic Tradition, and Ritual', *HR* 18 (1979), pp. 326-51.

Wall, R.W., 'The Acts of the Apostles in Canonical Context', in R.W. Wall and E.E. Lemcio (eds.), *The New Testament as Canon: A Reader in Canonical Criticism* (JSNTSup, 76; Sheffield: JSOT Press, 1992), pp. 110-28.

—'The Acts of the Apostles: Introduction, Commentary, and Reflections', in Leander E. Keck *et al.* (eds.), *The New Interpreter's Bible* (12 vols.; Nashville: Abingdon Press, 2002), X, pp. 1-368.

Walters, P., *The Assumed Authorial Unity of Luke and Acts: A Reassessment of the Evidence* (SNTSMS, 145; Cambridge: Cambridge University Press, 2009).

Walton, S., "Ομοθυμαδόν in Acts: Co-location, Common Action or "Of One Heart and Mind"?', in P.J. Williams, A.D. Clarke, P.M. Head and D. Instone-Brewer (eds.), *The New Testament in Its First Century Setting: Essays on Context and Background in Honour of B.W. Winter on His 65th Birthday* (Grand Rapids/Cambridge: Eerdmans, 2004), pp. 89-105.

—'Acts, Book of', in K.J. Vanhoozer, C.G. Bartholomew, D.J. Treier and N.T. Wright (eds.), *Dictionary for Theological Interpretation of the Bible* (London: SPCK; Grand Rapids: Baker Academic, 2005), pp. 27-31.

—'The Acts—of God? What is the "Acts of the Apostles" All About?', *EvQ* 80 (2008), pp. 291-306.

—*Leadership and Lifestyle: The Portrait of Paul in the Miletus Speech and 1 Thessalonians* (SNTSMS, 108; Cambridge: Cambridge University Press, 2000).

—'The State They Were In: Luke's View of the Roman Empire', in Peter Oakes (ed.), *Rome in the Bible and the Early Church* (Carlisle: Paternoster Press; Grand Rapids: Baker Academic, 2002), pp. 1-41.

Warfield, B.B., *Counterfeit Miracles* (New York: Scribner, 1918).

Watson, F., *Paul, Judaism, and the Gentiles: Beyond the New Perspective* (Grand Rapids: Eerdmans, rev. and expanded edn, 2007).

Weatherly, J.A., *Jewish Responsibility for the Death of Jesus in Luke–Acts* (JSNTSup, 106; Sheffield: Sheffield Academic Press, 1994).

Wedderburn, A.J.M., 'The "Apostolic Decree": Tradition and Redaction', *NovT* 35 (1993), pp. 362-89.

Wehnert, J., *Die Reinheit des "christlichen Gottesvolkes" aus Juden und Heiden* (FRLANT; Göttingen: Vandenhoeck & Ruprecht, 1997).

Weiser, A., *Die Apostelgeschichte Kapitel 13–28* (Gütersloh: Mohn; Würzburg: Echter, 1985).

Welliver, K., 'Pentecost and the Early Church: Patristic Interpretation of Acts 2' (PhD dissertation, Yale University, 1961).

West, M.L. (ed.), *The Contest of Homer and Hesiod in Homeric Hymns, Homeric Apocrypha, Lives of Homer* (LCL; Cambridge, MA: Harvard University Press, 2003).

—*Hesiod Theogony* (Oxford: Clarendon Press, 1966).

—*Homeric Hymns, Homeric Apocrypha, Lives of Homer* (LCL; Cambridge, MA: Harvard University Press, 2003).

White, H., *The Content of the Form: Narrative Discourse and Historical Representation* (Baltimore: The Johns Hopkins University Press, 1987).

Willetts, R.F., 'Ion', in *Euripides* (Complete Greek Tragedies, 3; Chicago: University of Chicago Press, 1992).

Williams, R., *The Wound of Knowledge* (London: Darton, Longman & Todd, 1979).

Winter, B.W., and A.D. Clarke (eds.), *The Book of Acts in Its Ancient Literary Setting* (Carlisle: Paternoster Press; Grand Rapids: Eerdmans, 1993).

Witherington, B., *The Acts of the Apostles: A Socio-Rhetorical Commentary* (Grand Rapids: Eerdmans, 1998).

—(ed.), *History, Literature, and Society in the Book of Acts* (Cambridge: Cambridge University Press, 1996).

Witherup, R.D., 'Cornelius Over and Over and Over Again: "Functional Redundancy" in the Acts of the Apostles', *JSNT* 49 (1993), pp. 45-66.

Wolter, M., *Das Lukas-Evangelium* (HKNT; Tübingen: Mohr Siebeck, 2008).

Wright, D., 'The Date and Arrangement of the Illustrations in the Rabbula Gospels', *Dumbarton Oaks Papers* 27 (1973), pp. 197-208.

Wright, N.T., 'Paul, Arabia, and Elijah (Galatians 1:17)', *JBL* 115 (1996), pp. 683-92.

Yamada, K., 'A Rhetorical History: The Literary Genre of the Acts of the Apostles', in S.E. Porter and T.H. Olbricht (eds.), *Rhetoric, Scripture and Theology* (JSNTSup, 131; Sheffield: Sheffield Academic Press, 1996).

Yamazaki-Ransom, K., *The Roman Empire in Luke's Narrative* (LNTS, 421; New York: T&T Clark International, 2010).

Yarbrough, R.W., 'The Date of Papias: A Reassessment', *JETS* 26 (1983), pp. 181-91.

Young, F., *Biblical Exegesis and the Formation of Christian Culture* (Cambridge: Cambridge University Press, 1997).

Young, K., and J.L. Saver, 'The Neurology of Narrative', *SubStance* 30 (2001), pp. 72-84.

Zacharia, K., *Converging Truths: Euripides' Ion and the Athenian Quest for Self Definition* (Boston: Brill, 2003).

Ziccardi, C.A., *The Relationship of Jesus and the Kingdom of God According to Luke–Acts* (Tesi Gregoriana Serie Teologia, 165; Rome: Editrice Pontificia Università Gregoriana, 2008).

Ziesler, J.A., 'The Name of Jesus in the Acts of the Apostles', *JSNT* 4 (1974), pp. 28-41.

Zwiep, A.W., *Judas and the Choice of Matthias: A Story on the Context and Concern of Acts 1:15-26* (WUNT, II/187. Tübingen: Mohr Siebeck, 2004).

INDEXES

INDEX OF REFERENCES

INDEX OF AUTHORS